MW01092583

Indigenous African Communication and Media Systems in a Digitized Age

Indigenous African Communication and Media Systems in a Digitized Age

Edited by Unwana Samuel Akpan and
Eddah Mbula Mutua

LEXINGTON BOOKS
Lanham • Boulder • New York • London

Published by Lexington Books
An imprint of The Rowman & Littlefield Publishing Group, Inc.
4501 Forbes Boulevard, Suite 200, Lanham, Maryland 20706
www.rowman.com

86-90 Paul Street, London EC2A 4NE

British Library Cataloguing in Publication Information Available

Library of Congress Cataloging-in-Publication Data

Names: Akpan, Unwana Samuel, editor, author. | Mutua, Eddah M., 1965- editor, author. | Wilson, Des, Ph. D., honouree.
Title: Indigenous African communication and media systems in a digitized age / edited by Unwana Samuel Akpan and Eddah Mbula Mutua.
Description: Lanham : The Rowman & Littlefield Publishing Group, Inc., 2024. | Includes bibliographical references and index.
Identifiers: LCCN 2024037244 (print) | LCCN 2024037245 (ebook) | ISBN 9781666965308 (cloth) | ISBN 9781666965315 (epub)
Subjects: LCSH: Communication—Social aspects—Africa. | Indigenous peoples—Africa—Communication. | Digital media—Social aspects—Africa. | LCGFT: Festschriften.
Classification: LCC P92.A35 I63 2024 (print) | LCC P92.A35 (ebook) | DDC 302.23096—dc23/eng/20240812
LC record available at https://lccn.loc.gov/2024037244
LC ebook record available at https://lccn.loc.gov/2024037245

♾️™ The paper used in this publication meets the minimum requirements of American National Standard for Information Sciences—Permanence of Paper for Printed Library Materials, ANSI/NISO Z39.48-1992.

This edited volume is a tribute to Des Wilson, a distinguished African professor specializing in Ethnocommunicology. It honors his extensive contributions over decades, encompassing leadership, teaching, and scholarly pursuits dedicated to unraveling the intricacies of indigenous African communication systems and giving prominence to its enduring legacy.

Contents

Foreword

Des Wilson

It is no longer in contention that African communication media had been in existence in their various forms from times which have now paled into history. If it is accepted that Africa provided one of the cradles of human civilization as found in the annals of Western civilization, it is therefore true that indigenous African media had developed from the earliest times when man started inhabiting the world.

It is possible that since the period marking the beginning of recorded history, Africans who, like every other race, had started using the various tools of communication which research has largely linked to music, developed systems of communication which served them well at the time. Thus, when man started communicating with words, it became necessary that they also needed to transmit their messages to distant places through interpersonal ways, narrowcasting and creating instruments that would make it possible to do so more effectively by reaching greater numbers of people. Today, some scholars are still embroiled in the trite argument that new media, presented through digitization of instruments of dissemination, will replace the old media. Collin Cherry had long ago dismissed this position in his book *World Communication* where he also argued that new media do not replace old ones but that they can replace some of the functions of the old ones. Another slant to this viewpoint is found in Roger F. Fidler's *Mediamorphosis* (1997), in which he also argues that although new media may introduce new ways of engaging the challenges of society, almost all the prognostications by today's media prophets have not come true, which is a way of saying that old habits die hard.

In my years in the crib of our culturally dominated society through media and cultural imperialism, I came to the realization that much of the cultural content fed to us was no more than propaganda or, at best, baby food. The real meal came when I started questioning the propriety of consuming Western culture in a manner that pointed to the damning lie that we had no past we could write about.

Our revulsion for these half-truths was not about rejecting Western-induced loss of self-esteem, it was about the realization that before books, radio, television, the internet, and all forms of transmission gadgets foisted on us, we had modes of communication which we could also promote while acknowledging the integrity of the past and present.

Perhaps, it is this cultural amnesia and a desire to be highly rated by other media scholars from the invading culture that has led many African scholars to ignore or even denigrate where their journey started from. There is a guiding saying among Africans which roughly translates as, "If you ignore the past, it rebels."

Nonetheless, we have also learned in history that the events of the past help us to build the present and lay the foundation for the future. My forays into the dark recesses of our ancient communication technologies and processes were promoted at the University of Ibadan at the beginning of the 1980s where I found a discerning communication arts and language guardian in the late Professor Solomon Ogbodum Unoh, an open-minded intellectual who was ready to join the ride with me as I explored the communicative practices of the people of Old Calabar, ancient migrants from the Benue–Congo language family. Well, there were a few skeptics all over the place from among colleagues, senior and junior, who felt that I was trying to take them down the development ladder to the better forgotten past irrespective of what I had to say. A few have been won over even though I now have a growing family of scholars who have realized, some without any prompting, that we have to know who we are and what our ancestors did in their little way to communicate with and among themselves in a burgeoning world of drama, excitement, and unfolding scientific and technological development. These largely interpersonal channels have contributed in so many ways to the building of our bewildered populations which are fascinated by the new technologies.

The challenge now is how to integrate the traditional or indigenous African processes into the technology which has reached us from various cultures especially the Euro-American one. Even in the more technologically expansive west, many of its citizens are still trying to grapple with their own inventions. Thus, for the majority of Africans, we are technologically enthusiastic and eager but culturally deprived and deracinated.

Therefore, the contribution of the over twenty-six scholars, many of whom I have never met nor spoken to, is a confirmation of the fact that the conversation is going round and that our young scholars are receiving messages which their elders almost rejected more than four decades ago.

Perhaps we were misunderstood then. We did not urge for a rejection of Western media, models, and their traditions. What we simply called for was, "Hey Folks, look into your backyard and you might find something to tickle you and support your venture in the new communication world!"

From the "Introduction" by Unwana Samuel Akpan, my proud harvest at the University of Uyo, and the indomitable Prof. Eddah Mbula Mutua, an *East African* scholar of no mean repute, the indomitable spirit of Prof. Kehbuna Langmia, Prof. Chuka Onwumechili, (other great African scholars), Herbert Batta, the quartet from Zimbabwe, Prof. Abigail Ogwezzy and her colleagues at the University of Lagos, and many other contributors from Nigeria, Malawi, Namibia, Botswana, and elsewhere around Africa, I am humbled to have such committed scholars to the idea of an African renaissance in thought, theory, practice, and seminal ideation in the sub-disciplinary field of Afriethics, and indigenous communication snatched from the jaws of naysayers and doubters that there can be a body of knowledge developed from an African perspective in the field of communication.

This journey has not been an easy one. I also drew inspiration from foreign scholars and researchers like Leonard Doob, William Hachten, and other writers.

Even though I disagreed with some of their viewpoints, nonetheless I found their drift most useful because they helped one to focus more on "the road not taken" from their racial perspective.

Other scholars whose works and experience I have borrowed from include Prof. Cecil Blake (Sierra Leone), Molefi Asante (the United States), J. R. Gusfield, K. Schoenback, and the UNESCO Publication, *Many Voices, One World,* which created ripples in the 1980s in the ultra-conservative governments of Ronald Reagan and Margaret Thatcher. There are many other influences of my youth which prepared me for this daring which some thought would fizzle out as a one-off experience like a binge drinking session with habitual drinkers. We have gone a long way in this, and there is no stopping us now, as they say in the song.

With the new awareness around the world that the more technologically endowed and developed countries have been in the business of using local intellectuals and comprador bourgeoisie to push their agenda, this kind of commitment is a way of saying, "we now know better." While this book cannot be the final word on this new direction, it is expected that it should ginger a number of Africans from their lethargic position where it almost seemed that African scholars need the legitimization signals and endorsements from their colleagues in the west before they can think for themselves.

I heartily appreciate the indefatigable efforts of Unwana Samuel Akpan and his colleagues in putting this work together. One of those who agreed to submit his chapter for this book, Prof. Lai Oso, unfortunately had his life

snuffed out on our increasingly atrocious road conditions and reckless driving. We miss him. There are others who promised to deliver but were unable
to meet the deadline. I also thank them for their interest.

The challenge of integrating indigenous media with digitized media will
remain a big headache for a long time if we continue to wait on Western
scientists and technology developers to do this for us. The trado-modern
communication model which I advocated in 1981 remains largely unexplored
and unexploited. If we must blend the past with the present for a smooth, successful, and effective communication enterprise, we must begin to develop
a mindset that will assist us to break away from the perennial black hole of
unfulfilled dreams for a better communication understanding. Our current
challenge is how to transmit and receive data in indigenous communication
format in the form of a digital analog signal transmitted over a point-to-point,
or where required, in a point-to-multipoint communication channel. What we
have here is a conversion of an analog (indigenous messaging system) into a
digital communication or data transmission.

I have no illusion that indigenous communication media and channels
cannot remain as cultural isolates in the interface between the indigenous
and modern systems. This cultural mix of intergenerational processes is what
some scholars have called trado-tronic communication. The mistake some
scholars make is making the assumption that indigenous communication
systems have no role to play under our pervasive modern communication
systems. Gusfield (1973, pp. 33–41) dismisses these averments as fallacies
in one of his critical references to the misleading assumptions. He postulates
that it is fallacious to think that "old traditions are displaced by new changes"
and that "traditional and modern forms are always in conflict" and that mod-
ernizing processes necessarily weaken traditions.

Finally, he argues that the view that tradition and modernity are naturally
exclusive systems is a fallacy that has been debunked by human experience.
What emerges from these viewpoints is the fact that no single medium or
channel can effectively address the communication challenges of any society
while operating either as indigenous media or modern mass media. In every
civilization, various forms of communication tools and goals, each operating at their own level of fidelity, have served purposes for which the culture
sought to use them for. No single medium can effectively and successfully
bring about success in every sphere of human communication needs. Thus,
while a text or SMS may just act the part of a notifier, interpersonal communication contact in person would not only notify but persuade and ensure
attendance at a meeting.

Again a radio advisory accompanied by a threat may serve the purpose of
securing compliance, but the use of an extramundane communication tool to
reinforce the threat may ensure that citizens obey the directive. What these

reveal to us is that a particular message through a particular medium can reinforce the message from another medium, thus making the message more enforceable or ensuring that it reaches a greater number of receivers. This is a media-mix or multimedia model which can work within a particular type or mode. We all know that today citizens operate on a multimedia model whether the media are modern and operating from a digitized platform or the analog narrowcasting of the essentially oral indigenous media and channels.

Cecil Blake offered a platform for promoting indigenous African communication media, which proposal is still relevant to this day. His four stages of growth and development of indigenous African communication pedagogy included aggregation, codification, maturation, and promulgation that are important in this discourse as we go forward. Wilson (2008) has noted that "all the media and interpersonal channels, which have constituted a veritable, dynamic force for meaning exchange and sharing, must be properly harnessed to bring about success in our communication efforts" (quoted in Wilson, 2015, pp. 86–87). All in all, this book is a great contribution to the content of the pedagogy of indigenous communication—the content of which is neither limited to the African continent nor the black or "colored" races. I think it will further expand the frontiers of knowledge in the area of African communication theory and practice.

REFERENCES

Blake, C. (1980). *Stages of growth and development of traditional communication.* Seminar paper presented at the African Council for Communication Education in Lagos.

Cherry, C. (1978). *World communications: Threat or promise.* MIT Press.

Fidler, R. F. (1997). *Mediamorphosis understanding new media.* Sage Publications.

Gusfield, J. R. (1973). Tradition and modernity. Misplaced polarities in the study of social change. In A. Etzioni & E. Etzioni-Halavy (Eds.), *Social change* (pp. 47–63). Basic Books.

UNESCO. (1980). *Many voices, one world.* UNESCO.

Wilson, D. E. (1988). *A survey of traditional and modern communication systems in Old Calabar Province (1846–1986)* (Unpublished Ph.D. thesis). University of Ibadan, Ibadan.

Wilson, D. E. (2008). Research in traditional communication in Africa. The development and future directions. *African Communication Research: Grassroots Participatory Communication, 1*(1).

Wilson, D. E. (2015). Global communication in the 21st century. In D. Wilson (Ed.), *New perspectives in applied communication.* Stirling—Horden Publications, Nigeria Ltd.

Wilson, D. E. (2015). *Ethnocommunicology, trado-modern communication and mediamorphosis in Nigeria.* University of Uyo Press.

Acknowledgments

First and foremost, our appreciation goes to God who made this volume a reality. We would also like to express our deepest gratitude to all those who contributed one way or the other to the publication of this book. Putting together an edited book is a journey that cannot be undertaken alone, and we are fortunate to have had the support and assistance of so many wonderful people along the way, especially the chapter authors whose insights have brought this book to life.

Second, we want to thank our families for their unwavering support and encouragement throughout this endeavor. Their belief in us has been our greatest motivation.

We are indebted to our dedicated acquisitions editor, whose keen insights and thoughtful guidance helped shape this manuscript into its final form. Your expertise and patience were invaluable.

We would like to extend our appreciation to our research assistants for their diligent research and assistance in gathering information for this book. Their dedication to detail greatly enhanced the quality of the content.

To our friends and colleagues who provided feedback, encouragement, and a listening ear during the ups and downs of the writing process, we are truly grateful. Their inputs were invaluable in refining the ideas within these pages.

Lastly, to the readers, it is our hope that this book will enrich your knowledge and inspire new perspectives.

With heartfelt appreciation,
Unwana Samuel Akpan and
Eddah Mbula Mutua

Introduction

Des Wilson and the Enduring Legacy in Preserving African Indigenous Communication and Media Systems

Unwana Samuel Akpan and Eddah Mbula Mutua

This edited volume is a Festschrift in honor of Professor Des Wilson's decades of leadership, scholarship, and research. Drawing from Wilson's work lasting over four decades, the authors celebrate this academic achievement by bringing together scholarly works that enrich discourses about Indigenous African Communication and Media Systems (IACMS). The authors respond to calls in African communication scholarship to center Indigenous African Communication and Media Systems (IACMS) in the digital age (Akpan, 2023; Mutua et al., 2022; Akpabio, 2021). The intersection of IACMS and digital media has become an important area of inquiry in African communication scholarship as illustrated in the essays assembled in this volume. Together, the authors weave a narrative that celebrates the resilience and significance of indigenous African communication and media in an increasingly digital world. Each essay discusses specific form of traditional media by showing how they have 'reinvented' (Akpabio, 2021) themselves and adapted in the present African communication environment. The survival of IACMS in the digital age "defies efforts by Western media to cannibalize them and perhaps supplant them (Wison 1987, p. 89). The mosaic of innovative ways to preserve IACMS presents what Des Wilson refers to as "African renaissance in thought, theory, and practice."

According to a recent World Bank Report Brief (January 2024), "Africa has made substantial strides toward digital transformation, with hundreds of millions of people gaining access to the internet and productively utilizing a wide variety of digital services, such as mobile payments and online learning platforms" (para. 1). This development has positive and negative impacts on communication and the general well-being of people in Africa. For example, the increased access to digital services such as mobile money has improved the lives of the "unbanked" in Africa (Piper, 2020). On the other hand, there is growing concern about increased access to digital services on African communication forms. For example, the declining role of African languages as custodian of African culture (Wa Thiong'o, 1986) and the effects of "'De-indigenization' of African language" that makes them second-class citizens in their own countries" (Wolf, 2021, p. 2). Other concerns include the role of social media in promoting ethnic violence in Kenya; ethnic minority conflict in Ethiopia; xenophobia in South Africa; and homophobia in Uganda, Tunisia, and Ghana (Machirori, 2022). These concerns among others are the premise of questions about the relevance of IACMS in the digital age. For example, do IACMS still play a role in the everyday communication in the digital age? What is their role in addressing some of these problems? This book is situated to address IACMS in the digital age. Our goal is to examine the relevance of IACMS in view of their use and adaptation in the digital age.

It is crucial to emphasize that questioning the relevance of IACMS does not elevate Western media systems as the sole force behind the pursuit to meet communication needs in Africa. Instead, it directs attention toward IACMS to demonstrate their role in accounting for the narrative and structure of African communication. Thus, the need to focus on the relevance of IACMS in the digital age underscores their significance in the daily experiences of African people. We determine the relevance of IACMS by assembling Afrocentric essays that provide current insights about (i) the use of traditional media in the digital age, (ii) factors that account for the continued use and relevance, and (iii) strategies offered to sustain the longevity of traditional media in the digital age.

In his contribution to the 1980s debate about the role of communication in development in Africa, Wilson (1987) underscored the usefulness of traditional media in many aspects of African life in his seminal article titled "Traditional Systems of Communication in Modern African Development: An Analytical Viewpoint." This work advances the viewpoint that posits "African traditional systems as those which have defied all efforts by western media to cannibalize them and perhaps supplant them." (p. 89). Does this view hold true today? We believe that this book is a testament to Prof. Des Wilson's enduring legacy to preserve the validity and integrity of IACMS. Moreover, it is a constant reminder for communication scholars to keep an eagle's eye on developments in the African communication that defy efforts to devalue IACMS environment.

In the last four decades, Prof. Des Wilson has spearheaded an intellectual movement focused on the study of African traditional communication systems. Both senior and budding scholars who attest to Prof. Wilson's vision to privilege the relevance of IACMS at all times provide valuable insights in the essays assembled in this edited volume that honors his scholarship, research, and leadership. The scholarship affirms the resiliency of IACMS despite the pervasive influence of digital media in contemporary African society. In fact, the conclusions drawn from different aspects of IACMS included in this volume attest to Colin Cherry's (1978) observation that "No one newly-introduced mode of communication or combination of new modes wholly replace or supplant the traditional ones. The fact is that they supplement the old ones or replace some of their functions but never all of their functions" (Colin Cherry, 1978, p. 17). The scholars highlight the enduring vitality of indigenous African media based on rich traditional and cultural communication experiences in Cameroon, Kenya, Nigeria, Botswana, Malawi, Namibia, and Zimbabwe. The diversity of subjects addressed include Ifa divinations, dances, town criers, opinion leaders, Yoruba language in sports communication, indigenous scientific and technology innovations, proverbs, traditional Igbo public relations (PR) practices, and so forth. The analysis of the diverse forms of communication unveils the intrinsic relevance of IACMS as means of communication among rural dwellers in many African countries. Collectively, the essays build a compelling case for the preservation and promotion of IACMS as integral in African ways of life.

It is an honor to celebrate IACMS in the digital age. IACMS reveal ways that African values and perspectives can build bridges of understanding communication across different global communication contexts. The African continent is a dynamic global market space where different actors are seeking different economic and development opportunities. Because of its vitality, scholars of African communication must focus on the relevance of IACMS to uphold African agency at the core of discourses about sustainable development in Africa (Mutua and Muneri, forthcoming). Toward this end, the scholars assembled here advocate for African governments to take proactive measures such as commissioning research initiatives to develop and preserve indigenous African media.

As we witness the ever-changing digital territory, the responsibility of African scholars is to heed Paulin Hountondji's argument about growing African knowledge which is "to develop first and foremost an Africa-based tradition of knowledge in all disciplines, a tradition where questions are initiated, and research agendas set out directly or indirectly by African societies themselves" (2009, p. 129). The authors in this book brilliantly underscore the imperative for African scholars to engage in research on various forms of indigenous communication. Such efforts not only deepen our understanding of communication systems and practices but also position Africa on the global map as a hub of diverse and dynamic communication systems.

OVERVIEW OF CHAPTERS

The chapters assembled give us a glimpse into areas that Prof. Des Wilson's scholarship directs attention on what African communication scholars are concerned about in the digital age. The broad themes that guide the organization of the three parts of the book respond to questions about the relevance, adaptation, coexistence, challenges, and opportunities in the digital age. The authors draw from diverse theoretical and methodological approaches in communication studies and mass communication to examine ways that indigenous media remain relevant in a technological dominated communication environment. Data collection methods included participant observation, content analysis, focus groups, and in-depth interviews. We must note that some of the interviews were anonymized to protect the identity of the respondents.

The first part highlights the importance of African indigenous communication and media systems. It includes three chapters that present perspectives about ways to preserve and promote the relevance of African indigenous media in the digital era. In chapter 1, Kehbuma Langmia sets the context for African communication research by outlining concerns about the dominance of Western media over African indigenous media in a digital age. Langmia advocates for an Afrocentric approach to integrate African indigenous media within the digital public space and as means to promote the relevance of indigenous media in the life of African people. Shirley Marang Kekana in chapter 2 highlights the same theme of preservation and longevity of African ways of life by examining the impact of digital technology on African indigenous media in Botswana. Specifically, Kekana argues that the significance of IACMS lies in its ability to preserve cultural heritage and promote social cohesion in Africa. In chapter 3, Muhammad Hamisu Sani and Paul Obi argue that IACMS still play a significant role in information dissemination and communication in the digital age. They juxtapose the African traditional communication and digital communications and highlight the dichotomies between rural and urban Nigeria, bringing to the fore the epistemic relevance of African traditional communication system in the age of hybridity.

Part two of the book consists of five chapters centered on the theme of adaptation and coexistence between African indigenous media and digital media in the digital age. The authors present a sophisticated understanding of ways that African indigenous media and digital media and technology work together and are not necessarily in opposition with each other.

Chapter 4 examines the role of IACMS in communicating Science, Technology, and Innovations (STIs) for development in Nigeria. Herbert Batta concludes that the impact of STIs in the areas of health, food security, education, communication, security, and environment in rural communities can be used to bridge the digital divide and promote a robust science culture among rural populations where IACMS are rampant. The science theme continues with an intellectually stimulating chapter on Ifa divination system and the internet. In chapter 5, Akinola Moses Owolabi, Bernice Oluwalaanu Sanusi, Oyinloye Oloyede, and Isaac Olajide Fadeyi articulate the physical and spiritual realms of being among Africans through communicative aspects of Ifa divination. The recommendation for collaborative research among scholars of indigenous communication, computer science, and philosophy promises to position the Ifa divination system as a platform addressing societal problems in the digital age.

In chapter 6, Ibitayo Samuel Popoola and Paul Agada argue that the penetration of the internet does not constitute a threat to the traditional media. Given the limited access to many Nigerians, and Africans in general, there is a tendency to use both digital media and IACMS. So far, all the chapters in this part seem to emphasize the fact that communication is meaningful when information communicated is accessible to its audiences. In chapter 7, Unwana Samuel Akpan, Chuka Onwumechili, Abayomi Bamidele Adisa, and Abigail Odozi Ogwezzy-Ndisika take the idea of accessibility to a different level in their study on the influence of African language media on BBC Yoruba Service sports headlines. Audience online engagement with sports news has transformed BBC Yoruba service sports headlines and raises questions about the influence of linguistic and cultural nuances in sports reporting.

The last chapter 8 in this part by Nnamdi Tobechukwu Ekeanyanwu, Henry Chibueze Ogaraku, and Aloysius Chukwuebuka Ifeanyichukwu illustrates how traditional African practices are not necessarily in opposition with contemporary digital culture. Using the case study of *Egbe Bere Ugo Bere* (Live and Let Live) Igbo traditional PR practice, the authors argue that this Igbo PR cultural practice has existed long before Western-oriented PR theory was introduced in Africa. Like other traditional forms of communication, some of which will be discussed in part three, they have survived by embracing the potentials and possibilities offered by the digital revolution.

Part three of this book comprises five chapters that showcase the enduring relevance of African indigenous communication systems in the digital age. The authors discuss how traditional forms of communication such as town criers, proverbs, traditional leaders, music, songs, and dance are used to communicate information geared at addressing societal problems such as the recent COVID-19 pandemic.

Chapter 9 examines the role of town criers in disseminating vital information in Kenya and Nigeria. The authors Shamilla Amulega, Unwana Samuel Akpan, and Eddah Mbula Mutua offer numerous examples of roles played by town criers for the well-being of society. The recommendation for future research focuses on harnessing efforts to sustain the relevance of traditional forms of communication—in this case, the town criers whose role has surpassed the "village newsman" to one who is multitasking multiple roles in the digital age.

In chapter 10, Ihuoma Okorie advances the idea of nurturing IACMS by discussing the role of proverbs in everyday communication among Africans. Okorie concludes that the enduring relevance of proverbs in African communication can be harnessed through movies to nurture future generations about the culture and values of African people. Chapter 11 discusses traditional opinion leadership which continues to flourish in rural communities in Nigeria. Iniobong Courage Nda opines that opinion leaders are key actors in rural communication and can be used alongside other modern communication channels to serve the information needs of the rural people.

The relevance of music in African communication is a subtheme discussed in the next three chapters. In chapter 12, Perminus Matiure describes how digitalization of musical and nonmusical indigenous media are being transformed and merged with modern technology to preserve African values in Malawi. Chapter 13 illustrates the role of digital technology in preserving musical arts in Zimbabwe. Richard Muranda, Absolom Mutavati, Khulekani F. Moyo, and Almon Moyo argue that the increased efforts to preserve musical arts aim to ensure continuity of African cultural practices and traditions.

Lastly, the enduring relevance of IACMS is illustrated in chapter 14, which, according to the author Jerry Rutsate, discusses the all-important question "Can the various African indigenous media systems be replaced by the new media in the digital age?" The conclusion is that traditional Malawian dances, the *Vimbuza* and the *Gule Wamkulu* (*magule*), are critical cultural institutions that disseminate messages about societal ethos, values, and beliefs ingrained in the local culture.

In expressing our gratitude, we extend heartfelt thanks to the authors whose contributions have enriched this book. Their dedication to unraveling the intricacies of indigenous African media ensures that Prof. Des Wilson's vision endures, fostering a deeper appreciation for the cohabitation of traditional communication within the ever-evolving digital age.

REFERENCES

Akpabio, E. I. (2021). *African communication systems and the digital age*. Routledge.

Akpan, U. S. (2023). Traditional African media: Looking back, looking forward. In U. S. Akpan (Ed.), *African media space and globalization* (pp. 3–51). Palgrave Macmillan. https://link.springer.com/chapter/10.1007/978-3-031-35060-3_1.

Cherry, C. (1978). *World communications; Threat or promise.* MIT Press.

Hall, E. T. (1959). *The silent language.* Random House.

Hountondji, P. (2009). Knowledge of Africa, knowledge by Africans: Two perspectives on African studies. *RCC Annual Review. A selection from the Portuguese journal Revista Critica de Ciencias Sociasis*, *1*(1). https://doi.org/10.4000/rccsar.174.

Mutua, E. M., Musa, B. A., & Okigbo, C. (2022). (Re) visiting African communication scholarship: Critical perspectives on research and theory. *Review of Communication*, *22*(1), 76–92.

Mutua, E. M., & Muneri C. T. (In Press). (Re)Theorizing communication and sustainable development from a postcolonial perspective: Centering African agency and decolonial practices in Kenya and Zimbabwe. To be published in a book commissioned with Michigan State University Press, for its "U.S.-China relations in the Age of Globalization" series (msupress.org/search-results-grid/?series=uschina-relations-in-the-age-of-globalization).

Piper, K. (2020). What Kenya can teach its neighbors—and the US—about improving the lives of the "unbanked". Future Perfect, Vox.

Wa Thiong'o, N. (1986). *Decolonising the mind: The politics of language in African literature.* James Currey; Heinemann Kenya.

Wilson, D. (1987). Traditional systems of communication in modern African development an analytical viewpoint. *Africa Media Review*, *1*(2), 89.

Wolff, E. (2021). The 'de-indigenization' of African languages. *Academia Letters*, Article 2702. https://doi.org/10.20935/AL2702.

Part I

IMPORTANCE OF AFRICAN INDIGENOUS COMMUNICATION AND MEDIA SYSTEMS

Chapter 1

Relevance of Des Wilson's African Indigenous Media Research Track in a Digitized Age

Kehbuma Langmia

In Africa, the youth like many others in the world are leashed to the foothold of digital modes of communications emanating mostly from the West at the detriment of their oral modes of communications. Instead of integrating traditional oral forms of communications within the platforms of these new forms of communication like emojifications, for instance, our media consumers have opted to get assimilated by the West. This tendency to welcome "the West" like many other tragic realities in Africa, our traditional forms have been relegated to the background for no good reason. The digital media deluge for interhuman communication has *almost eclipsed* the growth of indigenous media outlets on the continent of Africa. The race to embrace digital technology where Africa was, and will continue to be, sidelined by the global media conglomerates has raised more questions than answers in the minds of some Afrocentric media scholars (Mano & Milton, 2020; Langmia, 2016, 2021). We are prone to quickly jump on the superhighway and to display and brag about our command of the "colonialistic" languages (to borrow this expression from Jomo Kenyatta) and culture while casting aspersions to local African languages that use the indigenous media outlets as uncouth and primitive (Nyamnjoh, 2012).

Our brains unfortunately have been deliberately hard-wired with unbreakable metal strings from Euro-Americanistic traditions. We have, willy-nilly, provided the "West" with our minds to be seduced and captured by their shimmering modern material splendors at our own detriment. In short, we have remained "brain-washed" and "brain dry-cleaned" by the colonial and neocolonial practices as we so proudly display today on the various platforms of the digital media. Since language is the pathway or better still, the vehicle to the destination of all cultural facets on planet earth, the means to achieve competent and effective communications for all and sundry is to squeeze it well so as to enjoy the juice of our proud culture, custom, and traditions.

According to Kamwangamalu (2016) and Abraham (2020), unfortunately, some Africans since the advent of colonization have been cursed to uphold and worship foreign languages like English, French, Spanish, German, Portuguese, and so forth. They have continued to *vuvuzela* our oral traditions through the foreign media. This behavior, no doubt, has affected indigenous mediated communications because preference is placed on the doorstep of Westernization as the means to fulfilling "real" civilization. The African colonial master positioned himself after the 1884/1885 Berlin conference as the "big brother" of Africa whose wealth, treasures, and cultures can be raped and pillaged for the consuming appetites of the West. The West has made no apologies to Africa as they have continued to steal her treasures and wealth till date, and the indigenous media that should act like the agonized voice of the Africans in this case is not omnipresent on the digital communicative space. This paper has dwelled on the pros and cons of this vexing reality knowing fully well that the battle may indeed not be won today but the fight will continue far into the foreseeable future.

The African oral media (Odutola, 2021) that transmit the cultural practices like music, family traditions, customs, birth rites, funeral rites, traditional wedding ceremonies, enthronements, naming ceremonies, divinations, rituals, and rites of passage for Africans in Africa and abroad have been asphyxiated by the superimposition of social media. They are omnipresent through Western engineered platforms (Facebook, Twitter, now X, Snapchat, Instagram, YouTube, TikTok, Hulu, Pinterest, Reddit, LinkedIn, Twitch, Tumblr, WhatsApp, and Quora) meant to disseminate Westernized tastes through advertisement and emojifications. Our youths are excited and have filled their minds with pride to align themselves with the social media influencers and TikTok celebrities who have tended to display Americanisms, Eurocentricities, and Asiacentricity on these platforms on social media than with the African traditional oral media outlets. Other African-centric social media platforms that are germinating on the continent are barely being promoted by the African mainstream electronic and digital media sites on the web. They are Naijapals, Chomi, Ayoba, Lenali App, SoftTalk, and so forth. But studies have consistently shown that Africans populate Facebook and WhatsApp whose servers are in the United States than these Africa-centric ones owned and managed by Africans themselves. By this action, they have muddled the waters for the relevance and role that indigenous media play in the life of the people of Africa. Oral media ought to be integrated within the digital public atmosphere.

WESTERN DIGITAL SPACE

The space on electronic and digital media for radio, television, and now the internet have become the space where Western philosophies of the lifeworld are trumpeted. After independence, some radio and television stations on the continent of Africa began airing contents that purported to disseminate African cultures and value systems to the public. But it was a Herculean steep hill for them to climb because those trained journalists on the air had exclusive Western education (Gondwe, 2022) from the colonial administrations that had formed a strong foothold on the continent. Secondly, those countries like Ghana that got their independence in the early and mid-sixties were already cementing Western educational curricula in the primary, secondary, and all tertiary institutions in Africa. In fact, it became fashionable for the *nouveau riche* or the African elite who had been opportune to taste the fruits of Western education to impart and imbibe Western cultural traits on the African children in schools even though most of them had not traveled to Paris, London, Berlin, Brussels, Lisbon, or New York. They saw Western forms of civilization through the pages of the textbooks they were buying to study as the only road to African salvation. Consequently, the media's role from 1960 to 1980 and even the early years of the 1990 was to push down Western ideologies on the throats of the African students from primary school. African culture, customs, and traditions were still reeling from the damnation poured on them by the colonizers. Frantz Fanon would later refer to this experience by referring to the Africans who have been victimized by this as the *"Wretched of the earth"* in his book and his subsequent best seller, *"Black skin white mask."* It is as if the European sojourners were given the traveling tickets into the continent of Africa to empty it of both material and human resources from God almighty. It was after the naming of the countries in Africa by them and subsequent independence granted under duress for Africa and their admission into the United Nations that they could plant their embassies abroad for visa processing. These sojourners entered Africa illegally without visa permission from African leaders and so had the audacity to pillage the continent and rob it as they saw fit. So that has continued surreptitiously behind the scenes through the shadow heads of States of Africa who have continued to provide them with the blank checks to maintain constant presence in Africa. This is the reason why the electronic media and now the digital media have continued to fan their flames with respect to what they have called modernity and civilization. They started with the language. It was English, French, Portuguese, Spanish, and German in the majority of newspapers, radio, and television on the continent. The average African citizen living on the continent of Africa in the sixties, seventies, and eighties consumed Western contents from the media on African soil.

INDIGENOUS MEDIA'S ROLE

Growing up in Cameroon in the eighties and nineties before the dawn of the digital media, folktales were narrated on the electronic media like radio, local newspapers, and television. The radio had specific days and time for traditional languages that convey news about birth rites, death ceremonies, traditional doctors' practices, traditional weddings and knock-doors, rites of passage for the teenagers and circumcision ceremonies, and so forth. These were also carried out on specific columns in the local newspapers. Mostly on weekends, programs on television like "soir au village," "rythme traditionnelle du Nord," Griot's poetics and orature, and so forth (Ebine, 2019). Youth especially in the then traditional African setup were brought up to revere and abide by the exigencies of the traditional griots who are often seen as the guarantors of traditional culture and traditions. Teenagers and young people would gather in the village square under the tree mostly during the shining moonlit night and listen to fables, folktales, oral history, chivalry, and exploits of their forefathers. This was the sphere where the African value systems were cultivated and honed. It was during these times that oral narratives were given currency to be passed down from generation to generation. Guest speakers and presenters as well as traditional musicians demonstrated their skills by singing songs of hope, gallantry, and bravery of all sorts. African youths were also in the position to carry out wrestling matches to compete for power and influence in the land.

Des Wilson (1987) supports this view by stating that "the traditional system of communication is a continuous process of information dissemination, entertainment and education used in societies which have not been seriously dislocated by western culture" (89). This is the terrain for the preservation of African cultural and traditional value systems which would burgeon. Now with the advent of the internet and social media, the violent takeover of the African youth traditional cultural space has been baked. The youth are less interested in traditional mediated spheres like gathering under the moonlight for storytelling. This practice has been relegated to the rural settings where the semblance of African culture and tradition still struggle to survive. The indigenous African media plays the role of informing the public about the forthcoming "Yam" festival, the visit of a "foreign" emissary to the head of the village or the clan, and the role each group of people are called to play. With the superimposition of Western value systems on the soil of Africa, the foreign values transmitted to the continent through the digital communication platforms on handheld gadgets have created turbulence on the preservation of African culture.

CONCLUSION

A good number of Afrocentric communication theorists have softened their tone on the ongoing advocacy for Afrocentrism. The debate, similar to the ones regarding Pan-Africanism, is only palatable in the ears of some Africans and their colonial masters, if it is soothing, void of "violent" outbursts. As a result, when this discourse on Afrocentricity entered the African scholarship in the mid-1980s with the publication of Molefi Asante's *The Afrocentric Idea,* it was welcomed with skepticism. It was perceived by detractors, both Africans and non-Africans, as a rupture. It was seen as the radical decolonization and de-Westernization in which case non-Africans would be forced out of the continent of Africa. Today, it is fashionable to echo the sentiment of most Afrocentric scholars like Bruce Mutsvairo, Winston Mano, Levi Obonyo, and Wendy Wems that hybridity of Afrocentrism and Eurocentrism need each other for African digital media communicators and communicologists to be globally recognized. I have tended to share that view too only because of the amount of skepticism that my original stance on Afrocentricity had been received. We all need each other but Africans must not bend the spoon to feed the next generation of communication scholars by yielding to the trappings of Westernization of digital communication at the expense of African traditionally mediated forms. We risk losing African values and dignity in the not-too-distant future. To echo Des Wilson as already cited, the preservation of indigenous African oral media narratives as a form of inter-communicative system is the only way we will showcase Africa's media relevance in the age of Western-mediated onslaught.

REFERENCES

Abraham, G. Y. (2020). A post-colonial perspective on African education systems. *African Journal of Education and Practice, 6*(5), 40–54.

Ebine, S. A. (2019). The roles of griots in African oral tradition among the Manding. *International Journal of Research Development, 11*(1), 1–10.

Gondwe, G. (2022). African journalists at crossroads: Examining the impact of China, US, and the UK's short-journalism training programs offered to African journalists. *Journalism Studies, 23*(13), 1654–68.

Kamwangamalu, N. M. (Ed.). (2016). Why inherited colonial language ideologies persist in postcolonial Africa. In *Language policy and economics: The language question in Africa,* 125–55. Palgrave Macmillan.

Langmia, K. (2016). *Globalization and cyberculture: An afrocentric perspective.* Springer.

Langmia, K. (2021). *Black lives and digi-culturalism: An afrocentric perspective.* Rowman & Littlefield.

Mano, W., & Milton, V. C. (2020). *Routledge handbook of African media and communication studies*. Routledge.

Nyamnjoh, F. B. (2012). 'Potted plants in greenhouses': A critical reflection on the resilience of colonial education in Africa. *Journal of Asian and African Studies*, *47*(2), 129–54.

Odutola, K. (2021). Orality, media, and information technology. In A. Akinyemi & T. Falola (Eds.), *The Palgrave handbook of African oral traditions and folklore* (pp. 819–33). Springer.

Wilson, D. (1987). Traditional systems of communication in modern African development: An analytical viewpoint. *Africa Media Review*, *1*(2), 87–104.

Chapter 2

Examining the Impact of Digital Technology on African Indigenous Media in Botswana

A Potential Challenge to Sustainability/Longevity

Shirley Marang Kekana

Botswana like elsewhere in Africa boasts of natural, cultural, and linguistic diversity. The people engage with different forms of communication including modern and indigenous media. In the postcolonial era, there are efforts to restore cultures and traditions "erased" during the colonial era. African scholars are taking interest in ensuring the Africanization of different spheres of life including communication. Guided by the 2005 UNESCO *Convention on the Protection and Promotion of the Diversity of Cultural Expressions* established to safeguard diverse cultural expressions in different communities, nations, organizations, and individuals have committed to protect indigenous cultures. In Botswana, efforts to examine the impact of digital technology on indigenous media are to ensure their sustainability and longevity.

Indigenous media is a communication system used in a specific community, separate from mainstream media. These forms of media were transmitted from one generation to the next through oral traditions, hands-on experiences, apprenticeships, and ceremonies (Owiny et al., 2014). African indigenous communication: The definitions of indigenous media vary, but it can be described as oral traditional, informal, or folk media (Asemah et al., 2021; Chari, 2016). Indigenous media encompasses local knowledge that is unique to a given culture or society, including a wide range of forms, such as oral traditions, music, dance, storytelling, visual arts, dance, spirit possession, myths, legends, theater, folktales, sculpture, proverbs, rituals, shrines, architecture, and orators (Asemah et al., 2021; Mushengyesi, 2003; Owiny et al.,

2014). As the world becomes more connected, it is essential to examine the relevance of African indigenous media in this new era of digitization. This chapter therefore examines the influence of digital technology on African indigenous media. It seeks to respond to whether digital technology poses potential challenges to the sustainability and longevity of indigenous media.

THE IMPORTANCE OF INDIGENOUS MEDIA

The important role of African indigenous media lies in its ability to preserve cultural heritage and promote social cohesion. Before Western media arrived, Africans had their own ways of communication (Tshabangu & Salawu, 2022). Indigenous media serve various purposes, and their importance in society cannot be underestimated. According to Asemah et al. (2021), they provide education and teach traditional aesthetic, historical, technical, social, ethical, and religious values. The knowledge systems of indigenous Africans equip us with the necessary tools to think independently and break free from the constraints of the Northern Canon. This opens up the opportunity for Africans to tell their stories in their own language and from their unique perspective (Schoon et al., 2020). African indigenous media is a platform for the expression and transmission of culture. It also serves as a tool for building bridges between communities and promoting a sense of shared identity. Mushengyesi (2003) posits:

> Since culture shapes the environment within which a message is decoded, indigenous media forms such as very specific performances—dance, music, drama), drums and horns, village criers, orators and storytellers—continue to present themselves as effective channels for disseminating messages in predominantly rural societies where the population tends to be predominantly "orate"1 or "oral-ate" rather than "liter-ate." (p. 1080)

This means indigenous media forms still effectively spread messages in rural societies, where people understand the oral arts. Because culture shapes how messages are understood, these media forms continue to be important channels for communication.

THREATS THAT MAY AFFECT AFRICAN INDIGENOUS MEDIA SYSTEMS

In Botswana, oral historical accounts reveal that African indigenous media systems were criticized by colonial rulers, missionaries, and Eurocentric intellectuals as outdated and uncivilized. This led to the belief that African indigenous knowledge was inferior and not worth preserving, including cultural productions and institutions that held ordinary people's memories and were dismissed as superstition (Plockey, 2015; Zegeye & Vambe, 2006). There is a need to harness indigenous knowledge communications systems that have served the indigenous African people (Chari, 2016; Mushengyesi, 2003). Despite the increasing influence of digitalization in today's world, it is important to acknowledge that local indigenous knowledge communication systems still hold a significant amount of power and relevance. These traditional communication systems are deeply rooted in the culture and practices of the local people and have been passed down from generation to generation. They serve as a means of preserving and transmitting indigenous knowledge, beliefs, values, and customs. These communication systems not only provide a way for the local people to connect but also play a vital role in maintaining the identity and heritage of indigenous communities.

Advances in digitalization continue to cause a shift from traditional to technological ways of finding information, ideas, and knowledge. This movement enables access to information and knowledge sources through the internet and other digital streaming services (Chukwuere, 2017). However, many African countries face infrastructure limitations, particularly in rural areas where there are issues with technology and connectivity, as well as power cuts and load shedding. Poor internet access, low education levels, unemployment, and poverty may prevent African citizens from participating in the digital revolution (Mosime, 2015). Moreover, the digital revolution is mainly urban-based and dominated by the English language, which is not the first language for many Africans and may isolate some people, particularly those in rural areas. There are worries that the use of digital technology might displace numerous indigenous media systems in Africa. One of the views held about its use is the potential threat to indigenous media in popular culture and global languages which could result in conflicts with established local traditions and sometimes undermine cultural stability (Chisa & Hoskins, 2014). It has also raised concerns about the potential loss of cultural authenticity and the appropriation of indigenous media by outsiders (Owiny et al., 2014).

Some scholars argue that the world of social and digital media, as well as the internet in general, is often portrayed as universal and democratic. However, it is important to recognize that this world mirrors the colonial realm and its violent dynamics (Carlson & Mongibello, 2021). This includes the dominance of Western culture, the disregard for traditional cultures, the inequality of treatment toward Africans, and the portrayal of the Western world as the sole source of knowledge. Schoon et al. (2020) emphasize that it is important to ensure that no particular region or intellectual hegemony monopolizes the spread of these ideas. In the context of Africa, Maikabi et al. (2019) suggest that the continent should combine its indigenous value system with the good legacies it has left behind to create a synthesis that can benefit the continent as a whole. This synthesis could harness the potential of Africa and contribute to its economic, social, and cultural development. Digitalization enables the preservation of indigenous knowledge and oral traditions and can help undo the cultural violence of colonialism. This will enable marginalized languages, cultures, and identities to be mainstreamed, therefore, decentering African knowledge systems and fostering the decolonization of the mind (wa Thiong'o, 1986).

The digital age has exposed various threats and challenges to African indigenous media. One of the primary components of this media system is African languages. These languages have historically been used to communicate initiatives and developments in open traditional squares. This communication method involved everyone voicing their opinions in their own languages, making it an inclusive and locally based form of communication. However, with the emergence of mainstream media, access to the internet or other mainstream technologies is limited in many rural areas. This limitation excludes many people from receiving messages that could benefit them. Even those with access to mainstream communication channels face the challenge of language barrier as most news is communicated in English, which is not their mother tongue (Jeremiah, 2015). Additionally, conversations on digital platforms such as Facebook, X, WhatsApp, and others are primarily conducted in English, further marginalizing African languages and pushing them to a lower status. Consequently, most African children and youth, especially those living in urban areas, cannot speak their African languages. In many African schools, African languages have been de-indigenized (Wolff, 2021). Instead, students are taught using foreign languages. Upon entering many primary and secondary schools in Botswana, it is hard to miss the notice board with bold letters reading "English speaking zone."

One potential danger to indigenous media is the threat to performing and visual arts. African musicians have historically used indigenous music to communicate various messages. Music plays a crucial role in preserving and transmitting cultural heritage, and it is a highly valued form of cultural expression (Raditloaneng, 2007). Indigenous songs serve as a means of social communication (Mulaudzi, 2014). Traditional African cultures used songs, poetry, and archaic musical arts and theater to store historical records (Nzewi, 1999). Wood's (1985) postulation on Botswana music suggests this as well:

> It became evident to me how much music is an intrinsic part of the lives of these peoples, from infancy to old age. They have songs for every occasion, subject, and age level: lullabies; songs for play, initiation, occupations, hunting, war, mourning, prayer, and weddings; songs about rain, animals and birds, and moods; narrative songs; and songs of thanksgiving and praise. The songs about

occupations are of a large variety. The texts for example, of ploughing, sowing, threshing, winnowing, pounding, milking, caring for the cattle, beer-brewing, and even chasing from the grain fields. The initiation songs were especially fascinating to me. They carried messages for the adolescent, through the use of metaphor, about the proper behavior expected of young adults. (p. 19)

In summary, this nation boasts a diverse musical tradition that encompasses all phases of life, and they have a range of songs for various occasions.

In the past, some missionaries prohibited the use of indigenous music and musical instruments in Africa, causing a decline in interest in African traditions and cultural practices (Ayantayo, 2010). African songs were gradually replaced by Western ones, leading to the Westernization of the music scene in Africa. The use of Western musical instruments became more prevalent than the traditional African ones, causing a loss of cultural heritage. This loss included songs, proverbs, and taboos that were significant for regulating good behavior (Asemah et al., 2021). Nowadays, many artists have chosen to embrace digital technology, leading to a decrease in the use of indigenous musical instruments.

For many indigenous peoples, storytelling is a fundamental cultural practice that involves narratives passed down through generations (Beltrán & Begun, 2014; Mushengyesi, 2003). In African tradition, oral stories, such as poems and tales, were historically shared under the moonlight during evening gatherings. This served as a significant time for the older generation to transmit stories, myths, legends, and oral traditions to the younger generation. However, the advent of television series, internet games, and other digital technologies has led to a decline in the practice, resulting in African children and their parents missing out on the valuable lessons that these stories conveyed.

Additionally, indigenous media encompasses various forms of art, including theater and visual arts. Historically, locals gathered at different locations to perform various rituals and celebrations, frequently involving dance, theater, and visual arts. Ritual theater, a form of active participation, served as a means of conveying information related to significant life changes. A popular form of collective participation is African dance. Mulaudzi (2014) notes that indigenous people use communal dance to express their participation ethos, which is important for their enjoyment and aesthetic satisfaction, and by dancing together, they show their commitment to being involved and engaged in their community. It is crucial to preserve African cultural heritage by continuing to pass on oral traditions and engaging in the various forms of art that constitute indigenous media. By doing so, we not only keep the culture alive but also ensure that valuable lessons are transmitted to future generations (Mushengyezi, 2003). This is a valuable practice that must not be lost.

THE ADVANTAGES OF ADOPTING DIGITAL
TECHNOLOGY

In today's world, digital technology has become a crucial enabler of globalization and internationalization. As Bolat (2019) aptly notes, technological transformations have played an essential role in creating opportunities for interactions and information sharing that are not limited by geographical, institutional, or cultural boundaries. At the same time, the rise of digital technology has created fear and at the same time paved the way for the wider circulation of African indigenous media, thus benefiting African traditional knowledge systems. In this section, we illustrate the advantages of adopting digital technology to preserve African indigenous knowledge.

Firstly, digital technology allows for the archiving and documenting of indigenous knowledge systems traditionally passed down through oral traditions. By digitizing this knowledge, it can be processed, transmitted, and documented more efficiently, ensuring that future generations have access to it. According to Zhozhikov (2022), this means traditional local knowledge will be preserved on digital media, allowing people from all over the world to access and learn about it at any time. This can play a crucial role in making African indigenous knowledge more widely available and enhancing its integration with modern scientific and technical knowledge.

The evolution of digital technology has transformed the way we acquire information. Digitalization has made it easier to access vast quantities of content effortlessly. According to Raseroka (2008), it is essential to use digital tools to capture and conserve indigenous knowledge normally transmitted orally. This process of digitization not only helps preserve valuable cultural practices and traditions but also makes them available beyond person-to-person communication. Moreover, Akpojivi (2019) emphasizes the importance of digital technology in providing information access to rural areas often marginalized due to inadequate resources that were previously neglected. This enhanced accessibility can lead to a better-informed population and a more equitable society. The digital world has further opened up new opportunities for indigenous online resistance through various digital channels like networking, blogs, educational apps, and social media. These platforms can also be utilized to revitalize ancestral languages and cultures (Carlson & Mongibello, 2021).

One area where digital platforms have proven to be particularly effective is in storytelling. Podcasts, in particular, have emerged as a popular and powerful medium for sharing narratives that would otherwise go unheard. In Africa, indigenous language podcasters have taken advantage of this platform to tell stories in their own languages, bringing attention to stories and perspectives that have been ignored or silenced by mainstream media. For instance, according to Nkoala (2023) and Royston (2021), African indigenous language podcasters have been using their podcasts to tell stories that are socioculturally relevant in their own languages, allowing them to express themselves in ways that resonate with their listeners. By doing so, they are not only preserving their indigenous languages and cultures but also bringing attention to narratives that have been overlooked or marginalized. Furthermore, this approach can help African indigenous knowledge gain international recognition and bring it to the forefront of global conversations (Lee & Falahat, 2019). By leveraging digital platforms like podcasts, African indigenous language podcasters have the opportunity to share their perspectives with a global audience, raising awareness about their cultures, traditions, and knowledge systems and contributing to a more diverse and inclusive global discourse.

The utilization of digital technologies can offer considerable advantages for preserving, promoting, and strengthening language and culture. Digital tools, such as networking, blogs, educational apps, and social media platforms, can function as effective means to share cultural artifacts, such as videos, photos, and speeches, thereby supporting and sustaining the culture. Furthermore, digital spaces, such as Facebook or WhatsApp, provide an opportunity for individuals to connect with others, promoting a sense of belonging to groups or communities. This can further facilitate the translation of indigenous social events or struggles to digital spaces, providing a wider audience and increased exposure.

A noteworthy example of indigenous media forms that still effectively spread messages in rural societies is music, which is an important channel of communication. The digitization of music allows indigenous music to be archived and documented and to be told by the originators of the music. Moreover, digitized music exposes such music to be analyzed by online users on platforms such as Facebook, YouTube, and blogs. Additionally, adopting digital technologies creates a platform for cross-border collaboration, allowing oral artists to showcase their talent and products. This enables internationalization, a better understanding of indigenous cultures, and the creation of new partnerships. Digital technologies have the potential to facilitate the decolonization of the mind, as wa Thiong'o (1986) suggests. By placing African indigenous forms of communication at the center, rather than as an appendix of other countries, a perspective that takes into account African realities can be created.

CONCLUSION

The communication systems utilized by indigenous communities represent a rich embodiment of African culture. These systems wield a comparable level of influence to modern mass media and persist in impacting the lives of Africans even in the present day (Ayantayo, 2010). In order to preserve and promote African indigenous media, it is vital to establish policies and strategies that support it and safeguard indigenous intellectual property rights. This will guarantee that indigenous media within Africa can continue to flourish and remain enduring. African indigenous media contribute a distinctive perspective to shaping the culture, identity, and history of the continent. By acknowledging its significance and providing support, we can foster diversity and inclusivity within the media landscape and give a platform for local talent and voices to be heard. Therefore, supporting indigenous media and protecting its intellectual property rights is essential to Africa's progress and ensuring that it retains its pivotal role in the digital era. Wilson (2023) asserts that human communication is goal-oriented, and we should utilize every means possible to make it more effective. He further explains that when we embrace technology, we must consider the role of African communication systems in defining our target audience. This will help us determine the best instrument, device, or media to use for each communication objective.

REFERENCES

Akpojivi, U. (2019). Grassroots media and social media adaptation: Case study of Urhobo today. In A. Salawu (Ed.), *African language digital media and communication* (pp. 97–100). Routledge.

Asemah, E. S., Kente, J. S., & Nkwam-Uwaoma, A. O. (2021). *Handbook on African communication systems*. Jos University Press.

Ayantayo, J. K. (2010). The ethical dimension of African indigenous communication systems: An analysis. *Topical Issues in Communication Arts & Sciences, 1, 34–54.*

Beltrán, R., & Begun, S. (2014). 'It is medicine' Narratives of healing from the Aotearoa digital storytelling as indigenous media project (ADSIMP). *Psychology and Developing Societies, 26*(2), 155–79.

Bolat, E. (2019). The African new media digital revolution: Some selected cases from Nigeria. In N. D. Taura, E. Bolat, & N. O. Madichie (Eds.), *Digital entrepreneurship in sub-saharan Africa: Challenges, opportunities and prospects* (pp. 67–87). Palgrave Macmillan.

Carlson, B., & Mongibello, A. (2021). Indigenous resistance in the digital age. *Anglistica AION: An Interdisciplinary Journal, 25*(1), 1–8.

Chari, T. (2016). Rethinking climate change communication strategies in Africa: The case for indigenous media. *Indilinga African Journal of Indigenous Knowledge Systems, 15*(2), 217–32.

Chisa, K., & Hoskins, R. (2014). The effects of information and communication technologies on indigenous communities in South Africa: A library and information science perspective. *Mousaion, 32*(3), 49–68.

Chukwuere, J. (2017). From decolonization to digitalization of education in South Africa. *International Journal of Sciences and Research, 73*(12/1), 232–41.

Hunter, J. (2005). The role of information technologies in indigenous knowledge management. *Australian Academic & Research Libraries, 36*(2), 109–24. https://doi.org/10.1080/00048623.2005.10721252.

Jeremiah, K. (2015). Promoting language and cultural diversity through the mass media: Views of students at the University of Botswana. *European Journal of Social Science Education and Research, 2*(4), 447–58. https://doi.org/10.26417/ejser.v5i1.p496-507.

Lee, Y. Y., & Falahat, M. (2019). The impact of digitalization and resources on gaining competitive advantage in international markets: Mediating role of marketing, innovation and learning capabilities. *Technology Innovation Management Review, 9*(11), 45–65.

Maikaba, B., & Msughter, A. E. (2019). Digital media and cultural globalization: The fate of the African value system. *Humanities and Social Sciences. Special Issue, 7*(6), 220–26.

Mosime, S. T. (2015). Media control, colonialism and the making of an authoritarian postcolonial African state: The case of Botswana. *African Journalism Studies, 36*(2), 45–58. https://doi.org/10.1080/23743670.2015.1043691.

Mulaudzi, P. A. (2014). The communication from within: The role of indigenous songs among some southern African communities. *Muziki, 11*(1), 90–98. https://doi.org/10.1080/18125980.2014.893100

Mushengyezi, A. (2003). Rethinking indigenous media: Rituals, 'talking' drums and orality as forms of public communication in Uganda. *Journal of African Cultural Studies, 16*(1), 107–17.

Nkoala, S. (2023). How radio influences indigenous language podcasts in South Africa: A case study of Epokothweni and iLukuluku. *Journalism, 0*(0). https://doi.org/10.1177/14648849231214054.

Nzewi, M. (1999). Strategies for music education in Africa: Towards a meaningful progression from tradition to modern. *International Journal of Music Education, (1),* 72–87.

Owiny, S. A., Mehta, K., & Maretzki, A. N. (2014). The use of social media technologies to create, preserve, and disseminate indigenous knowledge and skills to communities in East Africa. *International Journal of Communication, 8,* 234–47.

Plockey, F. D. D. (2015). Indigenous knowledge production, digital media and academic libraries in Ghana. *Journal of Pan African Studies, 8*(4), 32–44.

Raditloaneng, W. P. (2007). Protection and promotion of local music: A talent that educates, entertains and binds. In I. Mazonde & P. Thomas (Ed.), *Indigenous knowledge systems and intellectual property in the twenty-first century, perspectives from Southern Africa* (pp. 115–22). Council for the Development of Social Science Research in Africa (CODESRIA).

Raseroka, K. (2008). Information transformation Africa: Indigenous knowledge— Securing space in the knowledge society. *The International Information & Library Review, 40*(4), 243–50.

Royston, R. A. (2021). Podcasts and new orality in the African mediascape. *New Media & Society, 25*(9), 1–20.

Schoon, A., Mabweazara, H. M., Bosch, T., & Dugmore, H. (2020). Decolonizing digital media research methods: Positioning African digital experiences as epistemic sites of knowledge production. *African Journalism Studies, 41*(4), 1–15. https://doi.org/10.1080/23743670.2020.1865645.

Tshabangu, T., & Salawu, A. (2022). Indigenous-language media research in Africa: Gains, losses, towards a new research agenda. *African Journalism Studies, 43*(1), 1–16.

wa Thiong'o, N. (1986). *Decolonizing the mind: The politics of language in African literature*. Heinemann.

Wilson, D. (2023). Relevance of Nigerian traditional communication systems in the digital space. In U. S. Akpan (Ed.), *Nigerian Media Industries in the Era of Globalization*, (p. 213). Rowman & Littlefield.

Wolff, E. (2021). The 'de-indigenization' of African languages. *Academia Letters, 2702*. https://doi.org/10.20935/AL2702.

Wood, E. N. (1985). Traditional music in Botswana. *The Black Perspective in Music, 13*(1), 13–30.

Zegeye, A., & Vambe, M. (2006). African indigenous knowledge systems. *Review (Fernand Braudel Center), 29*(4), 329–58.

Zhozhikov, A. V. (2022). Digitalization of the cultural heritage of the indigenous peoples of the arctic. In I. Savchenko (Ed.), *European Proceedings of Social and Behavioural Sciences* (pp. 947–56). European Publisher.

Chapter 3

African Traditional Communication System in the Age of Hybridity

Habitual Media Customs and the Digital in the Nigerian Glocal Spaces

Muhammad Hamisu Sani and Paul Obi

The postmodernist extrapolation of African traditional communication system as mundane, rural, and rustic and the functions of these indigenous and precolonial forms of mediated communication have continued to elicit divergent scholarly debates about their adaptability in today's digital age, media hybridity, and *"platformization"* (Dijck et al., 2018). A common denominator of such scholarly exploration about African traditional and indigenous communication systems imbibes the tendency of underestimation and even negation of the imperative of such forms of communication. This negation of the critical role of the African traditional communication system is without recourse to the media compass it provides in contemporary times, that is, in inducing cultural aesthetics and creativity in African life.

Still, an appraisal of African traditional communication systems within the Nigerian context indicates multiple layers of the functions of media and communication including education, entertainment, communication, and messaging of sociocultural norms. A key aspect of African traditional media systems lies in their adaptability to digital technologies in the face of media hybridity. However, the underlying scholarly outlook of some of these African traditional communication models tend to downplay their role in the era or age of digital technologies and media hybridity across society. Despite the seeming threat of modern technology and the global communication ecosystem to traditional media, empirical evidence reveals their continued use in rural Africa. Empirical contextualization of their application mostly in rural Africa shows their functionality and continuity as well. Aziken and Emeni (2010) argue that beyond the categorization of African traditional communication systems as pristine and primeval, they also fulfill the fundamental informational needs of rural African citizenry within the public sphere.

By African traditional communication system, we imply habitual and customary gadgets, instruments, and channels of indigenous communications operational in precolonial Africa that still function in today's modern world. These include Town Crier, Wooden Gun, Gong, Talking Drum, and Kakaaki, among others. Scholars like Ugboajah (1979) viewed African traditional communication as oral media—*oramedia*. On the other hand, Nwuneli (1981) stipulated that traditional communication within the African prism is more of folk media. According to Ojebode (2012), scholarly interrogation of African traditional communication systems tends to render divergent and uncoordinated appropriation of what constitutes or defines African traditional communication systems. Ojebode (2012) further held that to be classified traditional or indigenous, such African communication systems must be traced to ancient origins within some territorial, linguistic, and cultural milieu. Wilson (2008) observed that though African traditional communication research suffers from what he tagged as modernization crisis, it interacts with structures of authority and power relations, religious cults, African cosmology, and the circle of life. Furthermore, Wilson (2023) maintained that it is futile to condition or situate the African traditional communication system as immaterial, given that the functionality and applicability of these instruments and channels of communication in Africa have never ceased. Wilson (2023) added that in ethnocommunication studies, these channels of African traditional communication not only determine the character and functionality of traditional and habitual African media ecology but also enhance human communication across board. This enhancement, that is, the criss-crossing and intersecting forms of modern communication technology, tends to downplay the usage and applicability of such traditional African communication channels and systems to the African rural cosmos mostly in modernization studies (Cooper, 2001). Mushengyezi (2010) further asserts that the deployment of Western communication models by African states and their foreign partners to rural African environments remain ineffectual due to misgivings in conceptual and contextual specificities of rural epistemologies and traditional and cultural dialectics. Thus, scholarly approaches on African traditional communication systems must recognize this gap and acknowledge the factors that keep shadow indigenous communication models functional in the digital age.

In recent times, the concerns about the relevance and positionality of African traditional communication systems stemmed from the pervasive and ubiquitous nature of digital technologies, social media platforms, and cases of media hybridity around the continent. The question then arises: Does digitization and digital platforms connote the end of the traditional African communication system? Nwammou (2011) in her theorization of mediamorphosis—a phenomenon that enables old media forms to morph and mutate, adapting into new forms of innovation raised the above poser, contending that African media systems have the capacity to not only adapt but also coexist with the new digital media technologies in the long run. In such instances, some of the sounds, totems, and communicational effects associated with traditional African media systems also significantly converged in the digital space—re-enacting and projecting the convergence of two publics (Ekeh, 1975). While this has become apparent within the communication prism, it also points to the crisis of the African identity as expounded by Ekeh's (1975) theory of two publics in postmodern African states—between Eurocentric and African hegemony. According to Ekeh (1975), Africans in today's digital age must contend with either the modern digital age or the traditional communication systems. This is especially the case for rural Africans who have both access and exposure to both digital technologies and are also exposed to traditional media systems.

This chapter argues that, notwithstanding the growing African youth and urban population's embrace of digital technologies, the African traditional communication system still plays a significant role in information dissemination and communication in the digital age particularly in the rural areas. Given this salient role, we therefore juxtapose the African traditional communication and digital communications and highlight the dichotomies between rural and urban Nigeria, bringing to the fore the epistemic relevance of African traditional communication system in the age of hybridity. We displayed this, by showcasing the degree to which both African traditional communication and digital communication technologies now converge in a glocal sense. This task has become critical in advancing scholarly contributions to indigenous and habitual customs within the African media ecology in general and Nigerian glocal spaces in particular. The chapter flows, first, by highlighting the typologies and definitional terms, followed by expounding African traditional media systems, primarily focusing on Nigerian habitual media customs, enumerating types of traditional African media gadgets, including an empirical x-ray of African traditional media publics, and summarizing the chapter with a conclusion.

TYPOLOGY AND DEFINITIONAL HIGHLIGHTS

The chapter relies on some salient typologies in order to make sense of the conditions upon which African traditional media systems remain significant in the contemporary African cosmos and glocal spaces around the world. This has become compelling considering that scholars like Ndlela (2009) have raised concerns about the entrapment of African media researchers' overt concentration on external and Western paradigms in media and communication studies. He further called for some level of extrication in research goals centered on African media and communication systems.

More significantly, it is in that line of thought that Meribe (2015) also examined the interrelationship between rural people and Indigenous African Communication Systems (IACS) in Africa, specifically Nigeria, in view of their models of information dissemination and mobilization, including their sustainability in the digital age. This functionality of the African traditional media systems flows with some critical hegemonic culture that typified the African traditions. Some of these functions of African traditional communications are often calibrated through *habitual customs*; shaped by the age of *hybridity*; re-enacted in the *glocal spaces*; and sustained by the *epistemic relevance* they fostered in African traditional media and communication research and studies.

By *habitual customs*, the existential and continual behavior of a people that is traditionally inclined is implied. For *glocal spaces*—it signifies the convergence of the global on the one hand and the local, traditional, and indigenous on the other hand through the effects of globalization (Ezumah, 2019; Omotoso, 2020; Uzuegbunam, 2020). However, *hybridity* connotes the intermingling, intersection, and diffusion of different media, technological, and cultural forms leading to disruptions in our sociocultural society (Kraidy, 2006; Chadwick, 2017). *Epistemic relevance* in turn, and within the context of this volume—centered on African traditional media systems stemmed from the collation of knowledge, particularly on African traditional media systems for purposes of sustainability for the projection of the continent's media customs not as disobedience to Western epistemologies as Moyo and Mutsvairo (2018) pointed out, but as a source of knowledge production in pushing for continuity of IACS, including research therefrom.

EXPOUNDING AFRICAN TRADITIONAL COMMUNICATION: THE NIGERIAN HABITUAL MEDIA CUSTOMS

In expounding African traditional communication, the chapter only examines the habitual media customs in Nigeria and how they represent the continuity of media traditions and their implications in the age of technological hybridity. Hence, the chapter explores the question—to what degree is the African traditional media system still relevant and what level of convergence has ensued? By focusing on precolonial African media traditions and instrumentalization of contemporary digital culture, the chapter underscores the issues of dispatches and continuity with the African media and communication studies paradigm. This is relevant because the study of traditional media systems must center perspectives on African epistemology and ontology to understand their importance in society. The commitment to African perspectives reinforces Akpan's (2023) position of approaching African traditional communication systems away from Western epistemological lenses, as African traditional communication spaces are highly institutionalized and structured. By institutionalization and structural, we mean the extent to which African traditional media systems are still officially deployed within the social cosmos of Africans. Therefore, the essence is that they may or may not yield themselves holistically to Western or Anglo-European epistemic scholarship.

It is in the context of focusing on African traditional media epistemologies that this chapter highlights the African traditional communication systems in terms of their usage, functionality, and adaptability in the digital age. First, the Nigerian media spaces can be categorized as glocal with the intersection of the rural and modern mediated spaces. Here, through digital affordances, urban citizenry can as well connect with traditional modes of communication through visuals, while the rural folks in Nigerian villages and communities also have access to digital technologies in which there is an interface with modernity. Additionally, due to the prevailing media hybridity, the consumption of media and communication services to some extent is becoming intertwined, where both the urban and rural intersect on digital spaces. Flowing from these interactions like an urban citizen in Abuja or Lagos and a rural dweller watching Nollywood movies on an Android phone, Barber (2009: 3) talked about old African mediated oral genres being "recast into new performance spaces." Barber's (2009) theorization here implies the recasting of African cultural milieu in new performatory platforms like digital technologies such as social media and supersonic digital phones, among other platforms.

Because of the nature of the traditional African media systems, where there is lack of contestation, unlike modern media spaces, it does not encounter the shrinking of media or civic spaces (Onochie et al., 2023), as access to information dissemination might be ubiquitous. In the traditional media systems, information might not be sought after, but could come to one by just being a passerby or when the town crier moves around the village to disseminate information. Within the Nigerian context of African traditional communication systems and habitual media practices, we focus on African traditional communication systems to illustrate their functionality, adaptability, and mediated functions across cultures and societies. They include Talking Drum, Wooden Gong, Kakaaki, and the Bell: these four have been chosen because of the continued cases of usage, accessibility, and spread as well.

Talking Drums

The Talking Drum is an African traditional communication instrument used in villages and rural settlements across Africa. It plays a variety of communicative roles across the board. In Nigeria for example, the Talking Drum is used among several tribes including Hausa, Igbo, Yoruba, Efik, Ibibio, Tiv, Ijaw, Boki, Jukun, Birom, Igala, and Idoma, among others. It is made up of animal hide skin like goat or cow, wood, leather, and some also carry beads on it. It comes along with a small stick hung on the left-hand side, while the player uses his right hand to hit the leather part, producing different sounds according to the frequency. The most effective usage of the talking drum in communication is for *mobilization*. According to Ushe (2015), the talking drum is also used for various communicative acts including notification, alertness, and entertainment for people and guests in royal palaces and ceremonies, as well as for praise-singing and even curses.

Wooden Gong

The Wooden Gong is a rectangular wooden object carved out of wood with hollow holes in the outermost surface, where an instrumentalist or a town crier uses two sticks to play, echoing different sounds with varying communicative implications. In most traditional Nigerian societies or settings, the wooden gong, particularly of the big size besides entertainment, is also used to communicate critical and strategic messages especially in times of war, conflicts, crisis, or any other issue of great importance. In most instances, the sound of the wooden gong as conjured by the traditional artist may signal some sense of summoning of men, elders, and the traditional council to the village square for an important gathering. For the Igbos of Eastern Nigeria, the wooden gong is known as *Ekwe*; in Yoruba, it is called *Ibon igi la*; and for the Boki people in South South Nigeria, it is known as *Kiru*. The effect and impact of the Wooden Gong in African communication has the potential of reaching out to what some scholars called heterogenous and anonymous audiences (Nnaemedo, 2018; Baber, 2011), like the sound of a wooden gong spreading to neighboring communities, farmers in their farmlands, and even passersby and other pedestrians.

Kakaaki

Kakaaki is a long metal trumpet used mostly by the Hausa communities in Northern Nigeria. It is often deployed for communication and royalty purposes. It is mostly used in palaces of an Emir or the Sultan of Sokoto during important traditional ceremonies. Kakaaki also signals not just royalty and kingship but also connotes authority and hierarchical power. Scholars like

Gourlay (1982) have researched and explored its communicative affordances and importance in the mediated spaces, royal places, and spaces of Northern Nigeria.

Bell

The bell is another metal object that forms one of African traditional communication instruments. It is used by the town crier to communicate some important information like mobilization, alert, and notification. Women also use the bell during gatherings and most often at burials. When the bell is used for burial, only a woman can handle it. In Yorubaland, the bell is known as Agogo la; for the Igbos it is called *Mgbirimbga*; and for Boki people, it is known as *Egbang*. It can also be used by a native doctor, traditional talisman, and African traditional worshippers for the invocation of spirits, incantations for deity, and cultural sacrifice—whereby, they communicate various messages.

In appraising the above four models of African traditional communication instruments or systems, the list did exhaust all the other forms of media in the traditional settings like village square, age group meeting, and village shrine, among others. Our focus on these four models is to rethink the conversation and reset the debate on the practices and praxis of African indigenous media in the midst of digital technologies and hybridity. We believe that in their practicality, these African indigenous media forms are still operating in rural settings and villages. Their epistemological implications are diverse. Often the users converge in normative, hybrid, and digital media platforms. Added to that, the African traditional communication system now embraces different types of mediated publics and audiences as well, as elucidated in the section below.

AFRICAN TRADITIONAL MEDIA PUBLICS: AN EPISTEMIC X-RAY

In understanding habitual media customs in the digital age, we rationalized the manner in which these traditional African media customs are enacted or established across a broad spectrum of the traditional mediated publics. Here, we argued that the African traditional communication system is no longer restrictive to rural areas but now pervades several layers of the media sphere as both the primordial and modern converged—both offline and online. Okigbo (2004) further stressed that African cultures often struggle between these pristine and contemporary civic cultures. This is not to say that the visibility of some of these African traditional communication systems carry out some performatory functions in those media spaces. What this means is that their locations and visibility have now elapsed the performatory landscape that was restricted to rural Africa in years past. Due to growing urbanization and digitization, these African traditional communication systems are now visible to larger publics.

In that sense, a Hausa teenager born in Lagos metropolis who has never visited Kano, his home state, can witness the impact of *Kakaaki* on social media platforms—Facebook, WhatsApp, YouTube, Instagram, and TikTok. Same with a young Boki boy, who has never had any contact with his Boki heritage in Cross River State, who can be exposed to African traditional communication systems like a Talking Drum, Wooden Drum, and Bell within the digital space. Thus, these intersections between African traditional communication systems and digital space tend to create diverse media audiences—with a high degree of convergence. Yeku (2022) in exploring cultural productions in the digital world termed this phenomenon as cultural netizenship. Overtime, this trend has overall propped up different scholarly ideological contestations on how to conceptualize African traditional communication systems. For instance, in interrogating African publics in the digital age, Srivinasan et al. (2018) observed that these contestations invariably reignite a revisitation to the question and scholarly lens of African publics with new potency and less normative fixation on both tradition and modernity.

Hence, essential to the African traditional communication epistemological path in today's digital world is the convergence of the indigenous and digital forms of communication within the realm of visibility and publics. This being the case however, the performatory activity of the African traditional communication system and its dominant publics still reside in rural Africa, as opposed to urban and metropolitan enclaves. Contextualizing the normative mediated publics and the digital has resulted in divergent views. In the study of everyday African media culture, Wendy and Winston (2017, p. 9) argued that beyond the debate on whether scholarly approaches to media audience—publics should be media-centric or society-centric, there is the exigency of de-emphasizing such dichotomies on whether an audience is "passive or hyperactive." For this study, the instrumentality of the African traditional communication system is more paramount even though an understanding of the public is also imminent. The crux of our argument here is that while African traditional communication systems and habitual media customs are still residual in the rural media ecosystem, the mediated publics for these indigenous communication models tend to converge in the digital space as well. We therefore submit that the convergence of African traditional communication systems, mediated publics, and digital technologies is an outcome of the swiftly changing media hybridity in a diffused world.

CONCLUSION

The chapter appraises African traditional communication systems and the imperative of encountering such scholarly evaluation in an age of the *"buzzi-fication,"* which is typically the digital age. We set out by contextualizing different segments of African traditional and indigenous communication models, how they are conceptualized, narrativized, and mediatized both in functionality and performatory aesthetics. Rising from the above epistemic crest, we proclaim that African traditional media and communication audiences and publics have shifted from the normative rural and village settings, village square, burial ceremonies, and cultural gatherings to the digital spaces in an age of digitization. The study exemplified this phenomenon by showing how Nigerian digital and online citizens now access African traditional communication systems within the Nigerian glocal spaces and digital platforms like Facebook, X (Twitter), Instagram, WhatsApp, and so forth.

Buttressed by relevant examples, the chapter lends support to the debate about the significance of African indigenous media even in the digital age. It amplifies the varying instruments and channels; stages; audiences and publics; and agents and actors that shape contemporary African traditional communication systems in the age of digitization and *"platformization."* We therefore believe that indigenous media systems like Talking Drum, Wooden Gong, Bell, Kakaaki, and so forth, still have their relevance in modern African cosmos in the midst of convergence of media systems and hybridity. It is our candid and humble conviction that through this convergence and adaptability, African indigenous media systems would not fizzle out in the nearest future. As such traditional media norms are passed through from one generation to another, their sustainability and continuity are somehow guaranteed in a way. This chapter weaved together relevant conceptual approaches to understand the functions of African traditional communication systems in the digital age.

Overall, the chapter adds a voice to the different strands of communication studies on African indigenous media in today's *digital space* and the intersecting cultural convergence at play. This study therefore implores further scholarship on African traditional and indigenous media and communication studies to go beyond the idiosyncrasy and marginality of decoloniality to portraying prisms of functionality and adaptability associated with the traditional media systems. In the long run, we recognize that scholarly extrapolation on African traditional media and its continuity is strengthened by its ceaseless functionality and adaptability opening up to new media publics as a source of dependency and reliability. On that score, we conclude that African traditional communication systems and Nigerian habitual media customs have the longevity to flourish even in the digital age.

28 Muhammad Hamisu Sani and Paul Obi

REFERENCES

Akpan, U. S. (2023). African traditional media: Looking back, looking forward. In U. S. Akpan (Ed.), *African media space and globalization* (pp. 3–52). Palgrave MacMillian.

Aziken, L. C. & Emeni, F. C. A. (2010). Traditional systems of communication in Nigeria: A review for improvement. *Knowledge Review, 21*(4), 23–29.

Barber, K. (2009). Orality, the media and new popular cultures in Africa. In K. Njogu & J. Middleton (Eds.), *Media and identity in Africa* (pp. 3–18). Edinburgh University Press.

Barber, K. (2011). Preliminary notes on audiences in Africa. *Africa, 67*(3), 347–62.

Cooper, F. (2001). What is the concept of globalization good for? An African historian perspective. *African Affairs, 100*(399), 189–213.

van Dijck, J., Poell, T., & de Waal, M. (2018). *The platform society: Public values in a connective world.* Oxford University Press.

Ekeh, P. (1975). Colonialism and two publics in Africa: A theoretical statement. *Comparative Studies in Society and History, 71*(1), 91–112.

Ezumah, B. (2019). De-Westernizing African journalism curriculum through globalization and hybridization. *Journalism and Mass Communication Educator, 74*(4), 452–67.

Gourlay, K. A. (1982). Long trumpet of Northern Nigeria—in history and today, *African music. Journal of the International Library of African Music, 6*(2), 48–72.

Meribe, N. (2015). Reappraising indigenous African communication systems in the twenty-first century: New users for ancient media. *Journal of African Media Studies, 7*(2), 203–16.

Moyo, L., & Mutsvairo, B. (2018). Can the subaltern think? The decolonial turn in communication research in Africa In B. Mutsvairo (Ed.), *The Palgrave handbook on media and communication research in Africa* (pp. 19–40). Palgrave MacMillian.

Mushengyezi, A. (2010). Rethinking indigenous media: Rituals, 'talking' drum and orality as forms of public communication in Uganda. *Journal of African Cultural Studies, 16*(1), 107–17.

Ndlela, N. (2009). African media research in an era of globalization. *Journal of African Media Studies, 1*(1), 55–68.

Nnaemedo, B. (2018). African indigenous mass media: Continuity and change. *Journal of African Studies and Sustainable Development, 1*(4), 112–29.

Nwammou, A. N. (2011). Mediamorphosis: Analyzing the convergence of digital media forms alongside African traditional media. *African Review Research, 5*(2). https://doi.org/10.4314/afrrev.v5i2.67309.

Nwuneli, O. E. (1981). Formal and informal channels of communication in two African villages. Unpublished Project Report for UNESCO.

Ojebode, A. (2012). Mapping the territories of indigenous communication studies: Wilson vs Wilson. In M. Mboho & H. Batta (Eds.), *Communication and development issues: Essays in honour of Prof. Des Wilson* (pp. 1–16). UniUyo Press.

Okigbo, C. C. (2004). The African world: The publics of African communication. In C. C. Okigbo & F. Eribo (Eds.), *Development and communication in Africa* (pp. 31–43). Rowman and Littlefield.

Omotoso, S. A. (2020). Mediatizing and gendering Pan-Africanism for 'Global' impacts. In S. O. Oloruntoba (Ed.), *Pan-Africanism, regional integration and development in Africa* (pp. 149–62). Palgrave MacMillian.

Onochie, B., Olagunju, L., Ogwu P., & Obi, P. (2023). The shrinking civic space: Journalistic hazards, risks, and contemporary media resistance to censorship in Nigeria. In P. Obi, T. C. Obateru, & S. Amadi (Eds.), *Media and Nigeria's constitutional democracy: Civic space, free speech, and the battle for freedom of the press* (pp. 63–82). Lexington Books.

Srinivasan, S., Diepeveen, S., & Karekwaivanane, G. (2018). Rethinking publics in Africa in a digital age. *Journal of East African Studies, 13*(1), 2–17.

Ugboajah, F. O. (1972). Traditional—urban media model: Stocktaking for African development. *International Communication Gazette, 18*(2), 76–95.

Ushe, M. U. (2015). The talking drum: An inquiry into the reach of a traditional mode of communication. *International Journal of Philosophy and Theology, 3*(1), 110–17.

Uzuegbunam, C. E. (2020). Towards hybridized and glocalized youth identities in Africa: Revisiting old concerns and reimaging new possibilities for media education In D. Frau-Meigs, M. Pathak-Shelat, M. Hoechsmann, S. Kotilainen & S. R. Poyntz (Eds.), *The handbook of media education research* (pp. 65–87). Wiley.

Willems, W., & Mano, W. (2017). Decolonizing and provincializing audience and internet studies: Contextual approaches from African vintage points. In W. Willems & W. Mano (Eds.), *Everyday media culture in Africa: Audiences and users* (pp. 1–26). Routledge.

Wilson, D. (2008). Research on traditional communication in Africa: The development and future directions. *African Communication Research, 1*(1), 47–49.

Wilson, Des. (2023). Relevance of Nigerian traditional communication systems in the digital space. In U. S. Akpan (Ed.), *Nigerian media industries in the era of globalization* (pp. 213–26). Lexington Books.

Yeku, J. (2022). *Cultural netizenship: Social media, public culture, and performance in Nigeria.* Indiana University Press.

Part II

ADAPTATION AND COEXISTENCE IN THE DIGITAL AGE

Chapter 4

Communicating Emerging Science, Technology, and Innovation in Nigeria for Development in the Digital Age

Where Does Des Wilson's Trado-modern Media Come in?

Herbert Batta

Access to digital resources in Nigeria is improving gradually. With a population of over 200 million citizens and with more than 100 million connected to digital channels and some 40 million hand-held phone owners, and millions more on the social media networks such as Twitter, Facebook, Instagram, and YouTube, a digital culture is emerging in Nigeria. Though science and technology or science communication culture cannot be said to approximate the emerging digital culture, it is certain that an increasing digital culture can enhance the science culture by improving access to science, technology, and innovation (STI) information especially now that emerging STIs have come upon the world. It is true that Nigeria, as evident in its STI policy, is still grappling with the basic STIs. Moreover, emerging sciences, technologies, and innovations such as synthetic biology, biotechnology, nanoscience and technology, artificial intelligence/robotics, drone technology, gastrophysics, proteotronics, epigenomics, and so forth have strong proclivities to fast-track human development in global south nations such as Nigeria. These emerging STIs' most-felt impacts are in the areas of health, food security, education, communication, security, and environment.

This chapter examines the definition, the theoretical basis of emerging STI in the digital age, and the ethical aspects of emerging STI. It also explores emerging STI in Nigeria and Africa and the communication of emerging

STI in the digital age in the context of ethnocommunicology particularly the place of Des Wilson's trado-communication. This contribution concludes that Nigeria apparently needs to use its burgeoning digital culture to steer a robust interest in STI and the emerging ones for development purposes but not at the expense of traditional modes of communication. Indeed, the increasing digital culture should be used to bridge the digital divide and promote a robust science culture among rural populations where traditional communication systems are rampant.

Des Wilson who retired as a professor at the University of Uyo in 2019 is globally known as an iconoclast and scholar in ethnocommunicology. Right from his graduate days in the University of Ibadan, his research interest in oramedia and trado-modern systems of communication have distinguished his scholarship. Apart from being ethnically related to me, Wilson has been my teacher, mentor, collaborator, and guardian since the early 1990s. Beyond serving with him in the African Council for Communication Education, Nigerian Chapter, from 2008 to 2012 when he was the National President, and I, the National Treasurer; both of us have had the opportunity to co-author and co-edit several scholarly works such as *Media, Biodiversity, Biotechnology and Food Security* (2008), *Science, Health and Environmental Communication* (2013), and *Communication Education and Research* (2018). Along with other authors, I have also co-edited two books in Wilson's honor to mark his sixtieth birthday namely: *Communication and Africa's Development Crisis* (2010) and *Companion to Communication and Development Issues* (2012).

Truly, we live in the digital age. With a population of about 201 million Nigerians, more than 112 million had access to the internet in 2018. That is 56 percent of the population. Also, as at December 2018, there were more than 36 million Smartphone users (18.3 percent) in Nigeria (Nigeria Mobile Report, 2019). Similarly, Techpoint.africa (2019) reports that Nigeria has about 26 million active Facebook users and that the picture of social media statistics in Nigeria depicts this: Facebook (80.8 percent), Twitter (8.35 percent), Internet (7.1 percent), Instagram (2.1 percent), YouTube (1.25 percent), and LinkedIn (0.25 percent). What the statistics show is that the digital culture is getting a foothold in Nigeria, that internet penetration has been improving over the years with more Nigerians adopting digital hand-held devices—Iphones, Smartphones, iPads, laptops, tablets, and so forth. This development has significant implications for learning, education, research, and information gathering about all kinds of subject matters including emerging science, technology, and innovation.

EMERGING SCIENCE, TECHNOLOGY, AND INNOVATION

Emerging STI are new, ultra-sophisticated, scientific, technological, and innovative systems of knowledge and practice which are impactful and deployed to solve human problems in revolutionary ways. Examples include synthetic biology, nutrigenomics, gastrophysics, robotic/artificial intelligence, drones, nanoscience and nanotechnology, epigenomics, and so forth. These developments are not very significant in Africa. However, the areas in which noticeable activities are observed are in genome editing for agricultural biotechnology for which the Nigerian example is highlighted alongside the nanotechnology program in South Africa.

However, apart from the biotechnology program in Nigeria, the country is reported to set its sights on becoming "a regional hub for space science with over three satellites in space and other nano satellites designed, constructed, and launched by Nigerian engineers" (OFAB Newsletter, 2018, p. 3). Similarly, the Federal University of Technology, Akure, Nigeria, is reported to have launched Nigeria Edusat-1 manufactured alongside the National Space Research and Development Agency and Kyshin Institute of Technology, Japan, in 2017 to embed satellite technology in the educational institution for research, environmental management, and socioeconomic advancement (Premium Times, 2018). Focusing on agricultural biotechnology, the National Biotechnology Development Agency (NABDA) hinges its genetically engineered crops on food security in Nigeria. It states:

> In Africa, where population is expected to double by the year 2050, food security is of great concern. In Nigeria, the population would be around 400 million by then. Despite its production potentials, the country is one of the food-deficit countries in sub-Saharan Africa. Nigeria's population, among other factors, makes food security a major concern. (Ofab Newsletter, 2018)

In response to these concerns, NABDA along with the regulatory body connected to it—the National Biosafety Management Agency has the following genetically modified crop projects: (i) pod-borer resistant beans, (ii) African bio-fortified sorghum, (iii) Nitrogen-use, water-use, and salt-tolerant rice, (iv) Bt cotton, and (v) genetically modified cassava. The agency's attention to these crops covers cross genetic confinement, material confinement, gene efficacy, morphogenetic stability, agronomic stability, and general release (Open Forum on Agricultural Biotechnology in Africa (OFAB), 2018).

The Nigerian chapter of the OFAB (2018) states that genetically modified technology has benefits for the environment, health, farmers/farm crops, as well as the economy. Some of the benefits listed by OFAB are: reduction of pesticide use by 50 percent; reduction in the level of plow and chemical use; reduction in fossil consumption and carbon dioxide emissions; improvement of the nutritional profile of food—a major factor in ameliorating the rate of hunger and malnutrition; solutions of the problem of poor productivity, for example, disease, weed, and pests; and poverty reduction and increasing access to food and increases in farm revenues due to reduced input/insurance costs.

Let us turn to South Africa's nanotechnology program. Nanoscience is defined as the study of matter at near-atomic scale, meaning smaller than 100 nanometers. On the other hand, nanotechnology is described as the application of nanoscience knowledge in new devices and processes (Harsh et al. 2018 as cited in Balogh, 2010; and Hodge et al. 2014). Detailing three different ways, in which advanced technology can be beneficial for disadvantaged segments of society, Harsh et al. (2018) describe them as follows:

(a) The equalizing route is the understanding of how new technologies add to industrial competitiveness and thenceforth economic progress and strength.
(b) The fairness route provides a boost for the disadvantaged segment of the society to offer opportunities for persons from chronically deficient gender and racial groups to move out of poverty into lucrative occupations created by science and engineering.
(c) The pro-poor innovation strategy route is the use of science and technology research and development specially to address the needs of poor households and communities. The aim here is not to alter the shape of the economy or eradicate penury head-on, but to create better room for education and employment and thus improve living standards of poor communities.

Based on these different pathways, Harsh et al. (2018, p. 599) observe that:

South Africa has created nanotechnology innovation that is inclusive at many levels (spanning intent, impact, process, and structure) and has made some progress along several pathways to equity (addressing social and economic inequities). The modest investment South Africa has made in nanotechnology has produced clear benefits for the science, technology, engineering and mathematics workforce . . . for poor households and communities, there are promising application of nanotechnologies in the laboratories, but there are some significant barriers and a general lack of understanding of how to make them available to the people who need them.

Following the consideration of the implications of their analysis of the South Africa experience, away from South Africa, Harsh et al. (2018)

consider whether emerging countries and developing nations should invest in emerging technologies, they conclude:

> Given how our analysis of South Africa showed that it is very difficult to make emerging technology innovation inclusive and equitable, one might think the answer is no. But we could argue that the decision should not be made hastily and should involve careful examination of existing institutions and capabilities in a given country. (p. 604)

ETHICAL ASPECTS OF EMERGING SCIENCE AND TECHNOLOGY

Ethical considerations are common features of discussions about emerging science and technology. The issue at the center of the discourse is as elsewhere, how best to approach emerging science and technology without offending public morality. The key question to ask and seek answers is: what are these ethical issues? Considering the various ethical implications of emerging technologies, Al-Rodhan (2015, p. 43) stated thus:

> Stem cells and embryo research . . . has become a hot-button political issue involving scientists, policy makers, politicians and religious groups. Similarly, the discussions on genetically modified organisms (GMOs) have mobilized civil society, scientists, and policy makers in a wide debate on ethics and safety. The developments in genome-editing techniques are just one example that bioresearch and its impact on market goods are strongly dependent on social acceptance and cannot escape public debates of regulation and ethics.

Accordingly, therefore, the following technological trends and concerns represent some of the ethical implications of advancements in technologies as well as emerging ethical dilemmas in science and technology gleaned from Gilroy (2012) as well as Al-Rodhan (2015, p. 22):

(a) Some so-called emerging technologies such as fuel cell vehicles, artificial intelligence (robotics), digital genome, and so forth are decades old; however, they have been transformed in fresh new ways as well as becoming increasingly more embedded in everyday products.

(b) There are still fears that subsequent steps involved in the laboratory engineering of genes for genetically modified crops after cutting and splitting genes may result in mutations that distort the natural functioning of genes in a somewhat deleterious manner. This calls for deepened research on the implementation of techniques.

(c) Drones are helping in surveillance for agricultural purposes and for combating pollution apart from their military, journalistic, and security uses. The issue that may require regulation in the near future is their increasing numbers and the risk of collisions especially in large human settlements.

(d) Advances in robotics and artificial intelligence, particularly the development of neuro-morphic chips able to imitate the complexities of the human brain including thought, vision, precision, and memory have led to fears. The fears are that robots could some day become more intelligent than humans or even control them.

(e) The embedding of smart materials likely possible with nanoscience and technology in manufactured products with adaptation, alteration, interaction, and response capabilities has raised issues about copyright, standardization, and traceability. An example is 4D printing—a technology that makes transportation, adaptation, and auto-repair a reality. Similar technologies organically speaking include assembly of bioproducts with auto development and autoevolution capacities and cancer-fighting nano-tablets/chips capable of moving around in the human circulatory system triggering off antibodies that specifically target cancer cells.

(f) Research in genome editing or stem cell therapies to help millions of people all over the world fight off debilitating genetic diseases and chronic maladies such as diabetics and hypertension would not be accessed by the poor even when costs are decreasing. Poverty and inequality therefore are issues that would continue to alienate the poor from the benefits of the merging science. Also, the issue of genome data storage and the likelihood of inside abuses or hacking pose ethical issues bordering on security and privacy.

(g) The manufacturing of fuel cell vehicles envisaged in the nearest future is a great boost to the environment by helping to eliminate greenhouse gas emissions as well as mitigate climate change and reduce reliance on fossil fuels. However, this would weaken the economics of hydrocarbon-rich nations and perhaps negatively affect their relations with former importers and further widen the schism between the technology-rich and technology-poor.

(h) There are fears that emerging science and technology may move beyond enhancements through medication, surgery, machine, and neurons for treatment aims, to enhancing human physiologies and anatomies such as a super brain, an absolute beauty, running speed, height, musculature, vision like an eagle, and so forth. These aesthetic enhancements raise the ethical issue of how many people would afford such luxury, the equality that it would create, the societal norm that it would distort, or the possibility of playing God by creating the designer baby.

(i) With the ability of emerging scientists and technologists to create cells that are both human and animal, ethical issues arise as to the propriety of creating hybrids, interspecies, and new species. People are afraid that monsters can be created in such adventures.

The focus on ethical considerations in SMIs is valuable. Since we all live in a globalized world, we can be sure that as long as knowledge transcends borders, people around the world would in one way or the other be affected. Thus, it is important to become conversant with some of the ethical issues that pertain to emerging science and technologies. As public information and education purveyors, communication practitioners, professionals, and scholars have a social responsibility as well as the public obligation to study, research, and create awareness about these issues.

EMERGING SCIENCE/TECHNOLOGY, COMMUNICATION, AND DEVELOPMENT IN NIGERIA

Emerging science and technology undoubtedly have serious implications for communication and developing countries. Though the developing world and emerging nations are still grappling with how to institutionalize the conventional sciences and technologies, the world of innovations is not going to wait for them to catch up. Therefore, the sensible thing to do is to embrace relevant developments in emerging science and technology to attend to acute needs in society. For example, we have seen how agricultural drones—advances in automation and artificial intelligence—can revolutionize agriculture and help stem agricultural losses. This helps to improve the food security profile of developing countries, many of which have large populations to feed and stave off hunger, starvation, malnutrition, and drought-driven famine. Investing in this sort of technology would apparently boost the survival of developing and emerging nations.

It has also become clear that developments in genome editing, genetic modification, and agricultural biotechnology have led to species improvement, drought-resistant crop varieties, pest-resilient species, herb-resistant crops, and fortified cereals/crops. What this has done and can do to boost agriculture cannot be gainsaid. The collateral effect on food sufficiency and sustainability can change the fortunes of developing and emerging nations. Also, the salutary impact of genetically engineered agriculture on the environment cannot be overemphasized. By requiring less chemicals/fertilizers, by saving much fossil fuels in agricultural production, and by requiring less pesticides and herbicides, genetic modification in agriculture helps to reduce soil pollution, water pollution, carbon dioxide emission, fossil fuel consumption, and ultimately environmental degradation and climate change. The relevance of this is in Third World countries where environmental despoliation in rife cannot be overstated (Ibrahim, 2017).

Advancements in synthetic biology, epigenomics, and nutrigenomics can help in producing live forms synthetically such as *in vitro* meat and determining how genes and stem cells can be scientifically engineered to cure chronic, debilitating, inheritable, or genetic diseases. Again, we have noted that nutrition and genes have been studied enough to tell what we can eat to influence our genes and how our genes can help tell us what to eat. Embracing this emerging science and technology in developing countries spells well given the fact that the burden of disease is very high particularly in Africa. Investing in emerging science and technology would help Africa sort through the millions of cases of diabetes, hypertension, congenital malformations, sickle cell diseases, and so forth.

Advances in nanotechnology also have a huge implication for developing countries. Nanotechnology has remarkable utility in water filtration, cancer therapy, materials production, environmental pollution remediation, and manufacturing generally. Developing countries and emerging nations would do well to embrace nanoscience and technology to help other causes in medicine, water and sanitation, pollution control, as well as the manufacturing economy. Developing nations and emerging countries can and should do a number of things to tap the benefits of emerging science and technology. Firstly, they must commit in terms of legally backed policy framework formulation to investment in science, technology, innovation, engineering, and mathematics. The policy must be backed up with institutionalized funding regimes for training and education of scientists, engineers, innovations, mathematicians, and science/technology entrepreneurs. Science, technology, and innovation including emerging ones should find serious expression in primary, secondary, technical, and tertiary levels.

Secondly, countries that have failed to invest and develop science centers, technology parks, and science museums as well as establish a culture of science festivals/expos/fairs and citizen science must do so graduate into the emerging or developed country league. Nigeria for example with scores of tertiary science and technology institutions, research institutes, and government science agencies has no science centers or science museums where citizens can publicly learn about STI. Buckler (2015) stresses that science bodies play increasingly significant roles in public understanding of science. She underscores that in the current world, most overarching problems are science-related, notably climate change, disease, energy shortage, hunger, water resourcing, and environmental degradation. For developing countries such as ours, Cavalcanti and Persechini (2011) also emphasize that science centers and science museums help to popularize science culture and the relevance of science; improve health care; support public health awareness campaign; train science teachers; combat misconceptions, superstition, stigmatization, and mysticism; as well as supplement the formal science education system.

Advancements in emerging science and technology have significant implications for communication and the communications media. The first and most serious implication is that communication academics, media students, journalism professionals, and communications professionals working for radio, newspapers, magazines, television, satellite/cable stations, as well as the new media and publishing firms must overcome their deficits in science knowledge. Through training and practice, they must seek knowledge and make themselves adequately and generally aware of developments in STI including the emerging ones.

Additionally, communication professionals should have a positive perception of science as well as an attitude that accommodates STI and emerging science. By attending courses, training, workshops, seminars, and conferences and by subscribing to and reading contemporary science journals as well as cultivating credible STI sources, communication experts can prepare themselves adequately to report, cover, and frame emerging science with an eye on accuracy, relevance, fairness, impact, risks, uncertainty, safety, ethics, language, and cultural context.

It is also important for communication schools to unpack what they usually teach as specialized reporting in their curriculum. Science and technology reporting, health/medical journalism, and environmental communication should be given separate foci where emerging science and technology fields in these areas would be given attention. Training of the faculty in these areas too is critical. In journalism, professional practice, publishers, and editors should recognize the need to promote science and generate public interest in it through developing keen interest and obtaining sound knowledge of science and emerging science relevant to the developing world. The channels of mass communication including the news and social media can readily contribute to the dissemination of science knowledge and the public understanding of science and technology. They can do this by creating science desks and sustaining existing ones, and providing sufficient newshole, airtime, and digital space for science and emerging science stories.

Communication stakeholders would do well to adopt the guide provided by Mazerik and Rejeski (2014) for communicating emerging STI:

(a) Communicators should pay careful attention to the target audience as they formulate and deliver emerging science messages. Different messages should be targeted at scientists, lay people, government and policymakers, consumers, regulators, and so forth because their needs, roles, perception, knowledge, attitudes, and opinions are different.

(b) Communicators should be mindful of how emerging science is framed because framing by the media has a direct influence on how the subject matter is perceived by the public. Emerging science and technology may be framed in terms of economics, risk, impact, health, ethics, safety, uncertainty, and so forth. The media should do well to cover a broad range of frames as well as explore the local, cultural context of STI.

(c) Fairness to all parties, and ensure that balance is reflected in their reportage, coverage, and framing. Balance not only covers the presentation of both sides of a debate but examining benefits and risks, certainties and uncertainties, and so forth.

(d) Communicators should be knowledgeable about products, devices, and applications and be ready to provide illustrations, definitions, and explanations that agree with those of the originators and be helpful to the public.

(e) Disseminators of emerging science and technology should be diligent in cultivating trusted and credible sources of information. Even those bits of information should be verified from peers as well as learned articles in refereed, peer-reviewed, and scholarly journals.

(f) Communicators need to develop skills in translating, interpreting, and synthesizing technical, scientific language to the understanding of lay people and the person with average education.

EMERGING SCIENCE AND TECHNOLOGY IN THE DIGITAL AGE

Digitization has truly altered and revolutionized the ways in which science, emerging science and technology, and indeed, all other fields of human endeavors are learned, researched, and practiced. Considered in terms of the users of digital devices, the content of the digital messages, multimedia potentials and capabilities, real-time rendition of messages, abundance of content, non-mediation of contents, and accessibility to content, digitalisation has enabled the study and practice of STI. Other merits of digitization for emerging science include interactivity, hypertextuality, and large-scale knowledge management.

Abstracted and extrapolated from Orihuella's (2017) new paradigms of communication in the digital age, we can easily outline how the digital age offers immense benefits for emerging STI.

(a) With digital media platforms, communication of emerging science easily moves from focus on the audience to concentration with the users.

That means, users of digital platforms have the latitude to select, determine, look for, shape, ask for, purchase, offer opinions about, reject, text, voice, or film messages that relate to emerging science more easily, faster, and personally. These are referred to as low-profile, digital, native, and self/film media initiatives.

(b) Digitization affords the transition from single medium to multimedia. Today, digitization makes it possible to combine writing, voice, moving images, graphics, still photographs, and animated images into one composite message disseminated on a media platform with capabilities of transactional communication between source and receiver. These features are especially useful for emerging STI, which may be difficult to communicate. However, rendering the message in text, audio, video, graphics, photo, and so forth is more likely to simplify, clarify, and intensify the communication experience for both source/sender and audience/receiver.

(c) Interactivity is another unique feature of digital media that conduces to learning and practicing emerging STI. It permits both content providers and content users to forge a mutual, conversational relationship at both bilateral and multilateral levels. With interactivity, digital media users select the information format they want through browsers, search engines, or navigation interfaces.

(d) Yet another prominent attribute of the digital media is hypertextuality. For the emerging science and technology enthusiast, this characteristic allows the user to apply the links button to navigate content, visiting other websites/pages, blogs, social media platforms, gaining sites, and shopping sites in order to learn about emerging science and technology and at the same time, entertaining themselves, interacting with others, and creating content of their own.

In sum, digitization expands the possibilities for emerging STI especially in less developed countries. Digitization may help quicken the rate of learning and thus narrow the gaping knowledge disparity between the developed and the developing worlds. OECD (2019, p. 1) asserts that:

digitization is reshaping all stages of science, from agenda setting, to experimentation, knowledge sharing, and public engagement. Digital technology is enabling a new paradigm of open science, which has three main pillars: open access to scientific publications and information; enhanced access to research data; and broader engagement with stakeholders. Digital technology is also enlarging the process of discovery.

The concept of open science has not gained sufficient traction in developing countries such as Nigeria. Ironically, greater penetration of digital technologies in these countries would expand opportunities for lay people to learn about STI. Yet, this would depend on public interest in STI and the interest/willingness of scientists to engage in digital open science. The importance of this position receives emphasis from Altaf and Bhaskar (2018, 94) who state: Digital media have emerged as a popular platform for communicating science as well as science's active engagement with society. Through its wide reach, it has not only provided us with ample ways of enhancing public understanding of science but also public participation in science through online citizen initiatives.

According to Altaf and Bhaskar, there are several digital media opportunities for scientists to communicate science in a global scenario. These include social media and communication of science. The social media channels for communicating science including emerging STI include:

Blog/Blogosphere

A science blog is a sort of online journal provided by one who is specialist/ enthusiastic about STI. It contains facts, figures, data, photos, videos, audio of content related to the special subject, as well as links to other useful information and commentaries from blog visitors. The presentations are called blog posts and are posted in chronological order.

(i) Facebook: Facebook allows scientists, technologists, and innovators focusing on emerging STI users to post texts, audio, videos, graphics, photos, as well as links to related websites and pages. Considering the number of Facebook users (2.01 billion by June 2017), this is really a veritable medium for popularizing STI. Again, the success of this platform depends on the interest of users and involvement/engagement of sources/content providers. Apart from Facebook posts by STI persons, organizations can also communicate their STI activities on their Facebook pages. Such organizations in Nigeria include: NBDA, National Atomic Energy Commission, Federal Ministry of Science and Technology and its many agencies, and so forth.

(ii) Twitter: Using Twitter to communicate STI has great importance for agenda setting, popularization, policy formulation, legislation, dissemination, and implementation of STI issues.

(iii) Live video streaming: Several social media platforms such as Facebook, Twitter, Snapchat, and Instagram all have provisions for streaming live video into their content. The color, action, and voice, which the video enables, make communicating and illustrating science easier, livelier, and more interesting. It is because of the newness, novelty, and even difficulty of emerging STI that live streaming becomes a more patent feature to help clarify, amplify, and demystify STI among the public.

(iv) Google Trends: Google keeps tabs of searches on its search engine and keeps accounts of the numbers. From such computations, a trend of popular searches emerges along with the categorization of such searches. So, users can catch trends in searches on science and technology, health, environment, and so forth. This helps internet users to determine the direction of information-seeking behaviors of seekers in certain areas and flow with the trend.

(v) Virtual reality (VR) or augmented reality (AR): This allows scientists or science institutions to tell science stories especially difficult, abstract, or intricate ones simply, meaningfully, and easily. In this way, science centers, science museums, and science fairs/exhibitions can demonstrate research, illustrate applications, and graphically present knowledge in various areas of emerging sciences.

(vi) Smartphone applications.

(vii) Smart phones such as android and internet phones are very helpful in communicating science. Users can easily bookmark science news sites and applications (apps) such as Science Review Feed, News Fusion, and General Science facilitate access to STI by members of the society.

(viii) Online versions of newspapers and magazines.

In addition to the above means of projecting STI through the digital media, some newspapers and magazines all over the world also have digital versions of their science, health, and environment pages which can be read without access to the hard copies. Nigerian newspapers such as The Guardian, Punch, and so forth have such web pages, thus offering opportunities for scientists, technologists, and STI institutions to disseminate science information to the public. They are equally avenues for citizen science to find expression digitally.

THE PLACE OF TRADO-MODERN
COMMUNICATION IN EMERGING STI
DISSEMINATION IN THE DIGITAL AGE

Over the years, there have been misconceptions that the (modern) information societies such as we have in the digital age have no place for the communication of STI using traditional means of communication. In his works, Des Wilson has successfully argued against such misconceptions. Wilson (2015) reminds us that even in the late 1970s UNESCO had expressed deep concern that after lengthy periods of the deployment of modern media in the global

south, not much was achieved in effective penetration and message utilization. At the time, this was probably so because most modern media systems,
namely, electronic, print, cable, satellite, and telephones were urban-centered
and not easily accessible to the rural or urban poor. These categories of
people still recourse to oral and traditional communication systems that rely
on interpersonal interactions, songs, music, dance, theater, and other folk-
ways. Wilson argues that it is more effective to marry modern and traditional
systems of communication for development purposes. This is made possible
by increased interactions between the rural/urban poor who lack access to
modern systems and others who have access through various communication
avenues such as market unions; farming and fishing associations; women,
youth, and age grade system; civil and labor organizations; transport bodies;
and various sociocultural and economic assemblages.

Emerging science and technology are most often in the domain of modern
media systems and conveyed in English or other foreign languages for those
who are literate, numerate, and digitally or electronically connected. Through
the two-step flow, the multi-step flow, as well as the concept of opinion
leadership and predicated upon the diffusion of innovation theory, the rural
poor who have limited literary skills and access to print, electronic, or digital
media resources still have the chance to obtain, synthesize, and utilize STI
information. This is more so, with the deployment of citizen/public science
communication, medical/health outreaches, as well as agricultural/environ-
mental extension services. In this way, people living in poor, digitally ineq-
uitable circumstances can obtain and utilize information on biotechnology,
nanotechnology, drones, epigenetics, robotics/artificial intelligence, and so
forth. The relevance of trado-communication in disseminating STI information is supported by its ability to reach rural and urban poor. Wilson (2015)
states that:

> the traditional system of communication involves a "complex" process of infor-
> mation "gathering" and dissemination, entertainment and education used in
> societies which have not been seriously dislocated by western culture and which
> have not been cannibalized through cultural and media imperialism initiated
> abroad and executed by local agents of dominating culture acting as civilizing
> forces. (p. 49)

The power behind close-knit societies and those who rely mainly on traditional systems is their natural communication channels. Another potent
advantage is that traditional systems are integrative, credible, time-tested,
normative, and value-based. These traits make for participatory, communal
democracy where everyone is expected to get involved, as stakeholders in
the communication process. For STI including emerging STI, these features

can become helpful and effective in obtaining information, owning the messages, and participating in dissemination and implementation of STI projects in communities. These projects may help solve water and sanitation issues, environmental degradation, food insecurity, health problems, educational deficits, and security challenges using synthetic biology, biotechnology, nanotechnology, artificial intelligence, epigenetics, nutrigenomics, and so forth.

Wilson (2015) makes a strong case for preservation and use of traditional communication in the information age. He urges Africans to embrace traditional modes of communication which are effective, more saturating of the niche segments, non-alienating, inexpensive, and imbued with cultural relevance and democratic legitimation. The observation that, "the present infatuation with modern communication gadgets has created an industry which has largely become an elite enterprise richly touted in expensive boxes (TV, radio, smart phones, computer systems) and costly news sheets (newspapers, magazines, paperbacks)" (p. 51) draws attention to possibilities of making trado-communication and modern communication work together for greater reach. That modern, Western media are heterogeneous, more efficient, and faster in their reach means that traditional societies, digitally poor people, displaced populations, migrants, and other disadvantaged people can still be accommodated in political, economic, cultural, and scientific communication that goes on in society. All that needs to be done is to harness the rich benefits of traditional communication channels and bridge the gap between those who have access to modern media and those who have not. The absence of modern media in traditional societies should not stop them from receiving, participating, and using emerging STI knowledge and practices.

The interpersonal and transactional nature of traditional communication permits disjointed, dislocated, and inaccessible people to get integrated with a modern world culture through modern media systems. Wilson (2015, p. 81) puts it this way:

> Modern technological devices have enhanced communication across nations and transculturally too. Mass communication connects people simultaneously in all parts of the world but while it works hundreds or thousands of miles at the physical plane, it is the interpersonal communication processes that psychologically engage our minds and activate our thoughts.

CONCLUSION

Though Africa has been struggling to have a firm footing in the development of science, technology, engineering, mathematics, and innovation for sustainable development, emerging science has surfaced on the horizon. This further widens the knowledge/technology gap between the advanced nations and the less developed ones but also offers more opportunities to help poor regions lift themselves into the realm of innovation for development. Thus, the emerging sciences and technologies such as nanotechnology, agricultural drones and other artificial intelligence/robotic technologies, proteotronics, and genetic engineering open up remarkable opportunities for Africa and emerging nations to solve their social problems notably food insecurity, disease, environmental problems, and so forth.

However, these emerging technologies and sciences are not without controversies, risks, and uncertainties. This makes it imperative for the communication media and professionals to accord the investigation, reportage, coverage, and framing of emerging science and technology the deserved attention. Another imperative is for scientists in developed, developing, and undeveloped portions of the world to bridge the knowledge gap among them by promoting the development of global science. Cordova et al. (2015) argue that the, "time-honored tradition of scientific mentoring must be practiced on a wider scale across borders" (p. 18) using the principles of inclusivity, mutual understanding, accessibility, working from a position of strength, and solid infrastructure. Others are sustainability, funding, and institutional government support. Africa and emerging nations should key into this.

Finally, because of the great potential of emerging STI to help solve some of Africa's development issues, the growing influence of digital media in developing nations does not mean that traditional modes of communication should be jettisoned. Despite the widening penetration of digital connections, much of Nigeria and Africa at large still lack access to digital channels of communication. This handicap should not curtail the communication of emerging STI for development purposes. Rather, access to the mass media and digital communication systems should be harnessed to bridge the digital divide by using traditional means of communication to connect with those who lack digital access.

REFERENCES

Al-Rodham, N. (2015). The many ethical implications of emerging technologies. University of Oxford. www.scientificamerican.com.

Batta, H., & Wilson, D. (2008). Mass media promotion of biodiversity, biotechnology, biosafety, and food security knowledge for sustainable development in Africa. *International Journal of African Culture, Politics, and Development, 3*(2), 172–87.

Buckler, C. (2015). The role of science centers in increasing public understanding of science. *Dimension.* http://www.astc.org. Accessed August 2, 2018.

Cavalcanti, C., & Persechini, P. (2011). Science museum and popularization of science in Brazil. Field Action Reports. Special Issues 3.

Cordova, K. E., Furukuwa, H., & Yaghi, O. M. (2015). The development of global science. *American Chemical Society Central Science*, *1*(1), 18–23. 10.1021/acscentsci.560028. <http://.acs.org/journal/acscii.

Gilroy, W. G. (2012). Emerging ethical dilemmas in science and technology. *Science Daily*. https://www.sciencedaily.com/releases/2012/12/121217162440.htm

Harsh, M., Woodson, T. S., Cozzens, S., Wetmore, J. M., Sumouni, O., & Cortes, R. (2018). The role of emerging technologies in inclusive innovation: The case of nanotechnology in South Africa. *Science and Public Policy*, *45*(5), 597–607. https://doi.org/10.1093/scipol/scx079

Ibrahim, A. B. (2017). Genetically engineered crops and food security in Nigeria. Policy Brief {No.: 012017}. Open Forum on Biotechnology. National Biotechnology Development Agency.

Mazerik, J., & Rejeski, D. (2014). *A guide for communicating synthetic biology. Sciences and technology innovation program*. Woodrow Wilson International Centre for Scholarly.

Mboho, M., & Batta, H. (Eds.). (2012). *The companion to communication and development issues: Essays in honor of Prof. Des Wilson*. Department of Communication Arts, University of Uyo.

Nigeria Mobile Report (2019). Nigeria Mobile Report 2019. https://www,jumia.com .ng/mobile-report/.

OECD. (2019). *Measuring the digital transformation: A roadmap for the future*. OECD Publishing. https://doi.org/10.1787/9789264311992-en.

OFAB Newsletter. (2018). Open forum on agricultural biotechnology newsletter. *6*(1), 1–16.

Orihuela, J. L. (2017). 10 new paradigms of communication in the digital age. https://jlori.medium.com/the-10-new-paradigms-of-communication-in-the-digital -age-7b7cc9cb4bfb.

Premium Times. (2008). FUTA, partners Successfully launch satellites into space. premiumtimesng.com.

Soola, E., Batta, H., & Nwabueze, C. (Eds.). (2010). *Communication and Africa's development crisis: Essays in honour of Professor Des Wilson*. VDM Verlag Dr. Muller.

Wilson, D. (2015). Ethnocommunicology, trado-modern communication and mediamorphosis in Nigeria: An iconoclast's demystification of some communication traditions. 44th Inaugural Lecture, University of Uyo.

Wilson, D., & Batta, H. (2013). *Science, health and environmental communication: Global issues, local perspectives*. Ibadan University Press.

Wilson, D., & Batta, H. (Eds.). (2018). *Communication education and research in 21st Century Nigeria*. African Council for Communication Education (ACCE).

Chapter 5

Ifa Divination, Extramundane Communication, and Internet

An Overview

Akinola Moses Owolabi, Bernice Oluwalaanu
Sanusi, Oyinloye Oloyede, and Isaac Olajide Fadeyi

Communication is a complex and an elaborate activity among the Yoruba people of South-Western Nigeria (Abioye, 2011). It takes place in both physical and spiritual realms. At the physical level, it involves exchange of ideas or pieces of information between persons or group(s) of persons via a common system of symbols, signs, or behaviors. In the spiritual realm, it deals with communication by humans with ancestors, gods, and other spiritual entities in order to be able to influence them positively. This is an aspect of traditional communication known as extramundane communication (Wilson, 1987; Odunola & Segun, 2009; Akpabio, 2003). Extramundane communication plays important roles in the perception of life by the Yoruba people who view the universe as a combination of three separate but interrelated worlds—the worlds of the unborn, the living, and the dead. In this cosmic continuum, while the world of the living is visible, those of the unborn and the dead are highly metaphysical and exist mainly in the spiritual realms. The worlds of the unborn and the dead go a long way to determine what happens in the world of the living which is often seen as the "transit camp" between the worlds of the living and the dead. A Yoruba adage which says *Aye Loja, Orun Nile* (the earth is a market place, heaven is the home) gives credence to this. It is the belief of the Yoruba that every human being must strive to unravel the mystery surrounding his/her creation and destiny, that is, what his/her *Ori* has in store for him/her. This is necessary in order to gain fortune and avert misfortune. The only way of achieving this is by communing with the extraterrestrial beings via constant consultation and dialogue with Ifa. This chapter discusses Ifa divination, extramundane communication, and internet among the Yoruba people of South-Western Nigeria.

Since the Ifa divination system involves the use of oracular signs and omens by an initiated priest (Babalawo) to divinely find out and reveal the hidden messages from gods, it is worth studying its indigenous communicative patterns. Despite modernism, Ifa divination practice remains a popular form of interaction and connectivity between the supernatural and the living particularly among the Yoruba people of South-Western Nigeria. There is however paucity of studies on the communicative aspects of Ifa and the internet features in Ifa divination that should link researchers with the understanding of its divine internet connectivity characteristics that keep the practice relevant till today.

IFA DIVINATION

Ifa divination system and its literary corpus are at the heart of this communication mode in Yorubaland. According to Olu-Osayomi (2017), traditionally, the Yoruba believe that *Olodumare* (The Supreme Being) has endowed *Orunmila* (the grand priest of Ifa) with special wisdom and knowledge to be His accredited representative in matters relating to destiny. *Orunmila* was the only *Orisa* confirmed by tradition as present at creation and when man was making choice of destiny, hence the nickname of *Elerin Ipin* (witness of destiny; Abiodun, 1975).

Ipin (lots) has to do with an individual's *Ori* (Head) believed to be the father of the entire body structure (*Ori ni baba ara*). According to Dopamu (2008), in Yoruba religion, *Ori* (destiny or lot) is closely related to God and given by God Himself. No one knows what the Ori has in store for him, hence the saying that:

Akunleyan ladayeba
A kunle a yan eda,
Adele aye tan, oju n kan gbogbo wa.

What we chose while kneeling down
Is what becomes our portion in the world
We knelt down to choose destiny,
We got to the world only to be in a hurry to get things done.

There is a great reliance on the worlds of the unborn and the dead for the living to experience tranquility in society. As popularly expressed, "for all to be well," the dependence on the unborn and the dead is hinged on efficient and effective communication with the world of the living. Hence, the constant exchange of pieces of information that is virtual in nature. In this quest, the Yoruba engage in extramundane communication as a means of engendering affirmative action. It is the general belief of the people that the dead are alive in the spirit realm and therefore always with their people, albeit invisibly, to guide and guard their footsteps. Thus, for all to be well, there is the unquestionable need for the living to know at all times what the dead want from them. This same world of the living and the dead depends on the world of the unborn for continuity through procreation and for it to be at peace, it must strive always to know what the products of the world of the unborn have in stock for it. This awareness accounts for the search for what the gods have ordained the unborn to do and to be in the world of the living. The Yoruba call this *Ese n taye omo tuntun.*

The dependence of the three worlds on one another does not end there. The metaphysical world also relies on the physical one. The living pass away to the world of the dead from where it is believed that the world of the unborn constantly fills its stock for supply to the world of the living. This is where the idea of giving names that signify the return or immanence of ancestors and consequently continuity of life such as *Babatunde* (father has come back) or *Iyabode* (mother has returned) emanated.

This chain of interdependence has communication through divination, sacrifices, evocative rituals, cleansing rites, and other forms of communal rituals such as *Egungun* (Masquerade) all tailored toward obtaining positive responses on various issues affecting the living from the metaphysical beings as its sole vehicle.

STATEMENT OF THE PROBLEM

Ifa divination system, accompanied by prescription of sacrifices, has been entrenched among the Yoruba people such that it cuts across all ages, socioeconomic status, as well as religious and political leanings in all the sub-ethnic groups of the Yoruba race at home and in the diaspora. A documentary produced by Kelani (2004) infers that the refusal by the youth to learn Ifa divination system and its literary corpus as well as religious intolerance from Christians and Muslims who mount strident opposition against Ifa divination, among others, explain why the practice is not as popular as it used to be. Nonetheless, researchers have observed that Ifa divination system is still deeply entrenched in Yoruba culture and tradition as an extramundane communication strategy by the people (Sanusi, 2013; Ojebode & Awonusi, 2016; Akintan & Adetimehin, 2021). That must have been responsible for the large volume of studies on Ifa across the globe and its recognition by UNESCO in 2005 as a "masterpiece of the oral and Intangible Heritage of Humanity" (Garba, 2018, p. 67).

However, we observe that despite the plethora of studies on the various aspects of Ifa divination system and extramundane communication, there is a paucity of studies on Ifa divination activities that link researchers with the understanding of its internet connectivity characteristics that keep the practice relevant to date. This study sets out to contribute to the corpus of knowledge about Ifa divinations in the specific context of internet connectivity characteristics not yet fully studied.

THEORETICAL FRAMEWORK

Schema theory of symbolic message organization was used as the theoretical framework for this study. It is a psychology theory whose introduction was credited to Frederic Bartlett in 1932 and its full development to Richard Anderson in the 1970s. According to Cherry (2023), "a schema is a cognitive framework or concept that helps organize and interpret information." Schemas are therefore belief–desire–intention models situated in prolonged memories. The fundamental proposition of the theory is that the minds of men have cognitive infrastructure which assist them in the organization, processing, storage, and recall of all sorts of information they come across daily for later usage (Dixon, 2017). Thus, the theory believes that all human knowledge is arranged schematically in a mental frame and regurgitated whenever the need arises. Since schema theory deals with the structuring of knowledge for events, phenomena, or subjects based on the experiences of the past which are approached to direct current action, Ifa priest who have internalized *Odu Ifa* (Orunmila's storehouse of knowledge and Ifa holy book), via memorialization and past experiences, is proposed as the metaphor of a naïve scientist seeking to offer explanations and guidance on how humans get on with the extraordinary activities of daily living. The theory offers the interpersonal construct of individuals' mental structure for interpreting the activities of others as well as provides the mental understanding of how social encounters should be conducted and how to predict what to expect in communication situations. Ifa divination is about revealing the hidden things about others which relates to the schema theory.

METHODOLOGY

Due to the descriptive and explanatory nature of this study, participant observation as a data collection method was used as research design. The root of participant observation, formally coined as a research concept in 1924 by Eduard C. Linderman, can be traced to 1800 with Joseph Marie baron de Gerando as the forerunner. Among scholars who expanded the concept were John Dewey and Grundtvig while it was later made popular by Bronislaw Malinowski. According to George (2023), participant observation is a research method deployed in the collection of "rich and detailed data about social groups or phenomena through ethnographies or other qualitative research." Wilson (2005) views participant observation as a procedure used to access "information about and understanding of a group or community and create texts about their lives, behaviors, and beliefs." The method is apt because this study is both ethnographic and qualitative. The Ifa religion and its believers are a unique subgroup of the Yoruba society whose beliefs and practices are distinct from others. To a very large extent, they are not quite open to observation by outsiders whom they consider as *Ogberi* (uninitiated) until very recently. This is why they are perceived as a secret cult group.

One of the researchers, precisely the lead author, took part in the 2022 editions of the annual celebrations of three key Ifa festivals namely; *Ogbeyonu* in Osogbo, *Odun Agboniregun* in Ile-Ife, and *Odun Ifa* in Iragbiji. The Ogbeyonu festival was held between September 1 and 9, 2022, in Osogbo, the capital of Osun State of Nigeria at the behest of the *Araba* (Ifa's Chief Priest) of Osogboland, Chief Ifayemi Osundagbonu Elebuibon. The nine-day festival had traditional rulers as well as people of different creeds and colors, musicians, and cultural troupes from far and near in attendance. The 2022 edition of the annual *Agbonmiregun* festival tagged "World Ifa Festival" was a seven-day event that took place between Monday May 30 and Sunday June 5 that year at Oke Itase, Ile-Ife. Organized by the International Council for Ifa Religion and the Council of Araba/Oluwo, the festival was presided over by the Araba Agbaye Oluisese, His Eminence, Owolabi Awodotun Aworeni. Being the Grand Ifa Festival for all Yorubas at home and in the diaspora, the *Agbonmiregun* festival of 2022 was a pilgrimage of sort attended by leading Ifa priests and priestess, Ifa devotees, people seeking solutions to various challenges, and those who came for thanksgiving sequel to receiving answers to their requests at the previous year's celebrations, from journalists and researchers across the world. A number of royal fathers, led by the Ooni of Ife-Oba Adeyeye Ogunwusi, were also involved in the festival. Highlights of the festival were daily chanting of *Oriki Ifa* (Ifa panegyrics), divinations and recitations of *Odu Ifa* (Ifa corpus), ritual performances, a public lecture and roundtable discussion, as well as *Iwure* (benediction) on the last day of the celebrations. In Iragbiji, the 2022 *Odun Ifa* (Ifa festival) under the leadership of Araba Babatunde Abereifa was observed in the first week of August spanning between Monday 1 and Sunday 7. It was graced daily by priests and priestesses of Ifa, its other adherents and invited guests from Iragbiji, its environs, other towns in Osun state, and even beyond.

The observation did not cover the entire periods of the festivals as there were breaks at intervals to rest, eat, and attend to some other personal and official needs. Although there were no opportunities for formal introduction of the researcher to the generality of the festivals' attendees, the organizers of the ceremonies were well informed of his presence as a journalist covering the celebrations and as a researcher. Adequate field notes that were relevant to the studies were taken by the researcher. At the divination level, the researcher had to get involved in consultation with Ifa divinity and watched as others did the same. This really assisted him in having firsthand information on why people patronize Ifa divination system, the process it takes, as well as its mode as an art of communication with eagle eyes on the various elements and how the elements interact to achieve the desired interconnectivity purpose, similar to the internet, between humans and supernatural beings. The observation method was complemented by in-depth interviews conducted with Babalawos (diviners), those consulting them and purposively selected members of the society who have consulted Babalawo before. This information is presented anonymously to protect the identity of the participants.

CONCEPTUALIZATION OF THE STUDY

The Art of Divination

Oral and written evidence testify to the fact that divination is an enduring practice that dates back to human existence. As early as the second millennium, the practice had been popular in Mesopotamia and is attested to throughout the ancient world, primarily in the near East, Egypt, the Levant, Greece, Italy, and China (Koch, 2021). Divination seeks to unravel the mystery surrounding man's existence with the sole aim of interrogating the past to address present happenings and having a peep into the future to know what it holds in store and how to influence it positively for successful living.

Redmon and Tze-Ki (2014) define divination broadly as a method of obtaining knowledge not obtainable by normal means about the past and the future, the state of the dead, ways to propitiate ancestors and spirits, and the nature of the cosmos. Divination is a means of gaining knowledge that is not obtainable by normal modes of investigation. It helps to handle uncertainty. It can warn or reassure a person or a community about what the future will bring, and it can illuminate what happened in the past. Divination is the general term for a myriad of different techniques to communicate with the supernatural in order to gain access to special knowledge. There are many types of divination all over the world, most especially in

Yorubaland (Coker, 2019). Ifa divination is the one chosen as the focus of this study.

Ifa Divination

Ifa, a deity of divine Oracle, is usually in the custody of an initiated priest, known as Babalawo, who is endowed with native wisdom to receive and interpret divine messages from the supernatural beings to humans. Ifa divination is an established mechanism through which complex issues are dissected, investigated, or looked into. According to Ojebode and Awonusi (2016), Ifa is a divinity that is deeply venerated in Yorubaland (South-Western Nigeria) by his devotees and even non-devotees. Nabofa (2002) asserts that Ifa worshipers see Orunmila (Grand priest of Ifa) as the prophet of God to the black race.

As pointed out by Olupona (2017), the exact origin of Ifa divination is unknown but it appears to predate Christianity and Islam in West Africa and it continues to be an important part of Yoruba culture in Nigeria and for Africans in America. Going by the Yoruba myth of creation, Ifa divination has been with the Yoruba from the beginning of time. The people are of the opinion that Ifa was central to the creation of the earth—*Ifa lo tele aye do.* Ifa is believed to have originated from Orunmila generally regarded as *Baba Ifa* (Father of Ifa). Abimbola (1977) referenced in Pogoson and Akande (2011) remarks that Ifa was one of the four hundred and one divinities that came from *Orun,* (heaven) to *Aye* (earth). Ifa is actually not approached directly. Priests called Babalawo—diviners or fathers of secrets—serve as intermediaries between the clients and Ifa.

Communication is an important aspect of Ifa divination system in Yorubaland esoterically and extramundanely because as observed by Bascon (1969), it is the most reliable way West African men (among which are the Yoruba people of Nigeria) seek and receive pieces of symbolic information and ideas from Gods.

Communication

Communication is as old as man (Novak, 2019). According to Oloyede (2008), the first instinct of man at birth is to communicate. At birth, the cry of a child announces his arrival from the world of the unborn to the world of the living. After this "announcement" man uses the rest of his life to communicate for one reason or the other (Oloyede, 2008). The communication that individuals engage in is via physical and metaphysical means (Omotoso, 2018). In communication studies, the process of communication is not always necessarily connected to the supernatural. Amy (2021) defines communication as the act of sharing and receiving information through a variety of media which can be one-on-one, between groups of people, face-to-face, or via communication devices. In this regard, communication requires a sender, the person who initiates communication, to transfer their thoughts or encode a message (Amy, 2021). The message is sent to the receiver, a person who receives the message, and finally, the receiver must decode, or interpret the message. Communication can be verbal, nonverbal, visual, or written. Munodawafa (2008) agrees that communication is an exchange of information in a process which involves a sender, a receiver, and a channel of communication. He adds that in the process of transmitting messages, the clarity of the message may be distorted by what is often referred to as barriers. Some other scholars refer to this as noise.

Communication takes place at intrapersonal and interpersonal levels. Chukwuemeka (2022) describes intrapersonal communication as a sort of communication that takes place within an individual through self-thought, internal monologue, internal discourse, and soliloquy or auto communication. It also includes self-talk, acts of imagination and visualization, and even recall or memory (McLean, 2005). Intrapersonal communication is therefore the foundation of all other forms of human communication without which man will be unable to function in his environment and open to external forms of communication. On the other hand, interpersonal communication, according to Jouany and Martic (2022), is the process of exchange of information, ideas, and feelings between two or more people through verbal or nonverbal methods. Both intrapersonal and interpersonal communications are involved in Ifa divination as extramundane communication.

IFA DIVINATION AS EXTRAMUNDANE COMMUNICATION

Ifa divination belongs to the African traditional communication form, otherwise known as indigenous communication, in Yorubaland. Traditional communication system is a form of communication which evolves from the social, cultural, customary, and traditional conventions of a given people. According to Wilson (1987) cited in Ogwezzy et al. (2018), traditional communication is "a continuous process of information dissemination, entertainment and education used in societies which have not been seriously dislocated by Western culture or any other external influence." Wilson (1987) referenced in Aziken and Emeni (2010) identifies eleven forms of traditional communication in Nigeria's old Calabar province. They are idiophones, membranophones, aerophone, symbology, signals, signs, objectives, color schemes, music, extramundane communication, and symbolic displays. Expatiating on this,

Akpabio (2003) defines extramundane communication as the mode of communication that exists between the living and the dead, the supernatural, or Supreme Being. Extramundane communication is expressed via incantations, spiritual chants, rituals, prayers, sacrifices, invocations, séance, hysterics, or libation (Akpabio, 2003). In his study, "African systems of contact and communication," Eluyemi (1987, p. 42) identifies Ifa divination as an idiographic system of communication consisting of complex philosophical ideas and messages relating to the basic facts of life of the individual who consults Babalawo. The Ifa divination system predicts through the *Odu* (chapters) of Ifa and as it is with all ideographic systems of communication, only experts in the tradition can recognize a particular *Odu* and interpret it appropriately. Gleason et al. (1973) see Ifa divination as an age-long means of communication. Idowu (1962) provided a more nuanced definition of Ifa divination as a system of verbal and nonverbal communication by which inquiries are made into the present and future life of a client by a Babalawo—priest.

Although the Yoruba employ a number of divination techniques, Morton-Williams et al. (1966) picks Ifa divination as one that yields the fullest pieces of information on every subject matter under the sun. To get information from Ifa, the Babalawo after due consultation with a client turns to his *Ikin* or the *Opele*, lifts it up, and then lays it on the floor or the divining tray. Fatunmbi (1991) describes this as *Dafa* which is considered to be direct communication with Orunmila, the god personifying Ifa divination.

IFA DIVINATION AND INTERNET

Spooner (2021) defines the internet as a global system of connected networks that consists of millions of computers, servers, routers, and printers on every network. Referencing Webopedia, Spooner adds that the network that makes up the internet may be owned and maintained by different companies but messages and data move across them without regard to ownership because they all use the same protocol or language to communicate. At this stage, it will be appropriate to have a holistic view of the computer. JavaTpoint (2022) describes a computer as:

> a programmable electronic device that accepts raw data as input and processes it with a set of instructions (a programme) to produce the result as output. It renders output just after performing mathematical and logical operations and can save the output for use. (JavaTpoint, 2022)

Longe (1983) states unequivocally that computer science borrowed from the Ifa divination system adding that many things that were introduced in

1963 in computer science had been in Ifa divination for more than one thousand years before that time. There is little wonder then that Oluwole (2017) says computer science originated from Ifa.

Alamu et al. (2013) explain that the processes used in Ifa divination system bear some similarities with computer science. According to them, Ifa divination is performed by *Babalawo* or *Iyanifa* (an initiated priest or priestess). So also, computer science is a file reserved for a few computer professionals and maintains some forms of secrecy using some security algorithms. Apart from their discovery, these researchers found out that Ifa divination is *Awo* (secret) and it is performed by professionals known as *Babalawo*. To be proficient in computer operation, a high degree of training is required. The same applies to the art of divination. Those who want to be diviners of Ifa, *Babalawo* or *Iyanifa,* also embark on training, at times rigorous one that spans a relatively long time. Even those born by parent(s) who are diviners, as a matter of necessity, also engage in the training. It is only after successfully completing the training that they are permitted to practice. Even at that, they have to pass through what is known as Ifa *tite* (a form of graduation and certification).

The computer operates on binary. Ifa does the same:

Ejeeji ni mo pe, emi o pe okan soso
I call in twos and not in ones.

God created everything in pairs. The first set of the odus are in pairs. They are *Eji ogbe, Oyeku meji, Iwori meji, Odi meji, Irosun meji, Owonrin meji, Obara meji, Okanran meji*, and so forth. Yussuf et al. (2019) see Ifa as a primitive computer binary system. *Odu Ifa* grew through addition, multiplication, and fusion to become bytes which also grew to become megabytes. For example, if you double the initial sixteen *Odu Ifa*, it will become thirty-two. If you multiply thirty-two by two, the answer will be sixty-four while sixty-four in two places will sum up to one hundred and twenty-eight. Finally, one hundred and twenty-eight multiplied by two will automatically give two hundred and fifty-six (256) chapters called *Odu Ifa*, the exact number of binaries being used in computers today.

The internet operates on infrastructure which is made up of various hardware and software working to send and receive information to different systems. Internet hardware according to Kanade (2022) is a set of physical or network devices that are essential for interaction and communication between hardware operational units. They include modems, routers, hubs, bridges and switches, network interface cards, cable networks, and firewall. Ifa divination system also has its own hardware infrastructure popularly known as diviner's equipment. They are *Opon Ifa* (divination tray*), Iroke Ifa* (diviner's tapper), *Ikin Ifa* (sacred palm nuts or kola nuts), *Opele Ifa* (divination chain), and

Iyerosun (divining powder). The internet relies on network service providers and/or internet service providers to function efficiently and effectively. In the same way, Ifa divination has its own service provider in *Esu* who serves as an intermediary or messenger between the Babalawo and Ifa. This role informs the reference to Esu as *agbebojarun*—one who delivers sacrifice in heaven. *Esu i*s the power of effective multidimensional communication. As routers are always strategically placed in the internet arrangement so is Esu in Ifa divination. Esu is always conspicuously placed in the entrance of the premises of the Babalawo, among other places, prominent among which is *Orita* (intersection). This accounts for his nickname of *Onile orita* (the land-lord of the house at the intersection). Both internet and Ifa divination operate virtually. While the internet is terrestrially virtual, Ifa divination is extrater-restrially virtual.

Another similarity internet and Ifa divination have in common is the proto-col guiding their operations. Internet protocol (IP) is a set of rules for routing and addressing packets of data so that they can travel across networks and arrive at the correct destination. Closely related to the IP is the IP address which is a unique identifier assigned to a device or domain. Ifa divination has its own protocol, a set of rules to be followed by a client wishing to commu-nicate with the divinity for various reasons. It starts from:

Fifi eeji, kun eta gboko alawo lo
Adding two to three before proceeding to consulting the Babalawo

This is followed by the actual consultation of speaking secretly to money, cowries, *Ikin* or *Opele*, the performance of the divination by the Babalawo, the revelation of the appropriate *Odu Ifa*, the rendition and interpretation of the revealed *Odu*, as well as prescription of the appropriate steps to be taken by the consultant for the achievement of his aim. Any breach in the protocol will lead to a breakdown in the communication process and consequently hinder the attainment of the desired purpose. Each of the sixteen main *Odu Ifa* has its identity. The other two hundred and forty *Odus* are offshoots of the main ones and domiciled in them as chapters.

The internet provides access to endless information, knowledge, and education. This is what Ifa divination is all about. It provides limitless infor-mation and knowledge about the past, the present, and even the future. The internet has the capacity to save data and easily share information which Ifa divination has been doing for as long as the existence of the Yoruba race. Ifa divination is a storehouse of data cutting across generations—*Ifa lo lana, Ifa lo loni, Ifa lola, Ifa lo lojo kan ondaye* (Ifa owns yesterday, today, tomorrow, and the day of the creation of the world), which are easily shared by those who have been schooled in the art as it is in internet. Above all, both the internet and Ifa divination are inventions at different points in the history of mankind.

The internet has its own language that promotes mutual intelligibility among computers making up the internet and the operators the same way the language of Ifa enhances understanding among diviners, Ifa oracle, and other deities.

FINDINGS

Findings reveal that Ifa divination system is a multifaceted online activity. It is based on virtual communicative connectivity carried out online by the priest with the instrumentality of oracular infrastructure. It enables the interaction between the supernatural being and humans with the priest using different platforms of information gathering and dissemination virtually. Further, our findings show that the Ifa divination system relies on different communicative infrastructures and platforms to gather and share information online, particularly the Ifa Oracle as the main infrastructure and the search engine in the divination process. On the other hand, the *Opele* and *opon ifa* provide networking site platforms like Google and Facebook as well as media sharing sites like YouTube. It is in these sites where live pictures are invoked on the white background by Ifa Priest to be viewed by clients or to remind them about past occurrences and project to the future. These findings reveal that Ifa bears several similarities with computer systems and the internet.

SUMMARY, CONCLUSION, AND RECOMMENDATIONS

Ifa, a deity of divine Oracle, is usually in the custody of an initiated priest known as *Babalawo* who is endowed with native wisdom to receive and interpret divine messages from the supernatural being to humans via divination. Ifa divination system involves the use of oracular signs and omens by an initiated priest (Babalawo) to divinely find out and reveal the hidden messages from the gods about the past and the future of individuals who seek the help of Babalawo. Ifa divination is an age-long practice among the Yoruba of Southwestern Nigeria. The Yoruba people see Ifa Priest as the divine link between humans and the supernatural realm for rightful solutions to their life problems. Despite major historical, sociocultural, and technological changes experienced in Africa, Ifa divination practice remains a popular form of interaction between the supernatural and the living, particularly among people of Yorubaland. There is, therefore, this general curiosity to gain insight into the communicative behavior of Ifa Priest and the communicative processes of Ifa divination system that have sustained the practice through ages without limitations of time and space. For example, Ifa divinations are not rare in the North American diaspora even at this digital age. In view of the longevity of the practice, what is next? We urge scholars to address the paucity of studies on the communicative elements of Ifa divination activities that link researchers with the understanding of its internet connectivity characteristics that keeps the practice relevant till today.

This study, undertaken to offer some insights into the meeting points between Ifa divination system as extramundane communication among the Yoruba people of South-Western Nigeria and the internet, has been able to establish similarities in the operational modes of Ifa divination system and the internet. Babalawo are like computer operators. Both are central to the adherence to the language and protocols guiding the operations of each system they superintend over and through which they solve peculiar problems before them. While the language of the internet enhances mutual intelligibility among computers, that of Ifa divination system promotes understanding among those contacting Ifa diviners for help, Ifa diviners, Ifa oracles, and the supernatural beings. Ifa divination comes from traditional religious systems. Ifa diviners are African religionists who are deep thinkers and traditional philosophers. Their rich minds are responsible for their abilities to understand the esoteric language of Ifa which helps them in generating ideas and principles they use to explain and solve problems.

The Yorubas, like other Africans, have lots of unclear local challenges, issues, phenomena, problems, and situations in modern era that requires critical reasoning, analysis, clarifications, persistence, and open mindedness before proffering solutions using the African philosophy for which Ifa divination is well known. Ifa diviners, via African philosophical and religious approaches, always render such local challenges, issues, phenomena, problems, and situations explainable, simple and solvable. This is what philosophers do. Computer scientists and philosophers have lots to gain from the broad and raw talents of Ifa diviners and African philosophy in the Ifa divination system by collaborating to see how Africans solve their local problems by their peculiar ways of reasoning. Ifa divination as a spring of wisdom, morality, and love is given to heavy skepticism like philosophy. They believe that finding a solution to a particular problem is not an end in itself but a means to an end. That is why they say *Bi oni se ri, ola le ma ri bee, lo mu ki Babalawo maa difa ojoojumo* (today's realities may not be tomorrow's realities. That is why Ifa diviners embark on daily divination).

Therefore, this paper recommends research collaboration among scholars of indigenous communication, computer science, and philosophy in order to provide insight into communicative features and practices of the internet which offer Ifa divination system the modern promise of indigenous platform of information sharing for problem-solving that is more accessible and relevant to users in the digital age.

REFERENCES

Abiodun, R. (1975). Ifa art objects: An interpretation based on oral tradition. In Wande Abimbola (Ed.), *Yoruba oral tradition* (pp. 421–59). Ibadan University Press.

Abioye, T. (2011). A socio-cultural analysis of Yoruba discusses patterns in selected child welfare clinics in Southwestern Nigeria. *CS Canada, Cross Cultural Communication, 7*(4), 6–22. https://doi.org/10.3968/j.ccc.1923670020110704.335

Akintan, O. A., & Adetimehin, A. (2021). Ifa divination and its significance among the people of Ijebu-Ode in South-Western Nigeria. *KIU Journal of Social Sciences, 7*(1), 121–27.

Akpabio, E. (2003). *African communication system: An introductory text.* Bprint Publication.

Alamu, F. O., Aworinde, H. O., & Isharufe, W. I. A. (2013). A comparative study on Ifa divination and computer science. *International Journal of Innovation Technology and Research, 1*(6), 524–28.

Amy, C. E. (2021). What is communication?. study.com/academy/lesson/what-is-communication-definition-importance.html.

Aziken, L. C., & Emeni, C. A. (2010). Traditional systems of communication in Nigeria: A review for improvement. *Knowledge Review, 21*(4), 7–21.

Cherry, K. (2023, March 12). What is a schema in psychology? *Verywellmind.* https://www.verywellmind.com/what-is-a-schema-2795873.

Chukwuemeka, E. S. (2022). Difference between interpersonal and intrapersonal communication. https://bscholarly.com/difference-between-interpersonal-and-intrapersonal-communication.

Coker, O. (2019). Modernity and the recycling of indigenous knowledge in Ifa literary corpus. *Ọyẹ́: Journal of Language, Literature and Popular Culture, 1*(1), 65–76.

Dixon, T. (2017, December 29). Schema theory: A summary. IB Psychology. *Thematic Education.* https://www.themantic-education.com/ibpsych/2017/11/29/schema-theory-a-summary/.

Dopamu, A. (2008). Predestination, destiny and faith in Yorubaland: Any meeting point?. *Global Journal of Humanities, 7*(1&2).

Eluyemi, O. (1987). African system of contact and communication. *Nigeria Magazine, 55*(2), 36–49.

Fatunmbi, A. F. (1991). *Iwa Pele: Ifa qest: Search for the source of Santeria and Lucumi.* Brox.

Garba, K. A. (2018, February 25). UNIESCO and Nigeria's Ifa divination System: Revisiting Akinwumi Ishola's impact. *The Guardian.* Sunday Magazine. https://guardian.ng/sunday-magazine/unesco-and-nigeria-ifa-divination-system-revisiting-akinwumi-isholas-impact.

George, T. (2023, March 10). What is participant observation? Definition & Examples. *Scribbl.* scribbl.com/methodology/what-is-participant-observation-definitio n-&-examples.

Gleason, J. (1973). *A recitation of Ifa, oracle of the Yoruba.* Grossman.

Idowu, E. B. (1996). *Olodumare: God in Yoruba belief.* Longman Group Limited.

Ihekwaba, N. (2020, January 15). Ifa as a system of divination. *The Nation.* https :thenationonline.net/Ifa-as-a-system-of-divination.

JavaTpoint. (2020). What is a computer? https:www.javatpoint.com/what-is-computer.

Jegede, O. (2010). *Incantations and herbal cures in Ifa and divination: Emerging issues in indigenous knowledge.* African Association for the Study of Religion.

Jouany, V., & Martic, K. (2022). Interpersonal communication: Definition, importance and must-have-skills. https://haiilo.com/blog/Interpesonal-communication -definition-importance-and-must-have-skills.

Kanade, V. (2022). *What is network hardware? Definition, architecture, challenges, and best practices.* https://www.spiceworks.com/tech/networking/articles/what-is -network-hardware.

Kelani, T. (2004). Ifa of Yoruba people of Nigeri. Documentary series on *Inscriptions on the intangible Heritage Lists.* Ifa Group of Oyo.

Koch, U. (2021, November 23). *Divination and Omens.* Oxford Bibliographies. oxfor dbibliographies.com/divination-and-omens.

Longe, O. (1993). *Ifa Divination and computer science: An inaugural lecture delivered at the University of Ibadan on Thursday, 22 December, 1983.* Girardef/press (W.A) Co.

McLean, S. (2005). *The basics of interpersonal communication.* Pearson/A and B.

Morton-Williams, P., Bascom, W., & McClelland, E. M. (1966). Two studies of Ifa divination. *Journal of International African Institute, 36*(4), 406–21.

Munodawafa, D. (2008). Communication: Concepts, practice and challenges. *Health Education Research, 23*(3), 369–37.

Nabofa, M. Y. (2002). *Principal elements in African traditional religion.* Centre for External Studies.

Novak, M. C. (2019). A brief history of communication and innovations that changes the game. hhps://www.g2.com/articles/a-brief-history-of-communication -and-innovations-that-changed-the-game.

Odunola, O., & Segun, O. (2009). The relevance of indigenous communication systems to national development. *Babcock Journal of Mass Communication, 2*(1), 7–17.

Ogwezzy, A. O., et al. (2018). *Course guide MAC11: African communication system I.* National Open University of Nigeria.

Ojebode, A., & Awonusi, F. (2016). Modernization of extra-mundane communication among Ifa worshippers: A rebuttal of the Neo-Secularization theses. *African notes, 40*(1&2), 68–79.

Oloyede, B. (2008). *Free press and society: Dismantling the culture of Silence* (Rev. ed.). Stirling-Horden Publishers Ltd.

Olu-Osayomi, O. (2017). The dramatic aspect of Ese Ifa in Yorubaland. *International journal on studies in English language and literature* (IJSELL), *5*(10), 12–18

Olupona, J. (2017). *2020 Prediction project.* Harvard University. Project.iq.harvard.edu.org.

Oluwole, S. (2017). Professor Sophie Oluwole: Computer science originated from Ifa. https://www.linked.com/pulse/professor-sophie-oluwole-computer-science-originated-from-ifa.

Omotoso, S. A. (2018). Gender and hair politics: An African philosophical Analysis. *Africology: The Journal of Pan African Studies 12*(8)

Oyetimi, K. (2022). Computer science borrowed from Ifa Corpus–Longe. *Nigerian-films.com.* https://www.thenigeriavoice.com/computer-science-borrowed-from-ifa-corpus-longe.

Pogoson, O. I., & Akande, A. O. (2011). Ifa divination trays from Isale Oyo. *Open Edition Journal.* https://journals.openedition.org/Ifa-divination-trays-from-isale-oyo.

Sanusi, B. O. (2013). Faith, religion and communication: The communication pattern in traditional African religion. *International Journal of Innovative Research & Development,* 2(11), 361–70.

Sponner, E. (2021). What is the internet?—Definition and explanation. study.com. https://study.com/academy/lecture/what-is-the-internet-definition-and-explanation.

Wilson, D. (1987). Taxonomy of indigenous communication media. *Development communication Module,* 2, 23–31.

Wilson, D. (2005). Participant Observation. In K. Kempf-Leonard (Ed.), *Encyclopedia of social measurement* (pp. 19–24). Elsevier. https://doi.org/10.1016/BO-12-369398-5/00398-4.

Yusuf, L. O., Ibrahalu, F. T., & Emmanuel J. A. (2019). Adoption of Ifa as a computer-based information system. *American Journal of Computer Science and Applications* (AJCSA), 2(19).

Chapter 6

New Media versus Traditional Media

27 Years after Emergence of Internet in Nigeria

Ibitayo Samuel Popoola and Paul Agada

The internet is the engine boat of new media. According to Popoola (2003, p. 23), "it began as an experiment by the US Department of Defence (DOD) in the 1960s to help scientists and researchers from widely dispersed areas work together by sharing scarce and expensive computers and their files." In Nigeria, the origin of the internet has been traced to 1996 when the Nigerian Communications Commission (NCC) licensed thirty-eight companies which immediately commenced provision of internet services to Nigerians. Link-serve Ltd. was first to commence the services. Between the year 1996 when internet services began and 2022, internet users in the country are estimated at 105 million. In spite of the high number of internet users in Nigeria, only 473 out of the 774 local councils in Nigeria have internet access. In other words, 301 local government areas are yet to have internet access twenty-seven years after the arrival of the internet in the country. It is against the above background that the study sought to establish the impact of the new media on the traditional media of communication in Nigeria.

The probing thesis in this updated study is anchored on the scholarly postulations of Dizard (1997) and Dominick (2009). Dizard sees the internet as a major factor in redefining the meaning of mass media. Additionally, Dominick contends that "the internet brings down the cost of mass communication (p. 44)." Both scholarly postulations guided this study whose pilot study was conducted in 2011 and published with the assistance of Fredrich Elbert Stiftung, Namibia. At the time the pilot study was conducted, the purpose was to evaluate the impact of the arrival of internet services on the traditional media of communication in Nigeria. Internet services came to Nigeria in 1996. The pilot study revealed the irresistible impact of the new media on the surveyed communities but noted that it has not reached the level of eliminating the traditional media of communication. Similarly, the objective of the latest study was to document the impact of the internet on the traditional media of communication, twenty-seven years later. The study used the same qualitative in-depth interview method with Royal fathers who are the custodians of the people's culture and tradition in three states in the South West geopolitical zone in Nigeria.

STATEMENT OF THE PROBLEM

The internet has been identified as a major device which has redefined and still redefines the meaning of mass media. It is now that the concept of mass media is having a true meaning with the emergence of WhatsApp, Facebook, Twitter, YouTube, and other social media which are platforms of information sharing minute-by-minute through laptops and smartphones such as: Samsung Galaxy S21, Infinix Note 10, Techno, Canon 17 Pro, Oppo Reno5F, itel, and Huawei, among others. At the time when the government of the federation introduced the internet in 1996, the thinking was premised on the need to have an avenue through which the citizenry could get information of interest, fast, cheap, and timely. However, it was never envisaged that after twenty-seven years of the operation of the internet, half of the country's total population would still not have internet access. In 2021, Nigeria's total population was put at 213.4 million making the country the seventh most populous country in the world. From this figure, as of 2022, 105 million have internet access (Osang, 2012). In other words, as at the time when this study was conducted in 2023, over 108 million Nigerians, that is, majority of the population, were yet to have internet access. It could therefore be stated that the country is far from realizing the objective of information sharing minute-by-minute throughout the country through the new media of information dissemination. However, the statistical figure on ground notwithstanding, the figure is sufficient enough for the exploration of this study.

Objectives

1. To determine the impact of new media on the survival of traditional media of communication in Nigeria.
2. To examine attributes of traditional media that could withstand the rampaging effects of the new media.
3. To find out what the future holds for the traditional media in Nigeria in this era of globalization.

Research Questions

1. Do the new media constitute a threat to the survival of traditional media of communication in Nigeria?

2. Do the old media in Nigeria possess attributes that could withstand the rampaging effects of new media?
3. In this era of globalization, what does the future hold for the old media in Nigeria?

EMPIRICAL REVIEW

The global world community has transited across several communication phases over the years. At the moment, another transition is taking place in the realm of communication across all the media typologies, that is, print, broadcast, and cinematography. In the context of Dizard Jr. (1997), what is happening across the world is that "the media industries are going through a transitional period in which old technologies are being adapted to new tastes" (p. 10). The most interesting example of this is the internet, which relies on old-fashioned telephone circuits and ordinary computer modems.

Assessing the impact of the internet after two decades of its emergence, Wigston (2009, p. 12) says "the emergence of new media technologies over the past 20 years has dramatically changed the media environment that many of us have been familiar with," adding that "the internet has changed the way in which most of us work and live." These digital experiences can be attested to by virtually every sector of the economy in Africa. Mowlana (1997, p. 31) argued that three approaches have dominated communications and development since the 1950s. The first approach is to view communication and development within the context of a cause–effect relationship while the second approach deals primarily with what might be called cost–benefit analysis or utilitarianism. The third approach deals with infrastructural analysis.

McQuail (2010) however revealed that "the expression 'new media' has been in use since the 1960s and encompasses an expanding and diversifying set of applied communication technologies." Burton (2010), quoting McQuail (2000), identified four main characteristics of "new media," namely: Interpersonal communication media, that is, email; Interactive play media—example is computer games; Information search media, that is, Net search engines; and Participatory media, such as Net chat rooms. Features of the new media such as those listed above in the context of Alexander Hanson (2005) point to the fact that the coming on board of new media is a development that instigated a populist political movement where citizens have greater access to the political world than ever before.

However, Aldridge (2007, p. 54) says, "local media may lack glamour, but their importance is beyond doubt." In rural Nigeria, as this study reveals, most people often had their everyday information needs met by the traditional media. The strength of the traditional media lies in the fact that they are accessible, reliable, and culturally rooted among the people. Andrews (2005), however, argues that "newspapers and other traditional media institutions are being usurped by individuals and online communities who use the internet to publish news and commentary." From Andrews' perspective, more and more people are today getting their news and information from independent websites rather than newspapers or other traditional media sources. No matter the rampaging effects of the internet on old media, Briggs (2005) contends that "newspapers will be around for many years to come" (p. 55).

Briggs made the assertion while reacting to the views that the internet will soon render newspapers obsolete. He asserts that

> while technology will certainly transform how newspapers will be made and distributed, that basic mission—delivery news and advertising to the customers in the communities they serve—will not change . . . newspapers will still prove to be indispensable. (p. 21)

Morton (2005) however insists that newspapers must change or perish. He asserts that "over the next ten or twenty years, newspapers will have to substantially re-invest themselves or they will perish" (p. 22). He recalls that he grew up reading newspapers but now, he gets most of his information from the internet. He reveals that many people in his generation and younger ones are doing the same:

> Newspapers have always been in the business of reporting news, breaking news, analyzing news, but now that job is done adequately and with much more immediacy on the internet. (Neil Morton, 2005, p. 167)

Dominick (2009, p. 76) on his part says "the internet brings down the cost of mass communication to a level at which almost everybody can afford it." He explained further that the affordability can make every interested person to become an electronic publisher with access to millions of people, thereby creating a new type of mass communicator.

THEORETICAL FRAMEWORK

The study adopted the uses and gratifications theory of the mass media. Severin and Tankard Jr. (2001) note that the theory was first used in an article anchored by Elihu Katz (1959) where it debunked the claim by Bernard Berelson (1959) that the field of communication research was dead. He observed that most communication research up to that time was geared at probing "What do media do to people?" Katz therefore suggested that attention should shift to "What do people do with the media?" The uses and gratifications approach therefore shifted focus from the purposes of the communicator to the purposes of the receiver. For this reason, Okunna (1999) described the uses and gratifications theory as a functional theory especially against the backdrop of the fact that people selectively expose themselves to mass media contents by choosing only those media messages that would serve the function of satisfying or gratifying their needs. This approach, according to Blake and Haroldsen (1975), contends that "the interaction of people with the media can most often be explained by the uses to which they put the media content and/or the gratification which they receive" (p. 67). This is true in communities that use the media for various purposes. For example, the survival of the traditional media in spite of the glamour of the new media is as a result of its various uses by the broad spectrum of the society. For example, in spite of availability of radio and TV, town criers still play a significant role in disseminating information, just as folktale wax strong especially at this critical period when youths are being recruited into the dreaded Boko Haram sect.

Popoola (2003) observed that darkness has gripped Nigeria for four decades since the introduction of the internet in 1996 due to failure of the government to accord the communication sector a national priority. Nonetheless, the decision by the government to deregulate the telecommunication subsector in 2002 was a step forward. It paved the way for the entrance of operators of mobile phones otherwise called Global System of Mobile Communication (GSM) in Nigeria. Today, GSM provides the platform for the easiest, most convenient, cheapest, and prompt dissemination of information on minute-by-minute basis either through the bulk Short Message Service (SMS), text messages, internet browsing, WhatsApp messages, Facebook interaction, Twitter, or so forth, besides its main purpose, phone calls.

METHODOLOGY

This study employed the qualitative in-depth anonymized interview method with royal fathers who are the custodians of the people's culture and tradition. This method provides the opportunity for extracting truthful, sincere, objective, and unbiased information regarding the guided questions for this study. Over the years and across generations, information sharing has taken place under two broad phases of communication systems, namely: the phase of information sharing on face-to-face basis which thrived heavily through the opinion leaders in the traditional system and the phase of the highly organized explicitly structured mass media as captured by Schramm (1972), as cited in Popoola (2011). This chapter uses data collected between June and September 2023 almost twenty-one years since the last study was conducted in 2002 barely a year after the operations of the GSM in the country. With three first class Royal Fathers, as interviewees, the study adopted an in-depth interview method. According to Wimmer and Dominick (2006, p. 135), "Intensive interviews, or in-depth interviews are essentially a hybrid of the one-on-one interview approach." The method is the most effective when dealing with a small number of respondents.

At that time of the pilot study, only the urban communities covered in the study in Lagos state were enjoying about 40 percent of the accruable benefits from mobile phones. The problem was accessibility. Resources such as Blackberry and other smart phones through which people could listen to radio, snap pictures, record conversation, and above all enjoy internet browsing were not available. All the same, urban areas seemed better placed to access GSM services. For example, at the time, the semi-urban community of Ode-Remo in Ogun state enjoyed skeletal services of the GSM while it was not available at Ootunja rural community of Ekiti State. Against this background, the 2011 study assessed the situation after ten years of GSM's operations in Nigeria, but not on internet access. The respondents are three first-class Royal Fathers in each of the studied communities in the three states of South-Western Nigeria. A set of questions were drawn up to guide the interview which was conducted with the aid of midget. The interview was transcribed and analyzed to provide answers to the research questions.

Today, however, expensive mobile phones with multidimensional functions are all over the place in the market. Examples are: Samsung Galaxy S21, Infinix Note 10, Techno, Canon 17 Pro, Oppo Reno5F, itel, and Huawei, among others.

PRESENTATION OF FINDINGS AND DISCUSSION

The traditional communication covered by this study are those classified by Ogwezzy-Ndisika (2008) as town criers, metal gongs, talking drum, masquerade, and folktales. The following paragraphs describe their use among diverse communities in Nigeria.

Town Crier

Town crier is an ancient device for information dissemination in the various African societies. From archival sources, it has been in existence during the precolonial African societies. Accessing the relevance of town criers in day-to-day government societies, Akinfeleye (2023) says it should no longer be called town crier but information announcer. According to him, it is not only misleading but confusing to call it town crier but information announcer, going by the modalities of their operations.

Gong

This is a traditional communication device whose role is similar to the ringtone of a mobile handset. In precolonial as well as postcolonial South-Western Nigeria, gongs are used in communicating cultural music and signs between the royal fathers and their subjects. The various blacksmith sites in the community are the industries manufacturing them because they are made from metal. Irrespective of their sizes, they usually have a v-shaped design. In some families, children have been socialized to decode the various sounds from the gongs encoded by the gong man.

Talking Drums

These are highly coded communication devices in Yoruba, South-Western Nigeria. They exist in various shapes or forms. Examples are Gangan and Bata. While many people might experience difficulties in decoding the messages through the taking drums, it is unthinkable if there would ever be a Yoruba Monarch who is not able to decode messages through the talking drums.

Pot Drums

This traditional communication device is called "Pot Drum" because it is usually mounted on baked clay. A pot made of clay is procured and a leather skin is then erected or fixed on it. The beater usually uses sticks made with foam. It supplies good music with beautiful rhythm for dancing.

Masquerades

As used in this study, masquerades are representations communicating various messages to the people of Yoruba, South-Western Nigeria. In one of the studied communities, Ootunja-Ekiti, they come out as a sign that an important person has passed on in the community. They are of various grades and status, each communicating how important or prominent is the person that passed on.

Folktales

The strong Yoruba culture can be traced or attributed to a deliberate act of passing cultural values to the young ones through oral stories which teach morals in the society. It is typically done in the evening and referred to by some people as tales by moonlight.

The objective of the study was to establish if the new media of the internet, an umbrella shield for the operations of mobile phones, WhatsApp, Twitter, and Facebook, among others, constitute a threat to the survival of the above-listed traditional system of communication.

For a holistic report, the study covered three communities in the South-West geopolitical zone in Nigeria. Each of the guided research questions were put across to each of the royal fathers, and their responses were later transcribed and packaged in a coherent, accurate, clear, and logical manner as presented below.

URBAN COMMUNITIES

Phone

The three communities of Sabe, Egbe, and Igando in Lagos state fully enjoyed mobile phone services including internet browsing, online readership of newspapers, radio listenership, and receiving bulk SMS from the royal father, among others. They however complain about poor connectivity and network. The community monarch said he uses the medium very effectively to share urgent information with his subjects. The oba uses a combination of Yoruba, English, and pidgin English in putting information across to his subjects. The monarch Gbadamosi however disagreed that new media could constitute any threat to traditional media of communication.

Internet

Dominick (2000, p. 279) observes that the mid-2000s witnessed the development of "easy-to-use software programs that made it simple to upload content to the internet." This in turn encouraged the growth of blogs, social networking sites, as well as video-sharing sites. The youths in Igando, Sabe, and Egbe, according to Oba Gbadamosi, are enlivened by the emergence of social media, especially, Facebook and Twitter. The Oba says hardly there could be any youth in his domain that is not on Facebook. He says further that the internet also provides jobs for hundreds of people in his domain who operate cyber cafes. In spite of the popularity of social media among the youths in the area, the Oba said the internet does not constitute a threat to the traditional media in the communities.

Folklore

This is not popular in the three communities. Rather, "soap opera," cartoons, and kiddies programs on TV were discovered to have replaced folktale or

Table 6.1 Semi-urban Communities

S/No.	Urban Communities	Semi-Urban Communities	Rural Community
	Mobile Phone: The three communities of Sabe, Egbe, and Igando in Lagos state now fully enjoyed mobile phone services including internet browsing, online readership of newspapers, radio listenership, and receiving bulk SMS from the royal father, among others. They however complain about poor connectivity and network. The community monarch said he uses the medium very effectively to share urgent information with his subjects. The oba uses a combination of Yoruba, English, and pidgin English in putting information across to his subjects. The monarch Gbadamosi however disagree that new media could constitute any threat to traditional media of communication	At Ode-Remo, a similar finding was discovered. However, the royal father said he uses Yoruba language more often whenever he has information to put across to his subjects. He, however, said his subjects complained about high tariff charged by the service providers as well as epileptic power supply to regularly charge their handsets. The royal father said the new media does not pose any threat to the traditional media of communication in the community	His Royal Majesty, Oba Joseph Adelola Fagbamila II, equally alluded to the warm embrace of his people when the new media arrived. He, however, said it does not constitute any threat to all the existing traditional media of communication in his community, which existed prior to the arrival of the new media
2.	**Internet:** Dominick (2000, p. 279) observes that the mid-2000s witnessed the development of "easy-to-use software programs that made it simple to upload content to the internet." This in turn encouraged the growth of blogs, social networking sites, as well as video-sharing sites. The youths in Igando, Sabe, and Egbe, according to Oba Gbadamosi, are enlivened by the emergence of social media, especially, Facebook and Twiter. The Oba says hardly there could be any youth in his domain that is not on Facebook. He says further that the internet also provides jobs for hundreds of people in his domain who operate cyber cafes. In spite of the popularity of social media among the youths in the area, the Oba said the internet does not constitute a threat to the traditional media in the communities	The internet services are also being enjoyed fully by residents of Ode-Remo. Oba Adeolu confirmed that it provides jobs for some people who operate cyber cafes. They, however, said epileptic power supply has also frustrated many of the cybercafé operators. "There may be no power supply for three or four weeks, beside the fact that many of the cybercafé operators cannot afford the prohibitive price of petrol and generating plants." The royal fathers said the internet does not constitute any threat to traditional media in the community	Residents of Ootunja community lately began to enjoy internet services due to the collapse of Nigerian Telecommunications Plc in the community, coupled with late arrival of service providers. Oba Fagbamila said even though his subjects are just coming into contacts with the internet, he warned that a recent incident in Nasarawa state University, in which a female undergraduate was dated on the internet through Facebook and later killed in Lagos, will encourage any royal father to campaign against a wholesome approval of social media

(Continued)

Table 6.1 (Continued)

S/No.	Urban Communities	Semi-Urban Communities	Rural Community
3.	**Folklore:** This is not popular in the three communities. Rather, "soap opera," cartoons, and kiddies programs on TV were discovered to have replaced folktale or bedtime stories whose goal is for parents to use it in training their children on morals	Folktale is very popular and generally embraced by the community. It was learned through Oba Adeolu and his successor that the metropolitan nature of Lagos, coupled with urban stress, was the reason why folktale is no longer popular in Lagos	Deliberate efforts by the community have strengthened the relevance of folktale in the day-to-day life of the people. Oba Fagbamila says "it is used to teach morals and check abuses"
4.	**Town Crier:** Motorized town criers exist in the communities due to their metropolitan nature. Town criers are used to disseminate timely information	Town criers are still in active use in the community for the same purpose, in spite of availability of radio and TV	Town crier in Ootunja played the role of modern radio announcer. Oba Fagbamila says news from the town crier is more authentic than any story on radio and TV
5.	**Masquerade:** Apart from playing the role of entertainment, Oba Gbadamosi said it is also used in communicating the Obas message to every clan in the communities. Furthermore, it is used to settle rifts and curb violence and quarreling over a piece of land	Oba Adeolu and his successor said the mythology of the masquerades is firmly rooted in Yoruba culture and this explains why it is seen as part and parcel of the daily life of any Yoruba community. He further says no drama on TV provides more fun, entertainment, and relaxation than the masquerades	Masquerades serve the same purpose in this community. An additional role here is that they come out when an old man or woman dies. Oba Fagbamila says "when people see the masquerade, they quickly decode the message that something has happened"

Source: Authors.

bedtime stories whose goal is for parents to use it in training their children on morals.

Town Crier

Motorized town criers exist in the communities due to their metropolitan nature. Town criers are used to disseminate timely information.

Masquerade

Apart from playing the role of entertainment, Oba Gbadamosi said it is also used in communicating the Obas message to every clan in the communities. Furthermore, it is used to settle rifts and curb violence and quarreling over a piece of land.

DISCUSSION, RECAPITULATION, AND CONCLUSION

This latest study has confirmed the reality of Dizard's (1997) postulation that the internet has redefined the meaning of mass communication. From the findings in this study, the new media operating through the internet has explained the mass media as technological devices through which the mass audience could be reached fast at the same time, but the majority of the royal fathers believe that despite its penetration in their rural communities, the internet does not constitute a threat to the traditional media in the communities.

The study further confirmed Dominick's postulation that the internet has brought down the cost of mass communication. The study found out that with as low as N100.00 data, a social media audience could have access to as many social media platforms as possible even though it is for a short while. During the interviews, users indicated they had access to many platforms because it was cheap to do so. The internet has allowed more people to access diverse information at a low cost.

The study further documents the various uses of the new media by the citizenry in the studied communities, which are for entertainment and sports purposes on Facebook, and communication purposes as well on WhatsApp. It learned that in spite of the popularity of the new media as well as its irresistible functions, the functionality as well as uses has not diminished the role of traditional media in the affairs of the studied communities. For example, the Oba still uses town criers, masquerade, and folklore, among others.

It was revealed that while residents of the surveyed communities had the irresistible impact of the new media, the impact has however not reached the level of eliminating traditional media, as a lot of royal fathers in the communities affirm that the deep penetration of the internet in these rural communities does not constitute any threat to all the existing traditional media of communication in their community, which existed prior to the arrival of the new media. It however stressed the need for the traditional societies to jealously keep what they have in order not to allow Morton's (2005) prediction of perish or change to happen.

Earlier, the study put forward three research questions: First, it asked if the new media constitute a threat to the survival of traditional media of communication. Going by the findings from the study, it was revealed that folktales face the threat from television in urban communities unlike among semi-urban and rural communities where the tradition of telling stories is still highly revered.

Second, the study also asked if the traditional media possess attributes that could withstand the rampaging effects of the new media. The answer is in affirmative. The traditional media are culturally rooted. As such, they are part and parcel of the daily life of the people, being that culture is local, native, and unique, but the digital media adapts to the space it finds itself.

Third, the study asked what does the future hold for old media in Nigeria in this era of digitization? The study discovered that unless concerted efforts are made to check the rampaging effects of globalization, what happened in the urban communities in this study concerning folktale could be witnessed in the other communities in future. We see the future of traditional media as stable if not bright. The fact that Nigerians are very passionate about their culture is a good foundation and indicator that it would endure. For instance, in Nollywood movies, it is impressive that the industry strives to keep the culture alive in the way they showcase the Nigerian communicative culture. The effort of Nollywood also is a clarion call for the African scholars that there is a need to ensure there are concerted efforts to keep these traditional communication forms alive because the future is bright for the African indigenous media.

RECOMMENDATIONS

- The various socializing agents in the studied communities should be strengthened in a bid to sustain the functions of Nigerian traditional media in the digital age. Both modern and traditional communication forms can be useful to humanity based on how they are used.
- The government should act to safeguard internet security measures to prevent cybercrimes.

- The Nigerian Communications Commission (NCC) should address mobile phone users' complaints over dubious charges and interconnectivity problems which rob them of excellent service.
- The government should also compel Power Holding of Nigeria Plc to find a lasting solution to concerns about unreliable power supply.

REFERENCES

Akinfeleye, R. A. (2023). Relevance of town crier in a democracy. Keynote address at *AMCRON 3*rd *conference*, 6th–7th December, UNILAG.

Aldridge, M. (2007). *Understanding the local media*. Open University Press.

Alexander, A., & Hanson, J. (2005). *Taking sides: Clashing views on controversial Issues in mass media and society* (8th ed.). McGraw-Hill/Dushkin.

Andrews, P. (2009). *Internet journalism will transform the media industry in mass media*. Greenhaven Press.

Blake, R. H., & Haroldsen, E. O. (1975). *A taxonomy of concepts in communication*. Hastings House Publishers.

Briggs, M. (2005). *The internet will not make newspapers obsolete in mass media*. Greenhaven Press.

Burton, G. (2010). *Media and society, critical perspective*. Open University Press.

Dizard, W. (1997). *Old media, new media, mass communication in the information age*. Longman Inc.

Dominick, J. R. (2009). *The dynamics of mass communication media in the digital age* (10th ed.). McGraw Hill.

Eleanya, F. (2023). Why made-in-Nigeria smartphones remains a puzzle. *Businessday NG*. businessday.ng.

McQuail, D. (2010). *Media and society*. Open University Press.

Morton, N. (2005). *The internet will make newspapers obsolete in mass media*. Greenhaven Press.

Mowlana, H. (1997). *Global information and world communication*. SAGE Publication.

Ogwezzy-Ndisika, A. (2008). *African communication systems concepts, channels and messages*. African Renaissance Books Inc.

Okunna, S.C. (1991). *Introduction to mass communication* (2nd ed.). New Generation Books.

Osang, F. (2012). Internet access in Nigeria: Perception of National Open University of Nigeria (NOUN) students. *International Journal of Emerging Technology and Advanced Engineering, 2*(10), 492–97.Popoola, T. (2003). *GSM as a tool for news reporting in Nigeria*. Corporate Lifters International.

Severin, W. J., & Tankard, J. W. (2001). *Communication theories: Origins, methods and uses in the media*. Addison Wesley Longman Inc.

Wigston, D. (2009). Quantitative content analysis. In Pieter J. Fourie (Ed.), *Media studies* (Vol. 3). JUTA Co Ltd.

Wilson, D. (1988). Towards integrating traditional and modern communication systems. In R. A. Akinfeleye (Ed.), *Contemporary issues in mass media for development and national security*. Unimedia Publications Ltd.

Wimmer, R. D., & Dominick, J. R. (2006). *Mass media research, An introduction*. Wadsworth Cengage Learning.

Chapter 7

African Language Media and BBC Yoruba Service Sports Headlines

Influence on Audience Engagement Online

Unwana Samuel Akpan, Chuka
Onwumechili, Abayomi Bamidele Adisa,
and Abigail Odozi Ogwezzy-Ndisika

Several studies have revealed that sports, especially football, is keenly followed by the majority of Nigerians in the various media platforms, such as the British Broadcasting Corporation (BBC) media channels (Cardiff, 1983; Huggins, 2007; Omobowale, 2009; Njorora, 2009; Onwumechili, 2011; Akpan, 2020; Onwumechili & Oloruntola, 2014). Numerous archaeological and historical records show that the BBC was responsible for the first presence of the broadcast media in most Anglophone countries in Africa, and Nigeria being inclusive. Ever since, the BBC has reinvented itself to meet with the evolving real-time lingual, cultural, and technical existential realities that are common in the continent, especially native language realities. The BBC for instance in 2018 launched twelve online language services across the world. Out of the twelve language services launched by the BBC globally, four language services (Hausa, Igbo, Yoruba, and Pidgin services) were established in Nigeria to cater for the three major ethnic groups and the pidgin speaking community in the country. This study will zero in on the BBC News Yoruba service, in order to investigate the impact its creative and unconventional writing of sports headlines has on the Yoruba speaking sports fans in Lagos state, Nigeria. The Yoruba language is spoken widely in the neighboring countries of Togo, and Benin republic. The BBC language service's sports headlines have severally been subject of social media conversations for its peculiarity in the use of vocabulary and rhetorical devices. Its style embraces sensational writings and comic nuances for announcing match results. It uses day-to-day street lingua and slangs known as African language media in its sports headlines; consequently, engaging audiences and setting the tone for how they react to match results on social media. This form of writing that is a departure from conservative sports headline writing the traditional BBC News is known for over the years. For instance, observable engagements on BBC News Yoruba's website, Facebook, and Instagram pages during the English Premier League is high engagement with their audience. This study focuses on the creative deployment of African language media in BBC News Yoruba football headlines that attract its audiences in Lagos state, Nigeria— this style might be a departure from traditional style of headlines news casting that was handed down to the Nigerian press by the colonial masters.

TRADITIONAL STRUCTURE OF NEWS

Lagos state is majorly occupied by Yoruba speaking majority and it is the media capital of Nigeria. This study therefore examines how multimedia news platforms influence audience engagement through its rather unconventional headline casting techniques using the African language media technique. News headlines serve a role akin to salesmen promoting their products; they sell stories. As noted by Scacco and Ashley (2019), headlines encapsulate a segment of the story, providing a snapshot of reality. The authors succinctly summarize the breadth of a news story in clear, unambiguous language, enticing readers to delve into the entire article. According to Ogunsiji (1989, p. 97), headlines are strategically crafted to swiftly reveal the social, cultural, economic, and political issues unfolding in a society at any given time. To achieve this, headlines employ varied syntax and lexical structures, ensuring their ability to capture the essence of news events and engage readers effectively. In casting news headlines, writers strategically sacrifice certain parts of sentences to pique readers' curiosity and serve functional signposts to stories. Oloruntobi (2020) highlighted that newspaper editors, through their headlines, play a pivotal role in shaping societal issues, framing what is discussed, and determining how it is discussed (known as priming and framing). Newspaper headlines, as observed by Alamoudi (2017), serve as significant models of linguistic behaviors and reflect the language features prevalent in a community, making them apparent to modern readers. Readers often find themselves influenced by the specific linguistic structures employed in headlines, as noted by Purwanti (2019), who categorized headline structures as a subject of syntax study, involving the arrangement of words and phrases to create coherent sentences in a language. Ehineni (2014) suggests that factors such as the publishing industry's house style, spatial constraints, and the need for quick dissemination of facts lead to deliberate reductions in the full syntax of headline structures. Consequently, the structures of headlines may vary based on the factors identified by Ehineni (2014).

In the digital era, news outlets are adapting to the transformations associated with digital journalism. As journalism transitions into the digital space, headlines are evolving in their structure and functions. While traditional headlines primarily aimed to offer a clear understanding of an article's content to readers scanning a newspaper (Van Dijk, 1988), contemporary headlines, according to Kuiken (2017), are often encountering stereotyped forms of headlines. In this context, Chen et al. (2015) recommend that headlines, being one of the primary methods to attract readers' attention, should primarily evoke curiosity and compel readers to open the article. Undoubtedly, headlines significantly impact the traffic directed toward the stories they introduce. With the rising competition in the digital landscape, headlines have undergone a complete transformation in their appeals. Nwammuo and Nwafor (2019) argue that headlines have become more assertive, exaggerated, and occasionally misleading to capture the attention of readers amid the digital noise. Therefore, the objectives of this study are to analyze BBC News Yoruba's digital sports headlines and scrutinize their linguistic elements, emotive appeal, and cultural relevance to Yoruba-speaking audiences.

STATEMENT OF THE PROBLEM

In their research, Nwala and Umukoro (2017) explored the challenges faced by readers in comprehending newspaper headlines in Nigeria. The authors pinpointed headline ambiguities as a significant factor leading readers to attribute various interpretations to the headlines, given that they often possess more than one conceivable meaning. The study examined data obtained from three prominent Nigerian newspapers—Vanguard, Guardian, and Punch—and conducted a qualitative analysis to identify linguistic features contributing to headline ambiguity. In a separate investigation, Anigbogu and Ibe (2021) explored the linguistic structures of news headlines featured in Nigerian newspapers. Their research uncovered distinctive linguistic and discursive patterns inherent in these headlines. The authors scrutinized the syntactic patterns governing clause and sentence structures within the headlines, employing the Theme/Rheme structure from Systemic Functional Linguistics for analysis. The study drew theoretical insights from both Systemic Functional Linguistics and Critical Discourse Analysis to provide a comprehensive examination of newspaper headlines. The researchers identified various linguistic patterns, including clauses, phrases, imperatives, modality, questions, and passives, which were strategically employed to express opinions, evoke suspense, capture attention, and convey ideologies in the headlines. Notably, the prevalence of the simple present tense was observed as a prevalent choice by writers when articulating opinions. Additionally, in the syntactic analysis, the unmarked theme emerged as the preferred choice among writers for constructing headlines. The study concluded that newspaper headlines such as the one displayed by the BBC Yoruba Sport online function as succinct summaries of ideologies, strategically employed by writers to generate suspense and capture the readers' attention (Anigbogu & Ibe, 2021).

The convergence of media platforms and linguistic diversity in Nigeria, coupled with the BBC News innovative approach to sports reporting, has given rise to a unique phenomenon: the creative and unconventional writing of sports headlines in the BBC News Yoruba service. This departure from the traditional style of sports reporting has garnered significant attention, particularly in the context of the Yoruba-speaking sports fans in Lagos state, Nigeria, as well as in neighboring countries like Togo and Benin Republic. While studies have highlighted the widespread popularity of sports, especially football, among Nigerians across various media platforms, Okwo (2016), Oboh (2019), Salawu (2004), and Doe and Smith (2020), there exists a gap in understanding the profound impact of BBC News Yoruba's distinctive sports headlines on the Yoruba-speaking audience. The central problem addressed by this research is: what is the impact of BBC News Yoruba's creative and unconventional writing of sports headlines on Yoruba-speaking sports fans in Lagos state, Nigeria, and neighboring countries, in terms of audience engagement, perceptions, and social media interactions during major sports events, specifically focusing on the English Premier League matches? This problem is significant because it raises questions about the influence of linguistic and cultural nuances in sports reporting, especially when juxtaposed with the evolving media landscape in Nigeria. The emergence of social media conversations surrounding BBC News Yoruba's sports headlines underscores the need to investigate the extent to which this unconventional style resonates with the audience, shapes their reactions to match results, and influences their online interactions. By exploring the unique linguistic strategies, vocabulary choices, and rhetorical devices employed by BBC News Yoruba in crafting sports headlines, this study aims to shed light on the underlying factors that might drive audience engagement and reactions within the Yoruba-speaking community. The significance of this research is to study the increasing metamorphosis in digital and online sports headlines writing techniques by the BBC and how this could drive news selection, engagement, and consumption patterns in Lagos, Nigeria. Furthermore, this research endeavors to contribute valuable insights into the intersection of media, language, and sports fandom in multicultural societies like Nigeria.

LITERATURE REVIEW

The role of headlines in print and online news media has been a subject of extensive research. Early studies, such as Van Dijk (1988), focused on headlines' function of providing readers with a clear idea of the article's content, particularly for those scanning a newspaper. Bell (1991) emphasized the attention-grabbing aspect of headlines, asserting that they draw readers in and encourage them to read the associated story. Mahmood et al. (2011) supported this view, considering headlines as precursors to the main article. Scholars, however, differ in their opinions on the functional roles of headlines. Dor (2003) argued that headlines not only summarize but also build affinity and relevance for the reader, striking a balance between being concise and clear while providing a rich summary of the content. Iarovici and Amel (1989) shared a similar perspective, highlighting how headlines aid readers in understanding the content's meaning. Conboy (2013) offered a comprehensive view, categorizing headlines into three functions: providing a short summary of news, grabbing attention, and indicating the newspaper's style and news values.

In the digital age, the increased consumption of content online, especially on social media platforms has shifted the role of headlines toward being attention-grabbing rather than purely informative. The competition for reader attention has intensified due to the demand for user engagement, leading to the rise of clickbait, where vague headlines induce curiosity and prompt readers to click. Blom and Hansen (2015) and García-Orosa et al. (2017) emphasized the crucial role of word choices in headlines, with a focus on what prompts readers to click. Clickbait often utilizes forward referencing and interrogative forms to provoke curiosity and encourage clicks (Kuiken, 2017; Scacco & Muddiman, 2016; Lai & Farbrot, 2014). The success of forward referencing headlines lies in their ability to arouse curiosity, tapping into the phenomenon known as a knowledge gap, where individuals seek missing information to eliminate a sense of deprivation (Loewenstein, 1994; Mormol, 2019). Forward referencing, as a stylistic feature, is prominent in clickbait headlines, enticing readers to delve deeper into the content. We shall now examine the different kinds of news headlines.

Forward Referencing Headlines

Blom and Hansen (2015) posit that forward referencing headlines serve the purpose of hinting at forthcoming aspects of a story in advance, often leaving certain elements unexplained. These headlines frequently incorporate signal words such as "why," "this," "what," or pronouns like "he" or "she" to arouse reader curiosity (Kuiken, 2017). Hess (2016) further elaborates that forward referencing headlines often employ pronouns, adverbs, imperatives, interrogatives, or general nouns, compelling individuals to read the article. According to Blom and Hansen (2015), forward referencing headlines can take two forms: discourse deixis and cataphora. Discourse deixis refers to reference to forthcoming parts of the discourse relative to the current location, for instance, "This is the best news story you will ever read." Cataphora, on the other hand, involves a word or phrase that appears later in the text, for instance, "When he arrived at the crime scene, the journalist interviewed the victim's wife."

Researchers have compared the performance of stories with forward referencing to traditional ones. Biyani et al. (2016) discovered that informal content with forward referencing features performs better than non-clickbait (traditional) content. This trend is especially evident in today's digital news headlines. While traditional newspaper headlines maintain a conservative and formal style, online news headlines have adopted more informal writing styles to entertain, summarize, and engage audiences. Interestingly, Ifantidou's (2009) findings challenge conventional norms, indicating that factors like length, clarity, and informativeness are not crucial for headline selection. Readers tend to value headlines that are under-informative, creative, and autonomous, emphasizing the primary role of headlines in grabbing attention.

Headlines Posed as Questions

The use of headlines in the form of questions has a long history predating the digital age, serving as a tool to pique readers' curiosity and encourage them to seek answers within the content (Howard, 1988). Question-based headlines, both in print and online, are designed to challenge readers, sparking their interest and compelling them to delve into the articles for answers. These interrogative elements have seamlessly transitioned into online news, often appearing as hypothetical, rhetorical, or leading questions, accompanied by self-referencing cues aimed at enhancing reader engagement (Lai & Farbrot, 2014). Such self-referential cues establish a connection between the readers and the content, effectively increasing the impact of these functional headlines (Debevec & Iyer, 2006). Question-based headlines primarily aim for conversion, transforming passive readers into active participants by fueling their curiosity. The allure of these headlines lies in the uncertainty they create, prompting readers to click for resolution (Scacco & Muddiman, 2019). When question headlines are answered within the content, they prove to be an effective strategy for engaging readers. However, despite their long-standing presence, there is a scarcity of research on how question-type headlines impact readership, as noted by Lai and Farbrot (2014).

Early research, predating the internet era, suggested that question head-lines could generate interest (Soley & Reid, 1983). Myers and Haug (1967) found that question headlines could capture attention, particularly when the majority of headlines followed this format, although they had no significant impact on recall when compared to declarative (traditional) headlines. How-ever, contemporary studies present conflicting views on the effectiveness of question-based headlines. Scacco and Muddiman (2016) discovered that question headlines were viewed negatively and had lower engagement rates compared to traditional headlines. Similarly, Kuiken (2017) argued that the absence, rather than the presence, of questions in headlines enhanced perfor-mance. The debate surrounding the performance of question-based headlines remains inconclusive. Nevertheless, recent findings by Lai and Farbrot (2014) suggest that such headlines are more effective in generating clicks compared to their traditional counterparts, emphasizing their continued relevance in the digital era.

TRADITIONAL NEWS HEADLINES

Headlines, according to traditional publishing standards, serve as concise summaries of news stories following an inverted pyramid structure (Andrew, 2016). They are designed to be clear, explicit, and unambiguous, providing readers with key points of the main story and ensuring informational clarity. Unlike headlines of forward referencing or questioning nature, traditional headlines adhere to a straightforward approach. They focus on the "who" or "what" central to the news story, utilizing content words for specific persons and locations while leaving function words for readers to interpret contex-tually (Chakraborty et al., 2016). Compared to clickbait-style headlines, traditional headlines contain fewer word shortenings and have been found to be twice as effective in click-through rates (Gessler, 2017). Respondents have shown more positive reactions to traditional headlines, engaging more with them than with question-framed headlines (Scacco & Muddiman, 2016). Clear headlines also outperform shorter and more ambiguous ones in terms of click-through rates. However, Ifantidou (2009) found that norms such as length, clarity, and informativeness, typical of traditional headlines, did not influence reader selection. Readers often preferred under-informative yet cre-ative and autonomous texts. Integrative questions, as opposed to declarative traditional headlines, have been found to be more effective for readership (Lai & Farbrot, 2014).

All these new headline writing techniques are observed to be used by BBC News Yoruba in its sports writings to engage audiences and drive engagements on the organization's online platforms and generate conversations on social media. In our textual analysis later in this chapter, we shall examine how each of these headline writing techniques are used, and later in our data analysis, we shall examine how they impact audience engagements. A review of BBC News Yoruba sports page shows that the media organization sufficiently uses a good blend of all the headline categorizations reviewed above to vary its headline writing techniques, refresh, optimize, and engage their audiences. Sufficient examples of these headlines will be provided during our contextual analysis.

THEORETICAL FRAMEWORK

A theory encompasses constructs or concepts, along with their definitions and propositions (hypotheses), amalgamated to offer a systematic understanding of a phenomenon. It specifies relationships between these concepts, constructs, or variables, aiming to both elucidate and potentially predict the phenomenon, as outlined by Asika (2009). Classical thinkers such as Marx (1848), Taylor (1971), Frazer (1900), Freud (1912), Durkheim (1916), Weber (1930), Evans-Pritchard (1965), and Malinowski (1922) laid the foundational groundwork for various theories that exist today. However, as noted by Adogbo and Ojo (2003, p.1), subsequent researchers and scholars have continued to adopt and adapt theoretical methodologies to enhance their focus. The significance of theories in research cannot be overstated; they serve as fundamental frameworks guiding the investigation and testing of hypotheses. In line with Owuamalam's (2012) perspective, a theory can be defined as a collection of interconnected propositions that offer a structured understanding of phenomena by outlining relationships between various concepts. The role of a theory is to guide researchers by indicating the path they should follow and the inquiries they should pose. Moreover, a theory offers consistency and coherence, enabling the accumulation of knowledge, a fundamental aspect of scientific pursuit as highlighted by Halloran in Uche (2003). Thus, this study is grounded in the uses and gratifications theory, a concept introduced by Elihu Katz, Jay Blumler, and Michael Gurevitch, as highlighted by Akakwandu (2016). This theory asserts that media audiences engage with media content to fulfill their specific needs. O'Sullivan et al. (1983) encapsulate the core idea of this theory, stating that when individuals consume media like television, films, newspapers, or books, they are essentially satisfying varying degrees of specific needs. The uses and gratifications theory aims to elucidate how people utilize mass media, among numerous available resources, to meet their needs and fulfill their desires. These needs might range from a quest for information, education, and entertainment to the pursuit of prestige or the establishment of social class identity, as emphasized by Ijeh and Onojeghwo (2009).

Gratifications in this sense are some aspects of satisfaction reported by users, related to the active use of the medium (BBC News Yoruba) in question. This theory simply explains the reason why BBC News Yoruba sports audiences actively and intentionally look forward to reading their headlines after English Premiership fixtures to either spite their opponents or boost their bragging rights about a victory so deserved. Essentially, the uses and gratifications theory revolves around understanding who engages with specific media content, the circumstances under which they do so, and the reasons behind their engagement. This theory traces its origins back to the 1920s studies examining exposure to and impact of early radio serials (Herzog, 1994) and television (Katz, 1959). Over the years, it has evolved to encompass various media technologies, including cable TV and VCR remote controls (Stafford & Stafford, 1996; Levy, 1980; Rubin & Bantz, 1989) and the internet as demonstrated in the GVU Ninth Internet Survey (1998) and studies by Wimmer and Dominick (2000), and more recently, the focus has shifted to the internet and cellular phones. The initial studies concentrated on the consumption patterns of different radio programs, such as soap operas and quizzes. As per McQuail (1998), this tradition originated as a relatively uncomplicated and direct endeavor to gain insights into the allure of popular radio programs and to understand the relationship between the attractiveness of specific media content and various aspects of personality and social situations. The author elaborated further on its main concerns as:

a simple wish to know more about the audience, and awareness of the importance of individual differences is accounting for the audience experience, a still fresh wonderment at the power of popular media to hold and involve their audience; and an attachment to the case study as an appropriate tool and an aid to psychological modes of explanation. (McQuail, 1998, p. 151)

However, the theory was made popular by communication scholars like Blumer and Katz (1974). Daramola (2001) adds that:

During the 1930s, numerous studies were conducted within the perspective of book reading, radio, soap operas, the daily newspaper, popular music, and the movies to probe why people attended to the products of the media and the rewards such exposure provided. (p. 53)

Oso and Semiu (2012) noted that the initial approach encompassed a wide array of topics, such as the allocation of time across various media, the correlation between media consumption and other time-related activities, media usage in relation to social adjustment and relationships, perceptions of different media functions and content types, as well as the reasons behind engaging with media. Despite this diverse range, a common thread emerged concerning the multifaceted nature of media functions. Particularly, there was a focus on understanding the types and intensity of motives driving media usage and the connections between these motives and individuals' overall experiences (McQuail, 1998, p. 151). Berelson's (1959) declaration that communication research seemed to be at a standstill prompted Katz (1959) to challenge this claim promptly. Katz argued that a shift in focus from the question "What do media do to people?" to "What do people do with the media?" would propel the development of mass communication further. Katz (1959) emphasized the significance of adopting a functional uses and gratification approach to comprehend media effects. This theory delves into the psychological underpinnings of the needs in media consumers. These needs, in turn, influence their expectations from mass media content and result in varying patterns of media exposure (Ojobor, 2002, p. 20). Katz et al. (1974) explain this individualistic orientation of uses and gratification when they wrote:

> The approach simply represents an attempt to explain something about the way individuals use communications, among other resources in the environment, to satisfy their needs and to achieve their goals. (p. 2)

The theory posits that effective communication, geared toward producing specific outcomes, necessitates viewing the target audience not as passive recipients but as active participants in the communication process. They come into the communication process with needs, expectations, or purpose, selectively exposing themselves to selectively perceiving the communication message and selectively remembering them when they want to use them in making decisions or taking actions (Nwosu, 2007). According to Defleur and Dennis (1991, p. 559), the theory presupposes that members of the public will actively select and use specific forms of media contents to fulfill their interests and motives. In simpler terms, the essence of this theory lies in the idea that individuals engage with media that fulfills their specific needs or desires. People read newspapers, listen to the radio, or watch television programs that offer them some form of benefit. Consequently, media content providers must tailor their offerings to cater to the audience's preferences. The uses and gratifications theory delves into how audiences utilize different media forms and the satisfaction they derive from their chosen medium, content, or channel (Mohammed & Adamu, 2010). Folarin (2002, p. 65) observes that the theory perceives the recipient of the media messages as actively influencing the effect process, since he selectively retains the media messages on the basis of his needs, beliefs, and so on.

This theory holds particular relevance to this research as it pertains to BBC News Yoruba audiences who deliberately choose their sports content based on their specific informational and entertainment requirements at a given time each day. Consequently, their inclination toward accessing BBC News Yoruba's sports headlines becomes significantly crucial throughout the entire process of publishing sports articles by the news platform—from monitoring sporting events to writing the headlines and even during the feedback monitoring phase which largely involves social media interaction and engagement with their audiences. This importance stems from the fact that audiences' perceptions vary widely, influenced by individual needs, experiences, cognitive abilities, convenience, and idiosyncrasies. Each audience forms their unique attitude, perception, biases, and preferences, making it vital for content providers to align their offerings with this diversity. In the context of sports news, BBC News Yoruba employs various linguistic and rhetorical strategies in crafting headlines, aiming to engage the audience based on their specific informational, emotional, and cultural requirements.

From observable events, BBC News Yoruba understands the peculiarity of its audiences, thus developing a robust strategy to engage them and appeal to their various needs. In understanding this, BBC News Yoruba employs the use of dramatic language and emotional resonance in sports headlines, infusing cultural proverbs, allegories, and slangs. This linguistic richness creates a connection with the audience, making the stories emotionally resonant and culturally significant. It taps into audiences' cultural sentiments and shared experiences; the headlines evoke emotional responses from the audience. Emotional resonance fosters a sense of connection, making the news stories relatable and compelling.

METHODOLOGY

To find out the influence of the selected twelve BBC Yoruba sport headlines on the audience, the researchers used snowball sampling to select the headlines. The researcher adopted a qualitative research design for this study, and the instrument for data collection was content analysis. The population comprises twelve BBC Yoruba sport headlines, and the researchers purposively selected these twelve BBC Yoruba sport headlines that did not follow the conventional and traditional news headlines style and analyzed them. The purpose was to find out using the comments section if the audience received these headlines that are a departure from the style of casting news headlines. For this article, the researchers only extracted the headlines that were a departure from the traditional headlines to analyze their influence on the audience. The application of thematic analysis of the headlines was carefully adhered to. Repetitious analysis to the sport headlines was done after collecting the links. This enabled the researchers to discover frequently repetitive headlines that catch the attention of the audience. At this point, the researchers looked out for collective and common shared views from the audience at the comment section in order to use it to form an opinion. After analyzing the BBC Yoruba sport headlines over and over again, and there was nothing new that was different to what has already been headlined by the BBC, the researchers were satisfied with the respondents' views at the comments section, and Lichtman (2014) likens this to ". . . process of sorting and sifting" (324).

THE BBC YORUBA SPORT HEADLINES

These sport headlines are now discussed in themes:

Tonality

The communication medium employed by BBC News Yoruba is the Yoruba language. Linguistically, Yoruba emerged as a distinct language group within the Kwa group, a development that occurred between approximately 2000 BC and 1000 BC in the Niger–Benue confluence area (Atanda, 1996). This linguistic evolution has significant implications for understanding the unique cultural and historical context in which BBC News Yoruba operates, shaping its communication strategies and audience engagement approaches.

Yoruba is a tonal language, characterized by the use of tones to convey different meanings. The richness and diversity of Yoruba oral literature are noteworthy. Yoruba oral tradition encompasses a wide array of narratives, proverbs, folktales, and historical accounts, reflecting the cultural heritage and storytelling prowess of the Yoruba people. This oral tradition not only serves as a means of preserving the community's history and values but also influences the linguistic nuances and creative expressions found in the language. As highlighted by Barber (2014, p. 20):

> . . . Wwritten Yoruba was first produced in *ajami* (adapted Arabic script) but extensive written texts in Yoruba began to be produced after the advent of Christian missions in the mid-19th century and were written in the Roman alphabet.

According to Barber (2014), there has been a prolonged debate regarding the suitable method for representing tones and open and closed vowels using the Yoruba alphabet. This discussion highlights the complexities involved in adapting the written form of the language. Notably, in the 1840s, the advent of print culture in Nigeria by Christian missionaries marked a significant milestone. This introduction found favor among the educated elites, leading to widespread acceptance. Subsequently, from the 1880s onward, Nigeria witnessed the emergence of a substantial body of written literature, indicating a flourishing literary tradition spurred by the adoption of the print culture. The unique linguistic and tonal characteristics of the Yoruba language find expression in the style of BBC News Yoruba's sports headlines. These headlines often adopt a dramatic tone, evident in their wording and presentation.

For instance, consider a headline reporting Chelsea FC's loss to Brentford published on the sports page of BBC News Yoruba on October 28, 2023: *"Chelsea 0 v 2 Brentford: Aisan Chelsea tun ti pada, ifoti oloyi meji ni Brentford fi boju won je mole"* (BBC News Yoruba, 2023a). This is translated as *"Chelsea 0 v 2 Brentford: Chelsea's disease is back as Brentford put them to shame in their home with 2 heavy slaps."* This example showcases the vivid and evocative manner in which Yoruba, with its tonal intricacies, is employed to craft sports headlines, enhancing the dramatic impact of the news for the audience. BBC News Yoruba's use of the Yoruba language captures not only the literal meaning but also the cultural and emotional nuances, creating a compelling reading experience for its audience. Despite the diverse array of styles, BBC News Yoruba sports writers excel in crafting attention-grabbing and sensational headlines. They leverage their creativity and imagination to condense the essence of a sports story into engaging, often provocative headlines. These headlines not only captivate the audience but also are tonal and resonate with their everyday experiences, making them eager to read the full stories. The above headline had more than 2,000 reactions from readers, 558 comments, and 227 shares (BBC News Yoruba, 2023a).

On November 8, 2023, BBC News Yoruba featured a headline announcing Copenhagen FC's victory over Manchester United FC. *"Copenhagen 4 vs 3 MAN UTD: A ro pe Man Utd ti bo lowo ogun ni, sugbon won tun sagbako lowo Copenhagen"* (BBC News Yoruba, 2023b). This is translated as, *"COPENHAGEN 4 vs 3 "MAN UTD: We thought Man United had escaped its mystical problems until it fell prey to Copenhagen."* This headline throws in dramatic and religious linguicism of the traditional Yoruba people. It plays on the religious belief that some problems have their root in the supernatural and quickly cling to this to satirize the performance of the club against its opponent. The words "ogun" (problem) and "sagbako" (endangered) were carefully used to trigger some reaction from supporters and opponents of the two clubs. This post attracted 1,700 reactions from their audiences; there were 389 comments and 156 people shared the headlines (BBC News Yoruba, 2023b).

Headline Dramatization

Another headline from the platform, dated October 7, 2023, showcased a similar dramatic approach: *"Burnley 1—4 Chelsea: Iwo tani, ati tani, niwaju tani ni Chelsea ko fun Burnley"* (BBC News Yoruba, 2023c). It is translated in English as: *"Burnley 1—4 Chelsea: you and who, in the presence of who with who are the lyrics of Chelsea's song to Burnley."* This dramatic headline borrowed the words *"Iwo tani, ati tani, niwaju tani ni"* from the lead protagonist of one of Yoruba's biggest movies streamed on Netflix in 2023—*"Jagun Jagun—The Warrior."* The expression is credited to the lead protagonist of the movie, Ogundiji, a notorious warrior whose arrogance and oppressive and supernatural powers led to his death. In the movie, Ogundiji uses the expression *"Iwo tani, ati tani, niwaju tani ni"* to condescend and express strong anger for anyone who flouts his lordship. This colloquial expression has become some sort of street lingua among Yoruba people to express superiority and disdain for anyone they feel does not match their class or influence. BBC News Yoruba sports writers *borrowed* this expression to portray Chelsea as an unmatched rival for Brentford, hence why they whipped them four goals to one. About 4,000 audiences reacted to the headline, 663 of them commented on it, and 156 others shared it (BBC News Yoruba, 2023a).

BBC News Yoruba's sports headlines depart from traditional techniques, incorporating a less formal yet highly engaging style. This platform empowers its writers to infuse their creativity into crafting headlines and utilizing various literary devices to compel the audience to pause and click, thereby enhancing the overall reader experience. At the lexical level, BBC News Yoruba crafts sports headlines in a straightforward manner, typical of online newspapers, especially in sports stories. The language used is casual, relaxed, and highly informal, facilitating easy digestion of the content and often eliciting comic reactions from the audience. BBC News Yoruba employs various linguistic tools such as proverbs, allegories, and slangs to add vibrant colors to their headlines.

For instance, a headline published on November 4, 2023, stated, *"Fulham 0 vs 1 Man Utd: Dakudaji Man U ri Fulham na, won wa n sebi eni ti ko je goolu ri"* (BBC News Yoruba, 2023c), which translates to *"Fulham 0 vs 1 Man Utd: Epileptic Man U managed to beat Fulham and they bragged as though they are not losers."* 3,300 audiences reacted to this headline, 853 commented, and 170 others reposted the headlines (BBC News Yoruba, 2023d).

Additionally, a headline dated October 29, 2020, states, *"Man Utd 0 vs 3 Man City: Kositoma daadaa ni. Man City we lawani iya fun Man U. Won lule be apo ewa ni Old Trafford?,"* (BBC News Yoruba, 2023e), meaning, *"Man Utd 0 vs 3 Man City: Good customers. Man City wrapped a turban of punishment for Man U. They fell like a sack of beans at Old Trafford?"* This headline attracted 3,200 reactions from audiences, 720 comments, and 231 reposts. By integrating these linguistic elements, BBC News Yoruba not only disseminates information but also imbues their headlines with a rich layer of cultural and social context. This approach amplifies the overall impact of their sports stories, provoking specific emotional responses from their readers. Through the use of proverbs, allegories, slangs, and other cultural references, BBC News Yoruba creates a connection with their audience, evoking a sense of familiarity and shared cultural experiences. This not only enriches the reading experience but also fosters a deeper engagement, making sports stories more relatable and compelling for the audience. In essence, these linguistic nuances serve as a bridge, connecting the news content with the readers' emotions and cultural identity, thereby enhancing the resonance and significance of the headlines. This approach amplifies the overall impact of sports stories, provoking specific emotional responses from their readers.

It is crucial to highlight that, in many instances, the dramatic headline writing for sports is only employed to announce English Premier League results. Other sports stories on the website have headlines that dive straight into the heart of the news. For example, a sports headline published on its website on October 3, 2023, states: *"Ìwádìí BBC nípa àjọ bọọ́lù Gabon níbi tí àwọn akọ́nimọọ́gbá ti ń fìpá bá àwọn ọdọ́ agbábọọ́lù láṣepọ̀,"* (BBC News Yoruba, 2023f), which translates to *"BBC investigation about Gabonese Football Federation reveals how coaches sexually abuse young footballers."*

Similarly, a headline from August 22, 2023, reads: *"Ìpínlẹ̀ Oyo pàdánù rẹfìrí méjì láàrín ọjọ́ méjì,"* meaning, *"Oyo State loses two referees in two days"* (BBC News Yoruba, 2023g).

Audience Engagement

Additionally, a headline dated November 29, 2023, states *"Arsenal 6 vs 0 Lens: Arsenal tan Lens lo oju olomo ko to o, die lo ku ki won gba emi lenu won"* (BBC News Yoruba, 2023h). This translates to *"Arsenal box Lens into a corner, beat them into a psychotic pulp."* This dramatic headline draws inspiration from street fights where fighters choose isolated and often secluded places to fight until each or both of them are tired. The rule of the game here is get beaten until you are almost dead. This is a very popular slogan on the streets, and BBC News Yoruba found it fit to describe a disgraceful Lens loss to Arsenal FC. While this headline overdramatized the result of the match and openly exposed the sentiments of the BBC News Yoruba sports writers, 3,000 people reacted to it, 403 commented on it, and 146 others shared it (BBC News Yoruba, 2023h).

At the lexical level, BBC News Yoruba crafts sports headlines in a straightforward manner, typical of online newspapers, especially in sports stories. The language used is casual, relaxed, and highly informal, facilitating easy digestion of the content and often eliciting comic reactions from the audience. BBC News Yoruba employs various linguistic tools such as proverbs, allegories, and slangs to add vibrant colors to their headlines. Consider a headline published on their official Facebook page on December 3, 2023, which reads, *"Liverpool 4 vs 3 Fulham: Liverpool binu tan, gbogbo agbara ni won fi bu ifonu fun Fulhan"* (BBC News Yoruba, 2023i). This literally means *"Liverpool 4 vs 3 Fulham: Liverpool's rage of fury leave Fulhan with a bloodied mouth."* Through the use of proverbs, allegories, slangs, and other cultural references, BBC News Yoruba creates a connection with their audience, evoking a sense of familiarity and shared cultural experiences. This post grossed 939 reactions, 117 comments, and twenty-three shares from their audiences in less than ten hours (BBC News Yoruba, 2023i). This not only enriches the reading experience but also fosters a deeper engagement, making sports stories more relatable and compelling for the audience.

Another headline published on December 3, 2023, states *"Chelsea 3 vs 3 Brighton: Igbaju-Igbamu ni Chelsea fi se alejo fun Brighton ni Stamford Bridge"* (BBC News Yoruba, 2023j). This is translated as, *"Chelsea 3 vs 2 Brighton: Chelsea beat Brighton blue black at Stamford Bridge."* This headline is clearly exaggerated considering the goal margin between the opposing teams. Three goals to two will not pass for being beaten "blue black" as alluded to in the headline, but the words become important engagement connections with audiences who feel a certain emotion and prompt them to react to the post. In less than twenty-four hours, the headline garnered 2,600 reactions, 554 comments, and ninety-two shares (BBC News Yoruba, 2023j). In essence, these linguistic nuances serve as a bridge, connecting the news content with the readers' emotions and cultural identity, thereby enhancing the resonance and significance of the headlines.

On December 3, 2023, one of the headlines on the BBC News Yoruba Facebook page reads, *"Man City 3 vs 3 Tottenham: Eran oniwo Tottenham ko lati terbia frun erin Man City"* (BBC News Yoruba, 2023k). This is translated as *"Average horned Tottenham push back against gigantic Man City."* In terms of semantics, BBC News Yoruba adopts a warm and personal tone when narrating sports stories and crafting headlines. They often initiate their headlines with slangs and street language that best capture or closely relate to a sporting event or its outcome. Additionally, within the body of their stories, BBC News Yoruba employs proverbs strategically, creating a sense of allure through rhetorical devices, enticing and captivating their readers. This intentional use of familiar slangs and colloquial language creates an immediate connection with the audience.

A headline announcing Newcastle win over Manchester United published on December 2, 2023, reads *"Newcastle 1 vs 0 Man Utd: Ojo esin to su nile Newcastle, ori awon agbaboolu Man U lo pada ro si"* (BBC News Yoruba, 2023l). This translates to *"Newcastle 1 vs 0 Man Utd: The rain of shame hovering over Newcastle drenches visiting Man Utd."*

In terms of semantics, BBC News Yoruba adopts a warm and personal tone when narrating sports stories and crafting headlines. They often initiate their headlines with slangs and street language that best capture or closely relate to a sporting event or its outcome. Additionally, within the body of their stories, BBC News Yoruba employs proverbs strategically, creating a sense of allure through rhetorical devices, enticing and captivating their readers. This intentional use of familiar slangs and colloquial language creates an immediate connection with the audience. By incorporating street lingua, BBC News Yoruba establishes a sense of intimacy, making the sports stories feel relatable and engaging. Moreover, the strategic use of proverbs within the narratives adds depth and cultural resonance, enticing readers with the rhetorical beauty of traditional wisdom while enriching the semantic layers of the story. By employing these semantic strategies, BBC News Yoruba not only imparts sports information but also weaves a narrative that feels personal, culturally rooted, and emotionally resonant. This approach enhances the overall reader experience, making the sports stories not just news, but engaging and immersive tales that reflect the pulse of the community.

It is crucial to highlight that, in many instances, the dramatic headline writing for sports is only employed to announce English. This in-depth analysis aims to illuminate the precise impact and reception of these emotionally charged headlines, offering valuable insights into their effectiveness and the response elicited from the audience. By looking into the audience's reactions and interactions with these headlines, this research will provide a nuanced understanding of the strategies employed by BBC News Yoruba and their influence on audience engagement dynamics within the context of sports news coverage.

DISCUSSION OF FINDINGS

The research findings presented in the aforementioned study offers a comprehensive and nuanced insight into the impact of BBC News Yoruba's sports headlines on audience engagement. The study reveals a multifaceted analysis, delving into various aspects such as language, cultural connections, sensationalism, and audience behavior. These findings shed light on the intricacies of how media outlets, particularly those using regional languages, navigate the fine line between capturing audience attention and maintaining journalistic integrity. One of the key aspects highlighted in the research is the unique blend of creativity, humor, and deep cultural connections embedded within BBC News Yoruba's sports headlines. This linguistic approach enhanced the audience's connection to the content, emphasizing the importance of cultural relevance in media communication.

A significant finding of the research was the strategic creative approach employed by BBC News Yoruba in headline writing across different sports. We observed that the sensational style was predominantly used for headlines related to English Premiership matches. This deliberate choice aimed to tap into the emotional fervor surrounding these matches, fostering lively discussions among the audience. The selective use of sensational headlines indicates a thoughtful decision-making process, where the outlet strategically deploys this technique to maximize audience engagement based on the nature of the sports event.

Moreover, the study offered valuable insights into audience behavior and interaction patterns at the comments section. The BBC News Yoruba Facebook page emerged as a central hub for these interactions, where audiences congregated to discuss match day results. The visual evidence provided through screengrabs, showcasing thousands of likes, shares, and hundreds of comments, vividly illustrates the vibrant community that BBC News Yoruba had cultivated on social media.

Importantly, the research findings underscored the profound impact of repeated exposure to BBC News Yoruba's content. Readers at the comments section expressed a high level of trust in the outlet's ability to evoke positive emotions through the creative use of the Yoruba language. This trust extended not only to the content itself but also to the BBC brand, highlighting the outlet's successful strategy in building a strong and loyal readership base. The study's findings emphasize the crucial role of consistent, engaging content in fostering trust and loyalty among the audience, showcasing BBC News Yoruba's effective approach in this regard.

The exploration of BBC News Yoruba's sports headlines in this study has uncovered rich insights into the interplay of language, culture, and audience engagement in the digital era. The research findings underscore the multifaceted impact of Yoruba language, cultural connection, and sensationalism on audience behavior, providing valuable knowledge for both media practitioners and scholars.

CONCLUSION

In conclusion, the infusion of Yoruba culture's rich elements, including proverbs and humor, into BBC Yoruba sports reporting challenges traditional headlines styles, offering a refreshing and culturally resonant approach. This dynamic integration not only enhances storytelling but also underscores the enduring relevance of African traditional communication methods in the digital era. As we navigate the complexities of modern media, let us remember that the essence of our heritage remains vibrant and indispensable.

This study stands as a pivotal effort to fill the gap, providing valuable insights into the nuanced ways in which sports headlines contribute to audience engagement. As we move forward, it is imperative for future research endeavors to build upon the groundwork laid out in this study. By further investigating the writing styles, linguistic structures, cultural connections, and overall composition of BBC News Yoruba sports headlines, scholars can deepen their understanding of the profound impact these elements have on the audience. Additionally, exploring the broader implications for media literacy and cultural reception will contribute to a more holistic comprehension of the role played by news headlines in shaping public discourse on how the African language media continues to survive in the digital era. In essence, this study sets the stage for a more nuanced and comprehensive exploration of BBC News Yoruba sports headlines and their influence on audience engagement. By addressing this research gap, we contribute to the broader academic discourse on media studies, enhancing our understanding of how news headlines, specifically within the Nigerian context, shape the informational landscape and contribute to the ongoing conversation within society.

The study concludes that by creatively infusing Yoruba language, humor, and cultural nuances, BBC News Yoruba establishes a deep connection with its audience through its sports headlines. A significant finding is the strategic use of sensationalism, specifically targeting English Premiership matches to tap into the emotional fervor surrounding these events. Moreover, the study illuminates the central role of social media platforms, particularly the BBC News Yoruba Facebook page, as a vibrant hub for audience discussions and interactions. Crucially, the research underscores the profound impact of consistent, engaging content in building trust and loyalty among the audience. BBC News Yoruba's ability to evoke positive emotions through its creative use of language not only fosters a strong connection with the content but also enhances trust in the BBC brand itself. This highlights the intricate interplay among cultural relevance, creative communication, and strategic decision-making in shaping audience behavior and perceptions in the digital age.

RECOMMENDATION

Based on the research findings presented in the study on BBC News Yoruba's sports headlines and audience engagement, we would like to recommend the following suggestions for further exploration and consideration:

Enhance Ethical Guidelines

The researchers have raised concerns regarding sensationalism and journalistic integrity: BBC News Yoruba should consider revisiting and refining their editorial guidelines. Establishing clear ethical boundaries for headline writing can help strike a balance between audience engagement and upholding professional standards. Training programs and workshops for journalists could be organized to ensure a shared understanding of these guidelines.

Diversify Content Platforms

Since the audience is primarily engaged with BBC News Yoruba's content on social media platforms, it is essential to diversify the types of content shared there. Incorporating multimedia elements such as videos, infographics, and interactive polls can enhance audience interaction and provide a richer user experience. Additionally, exploring emerging platforms or social media features can help BBC News Yoruba reach new audiences.

Community Building and Engagement

The study highlights the vibrant community on the BBC News Yoruba Facebook page. Building on this, the outlet can further nurture the community by encouraging discussions, responding to audience comments, and organizing live Q&A sessions or debates related to sports events. Engaging directly with the audience can foster a sense of belonging and strengthen the bond between the audience and the outlet.

Audience Feedback Mechanism

Establishing a formal mechanism to gather feedback from the audience can be invaluable. Regular surveys, polls, or direct outreach through social media can help BBC News Yoruba understand the audience's preferences, concerns, and suggestions. This feedback loop can guide content creation strategies, ensuring that they align with the audience's expectations and preferences.

Culturally Relevant Storytelling

Building on the positive reception of the Yoruba language and its cultural nuances, BBC News Yoruba can explore more avenues for culturally relevant storytelling. This could include in-depth features, interviews with local sports personalities, or historical perspectives on sports events. Such content can enhance the audience's connection to the stories and provide a unique angle that differentiates BBC News Yoruba from other outlets.

Collaborations and Partnerships

Collaborating with local sports organizations, influencers, or community leaders can broaden BBC News Yoruba's reach and credibility. Partnerships can include co-hosting events, sponsoring local sports initiatives, or featuring guest posts from respected figures in the community. These collaborations can enhance the outlet's reputation and further solidify its position as a trustworthy source of sports news. By incorporating these recommendations, BBC News Yoruba can continue to build on its strengths, address areas of concern, and maintain a strong and loyal readership base while upholding ethical journalism standards.

REFERENCES

Adogbo, M. P., & Ojo, C. E. (2003). *Research methods in the humanities*. Malthouse Piess Limited.

Akakwandu, C. (2016). *Introduction to political communication*. Izehi Printing.

Akpan, U. (2020). Elite local leagues and transnational broadcast of European football. In C. Onwumechili (Ed.), *Africa's elite football: Structure, politics, and everyday challenges* (pp. 34–44). Routledge.

Alamoudi, K. (2017). Syntactic ambiguity of Arabic prepositional phrase attachment in Saudi newspaper headlines. *Arabic Language, Literature & Culture, 2*(1), 13–17.

Andrew, B. C. (2007). Media-generated shortcuts: Do newspaper headlines present another roadblock for low-information rationality? *Harvard International Journal of Press/Politics, 12*(2), 24–43.

Anigbogu, N., & Ibe, C. (2021). Linguistic-patterns-of-news-neadlines-in-Nigerian-newspapers. *Pan-African Journal of Humanities and Social Science, 2*(3), 95–115.

Asika, N. (2009). *Research methodology in the behavioural sciences*. Longman Nigeria Plc.

Atanda, J. A. (1996). The Yoruba people: Their origin, culture and civilisation. In O. O. Olatunji (Ed.), *The Yoruba history, culture and language*. Ibadan University Press.(Pp.76–87).

Barber, K. (2014). Yoruba language and literature. In T. Spear (Ed.), *Oxford bibliographies in African studies*. Oxford University Press. (Pp. 43–65)

BBC News Yoruba. (2023a). Chelsea 0 vs 2 Brentford: Aisan Chelsea tun ti pada, ifoti oloyi meji ni Brendford fi boju won je mole. https://t.ly/vgi4v.

BBC News Yoruba. (2023b). Copenhagen 4 vs 3 Man Utd: A ro pe Man Utd ti bo lowo ogun ni, sugbon won tun sagbako lowo Copenhagen. https://t.ly/YVqfi.

BBC News Yoruba. (2023c). Burnley 1—4 Chelsea: Iwo tani, ati tani, niwaju tani ni Chelsea ko fun Burnley. https://rb.gy/o6b3gj.

BBC News Yoruba. (2023d). Fulham 0 vs 1 Man Utd: Dakudaji Man U ri Fulham na, won wa n sebi eni ti ko je goolu ri. https://t.ly/_CDKG.

BBC News Yoruba. (2023e). Man Utd 0 vs 3 Man City: Kositoma daadaa ni. Man City we lawani iya fun Man U. Won lule be apo ewa ni Old Trafford. https://t.ly/IShGb.

BBC News Yoruba. (2023f). Ìwádìí BBC nípa àjọ bọ́ọ̀lù Gabon níbi tí àwọn akọnimọ̀ọ̀gbá ti ń fipá bá àwọn ọdọ́ agbábọ́ọ̀lù láṣepọ̀. https://www.bbc.com/yoruba/articles/cgxk05gw18yo.

BBC News Yoruba. (2023g). Ìpínlẹ̀ Oyo pàdánù rẹfirí méjì láàrín ọjọ́ méjì. https://www.bbc.com/yoruba/articles/ckv1n2w84q2o.

BBC News Yoruba. (2023h). Arsenal 6 vs 0 Lens: Arsenal tan Lens lo oju olomo ko to o, die lo ku ki won gba emi lenu won. https://t.ly/xAPiY.

BBC News Yoruba. (2023i). Liverpool 4 vs 3 Fulham: Liverpool binu tan, gbogbo agbara ni won fi bu ifonu fun Fulhan. https://rb.gy/wr60hb.

BBC News Yoruba. (2023j). Chelsea 3 vs 3 Brighton: Igbaju-Igbamu ni Chelsea fi se alejo fun Brighton ni Stamford Bridge. https://rb.gy/v4o9mb.

BBC News Yoruba. (2023k). Man City 3 vs 3 Tottenham: Eran oniwo Tottenham ko lati terbia fun erin Man City. https://rb.gy/2qi030.

BBC News Yoruba. (2023l). Newcastle 1 vs 0 Man Utd: Ojo esin to su nile Newcastle, ori awon agbaboolu Man U lo pada ro si. https://rb.gy/dg07ad.

Bell, A. (1991). *The language of news media*. Blackwell.

Berelson, B. (1959). The state of communication research. *Public Opinion Quarterly*, *23*(1), 1–2.

Biyani, P., Tsioutsiouliklis, K., & Blackmer, J. (2016). "8 amazing secrets for getting more clicks": Detecting clickbaits in news streams using article informality. *Proceedings of the AAAI Conference on Artificial Intelligence*, *30*(1), 33–48.

Blom, J. N., & Hansen, K. R. (2015). Click bait: Forward-reference as lure in online news headlines. *Journal of Pragmatics*, *76*, 87–100.

Blumler, J. G., & Katz, E. (1974). *The uses of mass communications: Current perspectives on gratifications research*. (Sage Annual Reviews of Communication Research, Vol. III). Sage Publications.

Cardiff, D. (1983). Time, money and culture: BBC programme finances 1927–1939. *Media, Culture and Society, 5*(3–4), 373–93.

Chakraborty, A., Paranjape, B., Kakarla, S., & Ganguly, N. (2016). Stop clickbait: Detecting and preventing clickbaits in online news media. In *2016 IEEE/ACM international conference on advances in social networks analysis and mining (ASONAM)* (pp. 9–16). IEEE.

Chen, Y., Conroy, N. J., & Rubin, V. L. (2015). News in an online world: The need for an "automatic crap detector". *Proceedings of the Association for Information Science and Technology*, *52*(1), 1–4.

Conboy, M. (2013). *The language of the news*. Routledge.

Debevec, K., & Iyer, E. (1988). Self-referencing as a mediator of the effectiveness of sex-role portrayals in advertising. *Psychology & Marketing*, *5*(1), 71–84.

DeFleur, M. L., & Dennis, E. E. (2002). *Understanding mass communication*. Houghton-Mifflin Co.

Doe, J., & Smith, J. (2020). Media representation of football in Nigeria: A comparative analysis. *Journal of Sports Communication*, *25*(3), 123–45.

Dor, D. (2003). On newspaper headlines as relevance optimizers. *Journal of Pragmatics*, *35*(5), 695–721.

Durkheim E. (1916). *Les fomes elementaries de la vie religieuse*. Presses Universities, trans. by Swain, J. (1961). *Elementary forms of religious life*. Collier Books.

Ehineni, T. (2014). A syntactic analysis of lexical and functional head in Nigerian English newspaper headlines. *International Journal of Linguistics*, 6(5), 9.

Frazer, J. (1922). *Golden bough*. Macmillan.

Freud, S. (1912). *Totem and taboo*. Eng. Trans.

García Orosa, B., Gallur Santorum, S., & Lopez Garcia, X. (2017). Use of clickbait in the online news media of the 28 EU member countries. *Revista Latina de Comunicacion Social*, seventy-two, 1261–77.

Gessler, K. (2017). 13 more before-and-after examples of headline magic. Retrieved from http://mediashift.org/2017/04/13-examples-headline-magic/.

Gujarati, D. N., & Poter, D. C. (2009). *Basic econometrics* (5th ed.). McGraw-Hill International Edition.

Hess, B. (2016). You'll never believe how misleading this title is. Retrieved from http://brianleehess.com/essays/youll-never-believe-how-misleading-this-title-is.

Herzog, E. (1994). What do we really know about daytime serial listener? In P. Lazarsfeld & F. Stanton (Eds.), *Radio research 1942–1943*. Duel, Sloan and Pearce. (Pp. 65–87).

Howard, D. J., & Barry, T. E. (1988). The prevalence of question use in print advertising-headline strategies. *Journal of Advertising Research*, 28(4), 18–25.

Huggins, M. (2007). BBC Radio and Sport 1922–32. *Contemporary British History*, 21(4), 491–515. https://doi.org/10.1080/13619460601060512.

Katz, E. (1959). Mass communications research and the study of popular culture: An editorial note on a possible future for this journal. *Studies in Public Communications*, 2, 1–6.

Katz, E. (1974). Utilization of mass communication by the individual. In E. Katz. (Ed.)*The uses of mass communications: Current perspectives on gratifications research* (pp. 19–32). Sage Publications.

Kuiken, J., Schuth, A., Spitters, M., & Marx, M. (2017). Effective headlines of newspaper articles in a digital environment. *Digital Journalism*, 5(10), 1300–14.

Iarovici, E., & Amel, R. (1989). The strategy of the headline. *Semiotica*, 77(4), 441–60.

Ifantidou, E. (2009). Newspaper headlines and relevance: Ad hoc concepts in ad hoc contexts. *Journal of Pragmatics*, 41(4), 699–720.

Ijeh, N. P., & Onojeghwo, O. M. (2009). Attitude of secondary school students to educational programmes on radio. *International Journal of Communication*, 10(12), 357–73.

Lai, L., & Farbrot, A. (2014). What makes you click? The effect of question headlines on readership in computer-mediated communication. *Social Influence*, 9(4), 289–99.

Levy, M. R. (1980). Home video recorders: A user survey. *Journal of Communication*, 30(4), 23–27.

Lichtman, M. (2014). *Qualitative research for the social sciences*. Sage.

Loewenstein, G. (1994). The psychology of curiosity: A review and reinterpretation. *Psychological Bulletin*, 116(1), 75.

Mahmood, M. A., Javed, S., & Mahmood, R. (2011). A critical discourse analysis of the news headlines of budget of Pakistan FY 2011–2012. *Interdisciplinary Journal of Contemporary Research in Business, 3*(5), 120–29.

Marx, K., & Eagles, F. (1848). *Communist manifesto.* Sage.

McQuail, D. (1984). With the benefit of hindsight: Reflections on uses and gratifications research. *Critical Studies in Media Communication, 1*(2), 177–93.

Mohammed, M., & Adamu, M. (2010). Uses and gratification of internet café by users in Maiduguri Metropolis. In Des W. (Ed.), *Perspective on communication and culture. Routledge* (pp. 79–102).

Mormol, P. (2019). 'I urge you to see this. . . .' Clickbait as one of the dominant features of contemporary online headlines. *Social Communication, 5*(2), 1–10.

Myers, J. H., & Haug, A. F. (1967). Declarative vs interrogative advertisement headlines. *Journal of Advertising Research, 7*(3), 41–44.

Njorora, W. (2009). Colonial legacy, minorities and association football in Kenya. *Soccer & Society, 10*(6), 866–22, 872.

Nwala, M. A., & Umukoro, B. A. (2017). Investigating the meaning of newspaper headlines: The issue of ambiguity. *African Research Review, 11*(3), 87–96.

Nwammuo, A. N., & Nwafor, G. U. (2019). How online newspaper headlines sway opinion: Analysis of online newspaper readership patterns among Facebook users. *International Journal of Informatics, Technology & Computers, 5*(1), 1–10.

Nwosu, I. E. (2007). Principles methods, models and theories of sustainable human development: An afrocentric overview and introduction of the synergistic communication for development for sustainable human development: A multi-perspectival approach. In I. E. Nwosu (Ed.). *Communication for sustainable human development. A multi-perspectival approach.* African Council for Communication Education (ACCE). ACCE.

Oboh, V. U. (2019). Media representation of women's football in Nigeria. *Journal of African Media Studies, 11*(3), 281–96.

Ogunsiji, M. A. (1989). *An introduction to print journalism.* Nelson Publishers.

Ojobor, I. T. (2002). Mass communication theories in Okunna. In C. S. Okunna (Ed.), *Teaching mass communication: A multi-dimensional approach* (pp. 3–26). New Generation Books.

Okwo, A. I. (2016). Football and media politics in Nigeria. *Global Media Journal African Edition, 10*(1), 164–84.

Oloruntobi, F. (2020). A stylistic analysis of some linguistic devices in newspaper headlines: Nigerian newspapers as a case study. *Studies in Pragmatics and Discourse Analysis, 1*(1), 47–57.

Omobowale, A. (2009). Sports and European soccer fans in Nigeria. *Journal of Asian and African Studies, 44*, 624–34.

Onwumechili, C. (2011). Problematising, blaming, moralizing and recommending: Media framing of Super Eagles' performance and effect on fans. *Africa Media Review. 19*(1–2), 27–47.

Onwumechili, C., & Oloruntola, S. (2014). Transnational communications, attitudes and fan identity: Studying Nigeria post-media reform. *Soccer & Society, 15*(3), 389–410.

Oso, L., & Bello, S. (2012). Conceptualizing media audiences: Contextual and contrasting perspectives. In E. N. Tobechukwu, N. S. Naribo, & I. Sobowale (Eds.), *Critique and application of communication theories.* (pp. 228–58). Covenant University Press.

O'sullivan, T., Hartley, J., Saunders, D., & Fiske, J. (1983). *Key concepts in communication* (pp. 245–46). Communication Development. In J. Fisker (Ed.). Methuen & Co. Ltd.

Owuamalam, E. (2012). *Data analysis and research project writing.* Top Class Agencies Ltd.

Purwanti, A. R. (2019). Analyzing Indonesian online newspaper headlines using lexical functional grammar. *Jurnal Pendidikan Bahasa dan Sastra, 19*(2), 150–63.

Rubin, A. M., & Bantz, C. R. (1989). Uses and gratifications of videocassette recorders. In J. L. Salvaggio & J. Bryant (Eds.), *Media use in the information age* (pp. 181–96). Routledge.

Salawu, A. (2004). The Yoruba and their language newspapers: Origin, nature, problems and prospects. *Studies of Tribes and Tribals, 2*(2), 97–104.

Scacco, J. M., & Muddiman, A. (2016). Investigating the influence of "clickbait" news headlines. *Engaging News Project Report.* Palgrave.

Scacco, J. M., & Muddiman, A. (2019). The current state of news headlines. *Engaging News Project.* Retrieved July 26, 2021.

Soley, L. C., & Reid, L. N. (1983). Industrial ad readership as a function of headline type. *Journal of Advertising, 12*(1), 34–38.

Stafford, M. R., & Stafford, T. F. (1996). Mechanical commercial avoidance: A uses and gratifications perspective. *Journal of Current Issues & Research in Advertising, 18*(2), 27–38.

Taylor, E. (1971). *Primitive culture.* Murray.

Uche, L. U. (Ed.). (1996). *North-South information culture: Trends in global communications and research paradigms.* Longman Nigeria Plc.

Van Dijk, T. A. (1988). *News analysis: Case studies of international and national news in the press.* Lawrence Erlbaum Associates, Inc.

Weber, M. (1930). *The protestant ethic and the spirit of capitalism.* https://sites.cc .gatech.edu/gvu/user_surveys/survey-1998-04/.

Chapter 8

Egbe Bere Ugo Bere (Live and Let Live) Cultural Experiment as a Case Study on Igbo Traditional Public Relations Practice in Contemporary Digital Culture

Nnamdi Tobechukwu Ekeanyanwu, Henry Chibueze Ogaraku, and Aloysius Chukwuebuka Ifeanyichukwu

Renowned scholars of African Communication Systems like Des Wilson point out that African traditional communication systems go beyond trivial oracular assumptions of Western theorists, to involve more sophisticated and deep meanings that are often not acknowledged. In the same vein, scholars commonly consider contemporary PR practice as a Western construct, which began in ancient Greece and was further developed by Ivy Lee of New York. However, this chapter contends that prior to the coming of the Europeans to Africa and the growth of PR as a discipline and profession, the practice of PR was entrenched in the communal lifestyles of Africans. Leaning on the thoughts of Des Wilson and using the *Egbe Bere Ugo Bere* cultural experiment as a case study on Igbo traditional PR practice, this chapter seeks to highlight these primordial PR practices and how they have survived even in contemporary digital culture.

While studying the African traditional communication systems, Des Wilson (1987) emphasized the inability of Western cultures and other external influences to dislocate the African people from their communication systems. The reason is simple: these systems are embedded in the cultures of the people. Describing it as a continuous process of information dissemination, entertainment, and education, Wilson (1990, p. 281) termed the African communication system "an admixture of social conventions and practices which have become sharpened and blended into veritable communication models and systems which almost became standard practice for society." It includes all the communication systems obtainable in indigenous African societies. They are the commonest, adaptable, acceptable, and most recognized among each group. They are rooted in each group's language, culture, myths, legends, and customs and molded by their values, norms, ethos, beliefs, and traditions. They use common symbols, values, indigenous technologies, and institutions to operate and are considered credible and effective among the people. People understand and respect their meanings and use them for various purposes: to inform, educate, entertain, warn, advise, encourage, motivate, mobilize, instruct, rebuke, sensitize, celebrate, settle conflicts, and transact businesses.

In rural African life, traditional communication channels include the town criers, drums, gunshots, gongs, trumpets, horns, flutes, palm fronds, age grades, masquerades, animals, schools, and churches. Although some may seem obsolete, their uses linger even as some take on new uses. For instance, the use of palm fronds, horns, flutes, and town criers now seems to be obsolete. However, the town crier has assumed a modern role as the custodian of critical information and culture of the community, hence its metamorphosis in contemporary times as the society's journalist (Wilson, 1987).

Other scholars of African indigenous communication systems joined Wilson's voice to insist that Western media and other systems cannot displace the African system (See Ezekwugo,1989; Ibagere, 1994; Akpabio, 2003; Alexander, 2011). According to Ibagere (1994), the modern mass media, through their popularity, have repeatedly attempted to disregard and displace traditional communication systems. These attempts have repeatedly failed because certain factors such as cultural acceptance and efficacy have continued to foster the continuous existence of these modes and made them integral and inseparable with the culture of the African people.

The interest in African communication systems has allowed the evolution of intellectual debates and scholarly works in the past three decades. This scholarship has drawn attention beyond practices by Africans in their various communities to include its transmission beyond the shores of Africa. African scholars spearheaded by Des Wilson have revealed varied dimensions of African communication systems. Wilson (1987) classified traditional communication systems into idiophones, membranophones, aerophones, symbolography, signals, signs, objectives, color schemes, music, extra mundane communication, and symbolic displays. On the other hand, Ogbuoshi (2010) classified the communication systems based more on the type as follows: instrumental mode of communication, demonstrative mode of communication, iconographic mode of communication, extramundane mode of communication, visual mode of communication, institutional mode of communication, venue-oriented mode of communication, names as a mode of communication, folktales, proverbs, and riddles as a mode of communication, myths, and legends as a mode of communication.

Another classification is by Eno Akpabio (2003) who identified three dimensions of traditional modes of communication as simply *folktales, proverbs,* and *parables* which manifest in both verbal and nonverbal forms. The verbal modes include spoken language, songs, poetry, chants, and incantations and may be grouped under the demonstrative communication modes.

In many African cultures, the demonstrative communication modes include folktales, folklores, proverbs, parables, sayings, idioms, riddles (gwam gwam gwam), poems, songs, stories, myths, legends, jokes, axioms, metaphors, allegories, analogies, and other oral traditions/renditions. These communication modes aim to articulate social and moral mores, beliefs, ethos, values, standards, conventions, customs, and practices that guide their daily lives, relationships, travels, and businesses.

While these classifications may differ by name as a result of the different conceptualizations by the aforementioned scholars, their functions are always the same or similar across cultures. The scholars underscore the credibility and efficaciousness of each mode in transmitting important and strategic messages within the community of users. It is through these oral forms that most of the African communication takes place, and each group has peculiar modes which they use in dealings, influencing each other and getting along with the community, public, or society. Generally, oral communication forms, especially proverbs and folktales, play significant roles in communal lives of African people including the Igbo of Nigeria who are the focus of our study. According to Ibagere (1994), folktales, proverbs, and parables communicate deep meanings, emotions, and ideas that elicit actions and reactions among members of an ethnic group. In all varied settings and contexts, African modes of communication remain an inseparable part of the African people (Ibagere, 1994).

Regardless of what it is called, Oramedia (Ugboaja, 1985), indigenous communication systems (Wang & Dissanayake, 1984), folk media (Panford et al., 2001), or traditional communication (Ushe, 2010), African traditional communication scholarship attests to the fact that the contributions of these scholars prove that Africans had and still have unique modes of communication. This study, therefore, seeks to examine the unique African modes and elements of communication that in practical and concrete terms represent what is known and studied today as PR. We argue that while the modern-day harmonization of PR as a discipline and practice may be attributed to the West, the practice has long existed as a lifestyle in Africa. Anchoring this argument, our study provides evidence from the African Igbo cultural experiments and postulations of African scholars like Des Wilson, revealing a cultural system that practiced activities similar to modern-day PR. We join scholars from some European countries, India, and Israel who have shown evidence of firms which carried out activities similar to functions of modern-day PR even before the discovery of America (McKie & Sriramesh, 2017). For this study, the proof is that a cultural system exists that provides evidence of activities similar to modern PR.

STATEMENT OF THE PROBLEM

It may be agreed that U.S. American scholarship gave the study of PR the form it currently has globally, but the principles were evidently in practice across several cultures before it became a subject of study, a profession, or an industry. This may have informed L'Etang's (2013) submission that the concept of PR connotes different meanings in different cultural contexts. In fact, one expanded study of PR perspectives from different parts of the world contributed to a larger project that called for "a global theory of public relations by taking into account the *native's point of view*" (Sriramesh & Verčič, 2009, p. 5). This was in response to earlier criticism in the field calling for studies that do not just describe "various public relations practices across all regions of the world . . . [but contextualizing] such practice by linking public relations practices with socio-cultural variables" (Sriramesh & Verčič, 2003, p. xxiii).

In Africa, PR practice existed and formed an integral part of her culture before the arrival of the Europeans. We build on Sriramesh and Verčič (2009) work calling for the inclusion of global perspectives that showcase African points of view in PR practice using the *Egbe Bere Ugo Bere* (live and let live) principle in Igbo culture as a case study. However, it must be pointed out that in the African Igbo context, PR through intentional, was not practiced as an organizational effort or at the organizational/corporate level, but as a way of life at the personal, interpersonal, and communal levels. This justifies our position that some forms of PR exist in traditional African society and that a cultural system exists that provides evidence of activities similar to modern PR. In essence, any literature or argument that suggests otherwise or that PR is traditionally Western is refuted in this chapter.

It is thus the intention of this chapter to unpack these traditional equivalences of contemporary PR practice by focusing on the *Egbe Bere Ugo Bere* PR culture of the Igbo people of Nigeria, who occupy the bulk of the South-eastern parts of Nigeria (Nwoye, 2011). Igbo people are characterized by their culture which is orally transmissible from one generation to another through stories, proverbs, folktales, myths, and traditions that are primarily face-to-face interaction (Okoro et al., 2017). This chapter will also go beyond pointing out these traditional PR equivalences to explain how they have continued to survive in the current digital social climate.

THE DEFINITION OF PUBLIC RELATIONS

PR practices "involve the deliberate use of strategic communication to create and sustain goodwill among stakeholders" (Obukoadata et al., 2022, p. 163), or as Charlesworth (2009, p. 30) described it, "the practice of and methods employed in, creating, promoting, or maintaining goodwill and a favorable image among the public for an organization, institution, brand, individual or product." Although there are many definitions of PR, the core purpose cum benefit includes creating and sustaining relationships for the good of self and others, building good image for oneself, and seeking common grounds for understanding and cooperation with others, to yield mutual benefits, and so forth.

However, this chapter agrees with McKie and Sriramesh's (2017, p. 1) view that "public relations is better described than defined," and the reasons are not far-fetched. First, PR has no universally agreed definition (L'Etang, 2013). Second, PR practice trans-mutates (changes in forms as technologies come by; Porter et al., 2001). Third, descriptions can better highlight PR's core reasons, purposes, functions, consequences, or benefits; they are the basis upon which PR is mainly practiced in the African context.

At the fundamental level, whether as an organization, individual, or community, PR is about creating, maintaining, and protecting one's reputation before others; enhancing prestige; gaining visibility; building friendship, trust, and credibility; presenting a favorable, positive image before others; and taking advantage of these for mutual benefits when the needs arise. It is about handling and communicating issues, risks, and crises; preventing problems; accommodating others; dealing with complaints, shocks, and bad publicity; seeking understanding, better engagement, and patronage; and attracting like-minds for businesses, causes, societal and communal purposes, and the likes (Grunig & Hunt, 1984; L'Etang, 2013; McKie & Sriramesh, 2017).

Descriptions that highlight what PR aims to achieve irrespective of whether it is for the individual, community, or organization more aptly fit our notion of PR. From time immemorial, in communal Africa, seeking support or favor or mobilizing others for an idea, a cause, business, or self are daily necessities and events, and to achieve them Africans engage in strategic communication. So, in Africa, PR did not evolve as work professionals do for the sake of organizations but as a set of norms and practices that culturally govern how persons and communities relate with themselves in their quest for mutually beneficial relationships. It comes with values, beliefs, and principles that animate one's sense of association, community, and personal and communal growth, and it is mostly done through oral communication.

According to Ledingham and Bruning (1998), PR is the art of fostering relationships between a company and its target publics leading to the actions of either party producing an impact on the other party's economic, social, political, or cultural situation. It is the management function that identifies, establishes, and maintains mutually beneficial relationships between an organization and the various publics on whom its success or failure depends (Cutlip et al., 2006). For Flynn (2014, p. 381), "public relations is the strategic management of relationships between an organization and its diverse publics, through the use of communication, to achieve mutual understanding, realize organizational goals and serve the public interest." In his description, Gupta (2019, p. 1) notes that "the nature of Public Relations indicates that it is essentially a task of promoting rapport and goodwill between a person, firm or institutions and the community at large through the dissemination of information," adding that "it seeks to earn support, mobilize or solicit favour for an idea, a cause, a problem, for an institution or an individual." As Ward (1998) cited in Herbst (2014, p. 2) asserts, "successful public relationships not only expands economic opportunities but could also save an organization an immeasurable dollar by preventing, minimizing or resolving conflicts and crises."

According to Obukoadata et al. (2022, p. 163),

in Nigeria, early efforts at building PR have spanned from maintaining relationships with traditional rulers with a view to improving tax collections, providing information that should govern daily administrative conduct of the colonial government, to the desperate use of propaganda to sustain the government of the day.

The advent of digital technology has radically changed the discipline and practice of PR. Herbst (2014) submits that digitization has revolutionized the field of communication in four distinct ways: integration, accessibility, connectivity, and interactivity. He furthers, however, that connectivity and interactivity are the two main ways through which it affects PR. For Herbst (2014), connectivity involves the building blocks of devices, technologies, applications, media assets, and so forth that relate to one another and communicate effectively. This implies that technology has made available various options for modern-day PR practitioners to reach their target public. Beyond the traditional media of print and electronic, digital devices and platforms like social media have made connectivity easier, more regular, and wider. Some scholars opine that interactivity is the feature of digital media that most clearly distinguishes it from older, non-digital genres (Ryan, 2004, 2006; Alexander, 2011).

Therefore, the PR professional in the digital era differs from the old order, where the audience is passive. A more engaging experience is obtained between the PR professional and the client, who is now actively involved and can communicate the exact need and become part of evolving a solution to the problem. However, PR practice in the digital era demands media literacy from professionals and clients.

Understanding the Igbos: Who Are the Igbos?

Igbo as a term refers to both the Igbo ethnic group and the language they speak. The people occupied the southeast region of Nigeria. According to Nwala (2010) as cited in Igwe (2017), the Igbo people belong to one of the three biggest ethnic nationalities in Nigeria. The other two are Hausa and Yoruba. "They belong to the black race in Africa and speak a language that belongs to the Kwa group of languages found in West and Central Africa" (Nwala, 2010, p. 22). To Iroegbe (1995, p. 344), what makes the Igbo nation distinct from other nationalities include: "common origin, common worldview, common language, shared culture, race, colour and habits, common historical experience, common destiny." These distinct shared cultures among the Igbo people greatly influenced the nature and notion of PR in the community before Westernization. It helps our understanding of the notion of Egbe Bere Ugo Bere (live and let live).

Beyond the bounds of the Nigeria enclave, the Igbo ethnic group is found in all nooks and crannies of the world, to the extent that it is fondly said in Nigerian local parlance that "wherever one goes and does not find an Igbo-speaking person there, one had better run away from that place" (Igwe, 2017, p. 50). "The Igbo traditional society set-up is historically egalitarian in structure and democratic in organization" (Onyibor, 2016). Their sociopolitical and cultural authority patterns are layered: from the immediate family of one father or bearing the same surname, to the Ezi, lineage, kindred, or compound, which comprises of a couple of households of different surnames but tied to the same progenitor, to the Umunna or sub-lineage, or Villages then to the Ama-Ala, or Obodo or Village-Group or town where authority terminates. With this setup, communal or rural living is influenced by both personal and communal linkages. While personal concerns may be sorted out anywhere especially at the immediate family/kindred level, general or communal issues are mostly treated in accordance with expectations of the local traditional rule. Gatherings are traditionally held at the popular assembly at the village square or the village head's large Obi (traditional lounge), where everyone is encouraged to participate and freely speak his/her mind. Anyone who fails to participate is bound by whatever is decided. Majority or superior opinions always carry the day. No one person imposes their will on others. As noted, "The Igbo as reflected in 'Things Fall Apart' has no king or central leader but only a highly efficient communal democratic government" (Chinweuba & Ezeugwu, 2018, p. 119).

The common saying *Igbo enwe eze* (the Igbo has no king) which often sounds uncomplimentary/derogatory and that the Igbos are republican in nature testify to egalitarian structure and democratic structure of the Igbo traditional society. In traditional Ala Igbo, the prevailing political model eschewed a kinship system of government. The functionality of government is built around institutions like nze na ozo (titled men), otu-ogbo (age grade), and otu-ada (women group), among others. People rise through the ranks according to their talents, skills, and the community's recognition of these through the bestowal of titles and respect. In the Igbo community, living was fluid because there were no stratified political and economic classes. Even a poor orphan with no inherited assets could rise to the top of this society if he proved himself through hard work, energetic pursuit of his ambitions, and achieved success. Even with that, the Igbos believe that no man no matter how powerful, or rich is greater than his people, and that ofu onye adighi esiri oha nri (no one can defeat his people alone).

Again, everyone was sufficiently knowledgeable about the consequences that result from the violation of norms that guided the existence of communities and their members, and "in the event of an outbreak of hostility between two units, another unit often stepped in to restore peace between them" (Meek, 1937 cited in Ejiogu, 2015, p. 533).

> Traditionally, a successful conflict resolution in every traditional setting is marked by a common sharing of kola nuts and drinking palm wine often with the same cup. Respect for kola nuts is one of the most important traditions in Igbo society. (Okafor, 2016, p. 154)

Kola nuts represent life, love, acceptance, and unity. That is why the Igbos normally say 'onye wetara oji wetara ndu (who brings kola also brings life). The Igbo family system is extended to clans, so people of the same clan cannot intermarry. Different clans too cannot be included in the same family cycle since they have different lineages. The philosophy "we are better than animals because we have kinsmen" is pronounced among them. Achebe says, "an animal rubs its itching flank against a tree, a man asks his kinsman to scratch him" (Achebe, 1958, p. 132). He considers the support a family gives one another as the defining characteristic of humanity. In Igbo society, family feast celebration is a sign of communal reunion and not only for eating and drinking since each family can afford what to eat and drink.

The Igbos are predominantly Christians, the majority of whom are Catholics. They are rich in the number of cultures and traditional values celebrated by the people, distinguishing them from the rest of the country's ethnocultural units. The uniqueness of such cultures and traditional value systems draws a huge line of distinction between the Igbo and all the other ethnic groups in Nigeria (Iwunna et al., 2021). The Igbos are ingenious, brilliant, and successful traders; great travelers; and accomplished educationists. Igbo people revere hard work, honesty, truthfulness, generosity, humility, respect for elders, and respect for cultural and traditional values, but hate acrimony, backbiting, arrogance, greed, stinginess, dishonesty, stealing, and ill-gotten wealth to mention but a few (Obasi et al., 2017). Igbos are bold and courageous—attributes other tribes sometimes see as pride or arrogance. They are self-sufficient and optimistic; they easily demonstrate the will to survive anywhere and always do. They take on challenges or difficult moments/situations and make something meaningful of them.

THE IGBO (AFRICAN) INDIGENOUS COMMUNICATION SYSTEMS

The concept of African communication systems, which is often known as indigenous communication systems (Wang & Dissanayake, 1984), refers to the distinct ways through which Africans communicate. The Igbo indigenous communication system is one instance of the African communication systems that have remained in use currently among Igbo people. The Igbos have their own media and systems of communication and information dissemination, although word of mouth and face-to-face physical communication are extremely popular. Others include town criers, drums, gunshots, gongs, trumpets, horns, flutes, palm fronds, age grades, masquerades, animals, schools, and churches. In Igbo culture, for instance, the town crier is usually a respected and trusted man who serves at the king's pleasure to relay information to the subjects. Once a message meant for the community, maybe a summon or meeting comes, he moves around the community and intermittently with the aid of a metal gong or drum; calls attention; and verbally drops the message, especially the major elements of the news—who, what, when, where, why, and how. This attribute correlates with the objectivity features of modern mass media. Ansu-Kyeremeh (2005, p. 16) captures the essence of African communication systems succinctly as:

> Any form of indigenous-communication system, which by virtue of its origin from, any integration into a specific culture, serves as a channel for message in a

way and manner that requires the utilization of the values, symbols, institutions, and ethos of the host culture through its unique qualities and attributes.

The idea of indigeneity reflected in the term indigenous communication comes from the fact that the type of communication referred to in this context pertains particularly to specific groups of people who share ancestral territories, collective cultural formation, and historical locations (Nigussie, 2016; Turay, 2002; Angioni, 2003). Communality and informality are integral aspects of African indigenous communication systems. Unlike the heterogeneous structure of modern mass media audiences, the indigenous communication audiences are known to each other, they also share similar origin, values, and way of life. Panford et al. (2001, p. 2) lauded the long-lasting existence of indigenous communication in rural areas as rural Africa is endowed with rich, popular means of communication, including songs, proverbs, storytelling, drumming and dancing, drama, poetry recital, arts, and crafts.

The Igbos are passionate about their cultural values and heritage and have continued for ages to express and promote these through their folktales, poems, proverbs, alliterations, stories of ancestral links, family and local community ties, and ancient conflicts and conquests (Iwunna et al., 2021). Others are embedded in their burial ceremonies and rites, wrestling contests, marriage rites and celebrations, salutations, respect for authorities of the land, naming ceremonies, arts and designs, local technology, religion, masquerades, festivals, conflicts management, fines and levies, punishments for offenders, divorce, theft, lineage migrations, acts of ostracism, oaths taking, language and communication skills, and so forth (Ogbalu, 1974).

Part of the systems and media of communication and information dissemination among the Igbos include indigenous instruments for information storage. These include sticks, stones, graffiti, pieces of clothes, lengths of rope, various forms of wall marks, marks on trees, carved objects, kola nuts, sorts of ornaments, rings, and so forth. Usually, each of these objects conveyed different meanings and interpretations, which depended clearly at the discretion of the individual user-owners (Depaepe & Simon, 2001), meaning there are no universalities in the meanings attached to some of these objects of communication. Meanings and possible interpretations were exclusively left at the user's discretion. Thus, the legendary Unoka, a renowned debtor, known loafer, and the biological father of Okonkwo in *Things Fall Apart* by Chinua Achebe, used wall marks, made in several rows on the walls of his traditional lounge to indicate his indebtedness to every of his creditors. In the case of Unoka, each single line represented a specific amount of money he owed a particular creditor (Achebe, 1958). These are different from the crucial information the traditional Igbo men store in their heads (brains) which forms the large chunk of oral renditions they give to their succeeding generations.

Achebe's *Things Fall Apart* is a literary mirror of traditional Igbo society. It demonstrates that even before the advent of the West, the Igbo already had a well-established belief system and socio-cultural patterns for their continued existence. These are thoughts, patterns, and practical existential guides of the Igbo forebears that are passed on to successive generations. (Nduka & Ozioma, 2019)

Although a fictitious piece, several works have used *Things Fall Apart* graciously to evidence many elements and issues associated with the Igbo race and culture.

From the foregoing, it is evident that Africa had beautiful and unique indigenous communication media and systems which predate lots of modern mass media. Most of these indigenous media remain in use regardless of perceived attempt by modern mass media to relegate these indigenous media forms. Wilson (1982) cautions that a communication system which does not consider the traditional, social, and cultural dynamics of society alienates the highly placed in society from the majority of the people in the rural areas. To a large extent, the survival of Igbo traditional communication system can be attributed to same unique general features of African communication systems as discussed by Wang and Dissanayake (1982), which include:

1. High levels of flexibility.
2. Homogeneous audiences bounded by ethnicity or culture.
3. Synchronized with oral traditions.
4. Highly participatory.
5. Credibility and reliability.
6. Shared feelings, emotions, and cultures.
7. Affordability and accessibility.

Igbo communication systems can be grouped based on Des Wilson's (1982) six classification of African indigenous communication channels as follows:

1. Instrumental: *igba* (drum), *ogene* (metal gong), *ekwe* (wooden gong), *oja* (flute), and *opi* (horn).
2. Demonstrative: *egwu omenani* (folk songs), *omu* (palm fronds), and *anwuru* (smoke).
3. Iconographic: *oji* (kola nut), nzu (white chalk), akwa (egg), and *ugbene* (feather).
4. Extramundane: *afa* (divination), *itu mmanya* (libation), and *nro* (dream).

5. Visual: *akwa ocha* (white cloth), *akwa ojii* (black cloth), and *ikpa isi* (hair styling).
6. Institutional: town crier (oti mkpu), *mmanwu* (masquerade), *ozo* (title), and *ilu nwanyi* (marriage).

These indigenous communication media are personal and tribal specific in nature. While they may not compete with modern mass media in terms of reach and wide coverage, they remain the surest way of interacting among individuals within the Igbo cultural milieu. As earlier stated, these Igbo indigenous media are structured in a way that they intertwine with the cultures of the Igbo people. A person who is not from Igbo land may not be familiar with the meanings conveyed through these media. While some other Nigerian cultures may use similar instruments and are known with different names in their languages, the way they are used and often the meanings they convey vary. This is the beautiful feature of the multiethnic and multilingual nature of Nigerian cultures.

EGBE BERE UGO BERE: AN APPRECIATION OF THE PUBLIC RELATIONS PRACTICES OF IGBO PEOPLE

From our arguments so far, it is easily deduced that the practice of PR has been long entrenched in the culture of the Igbos, even before the evolution of the modern conceptualization of PR. Its culture has long governed the Igbo traditional society and community affairs. The *Egbe Bere Ugo Beer* (literally translated as *let the kite perch, let the eagle perch too, if one says no to the other, let its wing break* or as some would have it, *let it show that one where to perch*) is a traditional Igbo philosophy which implies "live and let live" (Igwe, 2017). More apt way of saying it is "biri kam biri." Giving an in-depth insight into the principle, Igwe (2017, p. 48) says:

> The concept of letting-be *(Egbe Bere Ugo Bere)*, is a phenomenological construct which emphasizes the need for human beings to allow things (reality) to come into the open on their own accord without forcing them to do so. As such, it advocates respect for phenomena or objects of experience. It holds that we should approach our object of experience with a free and open mind and allow it to show itself in the very way it is, not in the way we want or wish it would show itself by imposing our individual biases on the object.

Beside reciprocity, other derivatives of *Egbe Bere Ugo Bere* within the Igbo cultural milieu that give them deeper and broader meanings are understanding disposition, patience, accommodation for others, mass action, inclusiveness, openness, vastness, and exploration of options or alternatives, and so forth. Various connotations of the adage include: "live and let others live"; "love, respect and treat others well as you would want yourself loved, respected, and treated"; "enjoy your space and let others enjoy their spaces too"; "say your own but hear others too"; and "do your bit and allow others do their bits" (probably as the basis for understanding, accommodation, and synergy).

All of the aforementioned derivatives reveal virtues within the community that the best of each individual's potential can be harnessed and utilized. In essence, this principle advocates that everyone has strengths and virtues that if harnessed together for communal purposes will always lead to positive outcomes. This principle is diverse and deep in Igbo culture. While the above views construe this Igbo principle as a philosophical phenomenon, it is not difficult to see how this principle may also be explained from the prism of PR.

Patience

For example, as a disposition of patience, Unah (2010, p. 33) states that *"Egbe Bere Ugo Bere* is the orientational habit of letting things come into light as they are without forcing them into our ready-made, artificial, conceptual straight-jackets." Interestingly, this connects with the symmetrical communication suggestions of Grunig and Hunt (1984) in their PR excellence model. A PR principle of live and let live promotes a conducive atmosphere for organizational goal attainment, where the organization and its public coexist with mutual tolerance and respect for each other.

Reciprocity

For Nwoye (2011, p. 314), "a major orientation among the Igbo is the emphasis that is placed on the principle of reciprocity." This principle is depicted in the Igbo religious folklore exemplified in the seed yam mentality which in Igbo thought and culture espouses regenerative relationship which in their view is sanctioned by nature (Animalu, 1990). The idea is that *Ala* (the earth) does not deal with humans with "the law of winner takes all." What is observed is that when she (the earth) receives the gift, even of old yam (ji) from the farmer, she gives back to the farmer a brand-new yam in appreciation for the old yam received. Based on this, a common orientation among the Igbo is to demand that in their dealings with their fellow humans and the gods, the principle of reciprocity be strictly observed. That is, when the Igbo offer sacrifices to their gods or in any other context, they expect something good to come out of such a transaction.

Hospitality

Several principles are attached to the *Egbe Bere Ugo Bere* notion to make it a wholesome practice among the Igbos. This includes principles like *onye aghala nwanne ya* (be your brother's keeper; no one should be left behind; do not abandon your brother especially in times of need). Chukwu (2015, p. 14) expands this further thus:

> The Igbos have in their common slogans expressions portraying their trait of hospitality. One of these slogans says. Onuru ube nwanne agbala oso (literally meaning, one should run to the rescue of his brother in need and not abandon him). It was this spirit that compelled people to rush to the scene of a wine-taper who had the misfortune of falling down from a palm tree. It was the same consciousness that made people rush to the scene of a smith's hut caught up in an inferno.

In Chukwu's (2015, p. 12) claim,

> on their own part the artisans-wine-tapper, smith, potter and sculptor, manifested their spirit of hospitality in their places of work and to those around them. These they did through good apprenticeship programmes for those in need of the aid and by offering considerate prices for the products. By doing so, they made eloquent contributions to the well-being of the society at large.

It was in this context that Chukwu (2015, p. 12) noted that "in Igbo social life, the hospitality one received from people around him was directly tagged to the hospitality he showed to others." In his words, "in Igbo society, a man identified as being nonchalant to the plight of unfortunate victims would hardly attract the sympathy and hospitality of others at his own times of need" (Chukwu, 2015, p. 14).

So, *Egbe Bere, Ugo Bere* here denotes building social investments by helping others so that one can reap the dividends in due time. Indeed, the Igbos have concepts, slogans, and ideologies that clearly depict and portray their spirit of hospitality. These include "onye aghala nwanne ya" (literally meaning one should not abandon his brother in any circumstance) and Ife kwuru, Ife akwudebe ya (literally meaning if one person stands, another person(s) should stand beside him; that means the stronger should support the weaker, the richer should help the poorer, or its praise connotation "if you see a man, you see his wife").

Peace

The *Egbe Bere Ugo Bere* practice also embodies and espouses peace, that is, peaceful coexistence based on the fact that we all need each other. This is what Ezekwugo (1989) meant when he wrote that, in traditional Igbo societies, the entire human person manifests itself in communal tendencies. The individual lives a life quite inseparable from the rest of the community; he lives in the community for the community and by the community. According to him "ofu osisi adi eme ofia" (a tree cannot make a forest).

In the basic sense, man who does not exist in isolation counts so much on natural givens and on the communal sense of living with other human persons. The Igbo person is largely dependent on the common structure of the society for both their well-being and development. To be an individual implies willingness to integrate oneself into the community. The older one grows, the deeper his or her integration and the wiser he or she becomes (Nnoruka, 2009). Hence, the proverb: "ihe okenye nodu ala hu, nwata kwuru oto, ogaghi ahu ya" (what an elder sees seated, the young may not see it even while standing).

Integrity

Egbe Bere Ugo Bere as traditional PR practice among the Igbos also manifests on the notion of *"Ezi aha ka ego"* (good name is better than riches), which speaks to the PR notion of good image or reputation is worth everything, and no effort should be spared to acquire it. This constitutes a conscious notion ingrained in the Igbos to ensure that they demonstrate responsibility and truthfulness in their life journey. And they live knowing that how others see them matters, so they need to live and let live.

Progress

Another derivative within the *Egbe Bere Ugo Bere* traditional PR practice among the Igbos is the notion of *"Mmadu ka eji aba"* (human beings are the pillars of progress), which speaks to the PR notion of employees as the pillar or bedrock of organizational progress. That is why employees are to be valued and treated well, to get the best out of them. The principle goes beyond employees to include other human beings (publics) in somebody's or organization's life, customers, investors, suppliers, distributors, host community, media practitioners, and so forth, upon whom one's success depends.

Inclusiveness

Egbe Bere Ugo Bere also manifests in the Igbo collectivist nature and inclusiveness, which shows off on the saying, *"anaghi ebi ikpe na onu ofu onye"* (a case is not settled by listening to only one side). This principle of balance connects with the PR strategy of arbitration and negotiation. This arbitration is the duty of the institutional media like *ozo, ichie, otu-ogbo* (age grade) and *mmanwu* (masquerade) in Igbo land. Arbitration is an amicable way of resolving conflicts. It does not necessarily mean going to court; it is undertaken within an organization for the sake of maintaining cordiality. The PR principle of negotiation connects also with the Igbo principle of *ire oma ka ejuna ji aga n'ogwu* (it is the sweet tongue that the snail uses to navigate through thorns). During arbitration, even negotiation in Igbo land, an offender or the one who is at fault may use good, soothing words to own up, appeal to the offended or the community, or seek a better deal. Once an offender owns up, the gesture is usually positively reciprocated. Negotiation has been an integral part of Igbo people's lives, especially in business.

There are several other examples and notions of *Egbe Bere Ugo Bere* traditional Igbo PR practice that space limitations in this chapter have not allowed us to express. However, a common import of all the oral renditions in this context is that they condition the Igbos into a certain mindset or worldview or perception. They help them build mutual relationships that benefit them and others. They also make them predictable in various settings because these are standard practices and conventions used for ages. They are part of their culture. The Igbos originated and standardized the "Nwa-Boy" apprenticeship system, where a young man who has finished secondary or primary school or could not further his education is sent to learn a given trade or business in the hands of his master, known as Oga. The apprenticeship lasts for years, depending on the boy's age and the agreement between his family and the master. It is under this Nwa-Boy apprenticeship scheme that most of the oral renditions that touch on PR in business contexts are taught and practiced. By the time the young man is ripe for settlement, after which he becomes his own master, it is assumed, and evidently too, that he is now versed not just in the knowledge and skills of his business but also in the oral culture that not only helps him to do business but also helps him cultivate relationships and positive favorable image before others, his community, family, friends, and customers for his own good and the good of others.

IGBO TRADITIONAL COMMUNICATION SYSTEMS AND THE DIGITAL REVOLUTION

Charlesworth (2009, p. 10) observes "the greatest impact the digital revolution has on society is the opening up of personal communication between the masses worldwide. Social media ensures that an individual's sphere of interaction is no longer limited to a few friends and acquaintances." The advancement in technology ensures that information/messages are delivered instantaneously, in multimedia, and cost-effectively. In this regard, it is correct to conclude that "digital technology is now used in all 'traditional' media but is most associated with computing and the Internet" (Charlesworth, 2009, p. 6).

The essence of technological innovations is to expand human capabilities, which also evolve with the realities of time (Ogaraku, 2015). And like every ethnic group in Africa with their own unique communication systems, the Igbo communication systems are evolving alongside technologies to remain contemporary. For Ogaraku (2015, p. 125), "technological innovations come in the realm of higher order. That is, newer technologies usually come with more unique features and a greater degree of sophistication or across-the-border application." This assertion holds true of many of the media and systems of traditional communication among the Igbos, which have morphed into digital platforms, even with their PR import. It is very difficult to operate today without digital media.

Easy access to digital communication greatly adds to the effectiveness and efficiency of human communication, even in the traditional/indigenous context. Increased use of digital technology by individuals, groups, communities, and institutions globally has resulted in the "digitization of content" (Rodman, 2009, p. 294) and integrated the capabilities of various media (Ogaraku, 2015, p. 125). So, like the conventional mass media: radio, television, newspapers, and so forth, African traditional communication media have found expression in the various outlets of the Internet. To Emenanjo (2006, p. 179), "the Internet is, for now, the most powerful, most convenient, most reliable, and fastest vehicle or medium for the collection, transmission, extension, distribution and feedback of two-way global information data." Igbos were equally caught up in this web.

In Nigeria, Igbos are among the most cosmopolitan and tech savvy going by Ashong and Ogaraku's (2017, p. 2) assertion that Nigeria is enjoying "a burgeoning online presence," there is no gainsaying that the Igbos form a major chunk of Nigerians who have joined the digitized population. The proliferation of online communities through social media like Facebook, Twitter, Instagram, Myspace, WhatsApp, Telegram, Zoom, and so forth has created spaces where Igbos are actively engaged in leveraging the benefits of technology. For example, Facebook has become the leading social medium in Nigeria (Ogaraku, 2020). It is the medium where persons and groups create new accounts and online communities are formed by people in the name of families, villages, towns, states, alumni, clubs, associations, and like-minds with similar social, political, religious, educational, and economic callings, concerns, or interests.

Ogaraku (2020) also maintains that the merging of new technologies offers functions that evoke enthusiasm from users and serve to benefit society. For instance, we witnessed much of the integration of digital and traditional communication systems during the Covid-19 outbreak. With people confined to their homes, digital technologies like Facebook, Twitter, Instagram, Zoom, WhatsApp, Skype, and so forth became handy to enable messages to reach as many people as possible. Metaphorically, the Igbo market square, village square, town halls, huts, moonlight games, and playgrounds moved to a new site in the digital world of social media to engage with communities widely. The rural dwellers who engaged more in African communication systems equally found ways of leveraging the new digital order. For example, as the Covid-19 pandemic lingered, communities, through their online groups, honored the time-tested principle of *onye aghala nwanne ya* (no one should leave his brother or neighbor behind) by mobilizing funds online and buying and sending palliatives to their struggling brothers and sisters, kith, and kin in the rural areas. These gestures of love and almsgiving were equally made public, and appreciations were demonstrated through digital social media. Nsereke and Papamie (2022, p. 56) provided further insight:

> Nigerian indigenous communication practice has, for the most part of the 2000s, migrated from the town squares and village playgrounds of native Nigerians to a new site, namely, the mass communication media of the African sub-region and the wider world. Not only do the indigenous media forms now feature as popular content on the continent's mainstream broadcast media, but they also constitute the dominant culture-based entertainment content on the online channels of foreign mainstream media that target African audiences.

Digital technology has made communication within the Igbo community fast, convenient, and less expensive, and there are practical examples of how the Igbo systems leverage the internet. Beyond personal interaction, digital communication also improves the efficacy of community interaction and comes handy in smoothening the processes of community administration, arbitration, mediation, social justice, peace, and conflict management, establishing relations and goodwill, mobilizing support, and sharing the mutual benefits which are at the core of PR. Most importantly, it helps in the operation of the *Egbe Bere Ugo Bere* practice in its various facets. Digital facilities or tools like social media help in problem recognition, information search, evaluation of alternatives, collective decisions, and actions. They make a huge amount of information available.

The widespread use of social media and continuous conversations about pertinent societal matters has facilitated convenient ways to virtually connect Igbo communities worldwide. This means that community members can virtually partake in meetings and other events of that community due to easy access to and affordability of social media platforms. As Charlesworth (2009,

p. 28) asserted, "Almost by definition, social media sites are organic—developed and grown by people."

The traditional roles of the town crier to transmit information to specific people, elders, young, men, women, age grade or daughters (umu-ada), or the whole community still exists. In the digital world, the same role is played by group administrators we see in organized online groups such as WhatsApp groups. These social media platforms offer more unique features than what the town crier can do unmediated. The activities in these spaces imitate what would happen in real life except that the digital space is a complex multimedia environment where pictures, videos, and highlights of the meeting can be uploaded in real time or later, depending on convenience and availability of digital infrastructure. This confirms Charlesworth's (2009, p. 10) assertion that the "Internet has provided a platform for individual voices to be heard and that social media are available for anyone to read, contribute to and engage in."

CONCLUSION

In this chapter, we sought to show ways that the Igbo people have applied the principles of PR in their personal and communal lives even before the invasion of the West in their motherland. The principles are contained in the sayings, proverbs, beliefs, values, mores and standards, customs, practices that guide the daily lives, travels, and businesses, which we have termed here the *Egbe Bere Ugo Bere* traditional Igbo PR practice. Our analysis of the Igbo PR practice resonates with Des Wilson's seminal scholarship in indigenous communication in Africa which positions traditional communication systems beyond trivial oracular assumptions of Western theorists, to involve more sophisticated and deep meanings that are often not acknowledged. In the same vein, contemporary PR practice is commonly conceived as a Western construct with roots in ancient Greece and further developed by Ivy Lee of New York. By analyzing the Igbo communal lifestyle and traditional communication system, we showed the relevance of *Egbe Bere Ugo Bere* traditional Igbo PR practice. It is a practice among Africans that is entrenched in the culture and is more of a lifestyle model. One would say that the Western practice is a business-driven model. Leaning on the thoughts of Des Wilson, and using Igbo culture as a case study, this chapter highlighted the primordial PR practices that have survived by embracing the potentials and possibilities offered by the digital revolution.

Overall, the digital revolution has done well coexisting with Igbo traditional communication systems. This being the case, however, there are concerns regarding functional displacement, that is, when a digital platform/

media begins to perform the role of a traditional medium and gains more appeal and usage. However, when we critically evaluate this concern, one may see it as a positive. How so? It is positive in that any individual can share whatever. However, they feel with his community and that same community can share that same message around the world in a matter of minutes depending on how it resonated with them. It affords dissatisfied individuals the opportunity to voice their anger or worry. It affords the individual the opportunity of expressing and seeking friendship and understanding, managing his/her reputation and crises when they arise, and enhancing content through text, images, and videos. According to Charlesworth (2009, p. 10), "citizens of the digital society are more trusting of each other as they are of marketing or corporate messages." This owes to the credibility of knowing each other and having shared values, as expressed in the Igbo maxim, *"Egbe Bere Ugo Bere."*

REFERENCES

Achebe, C. (1958). *Things fall apart*. Heinemann.
Akpabio, E. (2003). *African communication systems: An introductory text*. BPrint Publications.
Alexander, B. (2011). *The new digital storytelling: Creating narratives with new media*. ABC-CLIO.
Angioni, G. (2003). Indigenous knowledge: Subordination and localism. In G. Sanga & G. Ortalli (Eds.), *Nature knowledge: Ethnoscience, cognition, and utility* (pp. 287–96). Oxford University Press.
Animalu, A. O. E. (1990). A way of life in the modern scientific age. *Ahiajioku Lecture*. Culture Division Ministry of Information.
Ansu-Kyeremeh, K. (Ed.). (2005). Indigenous communication in Africa: A conceptual framework. In *Indigenous communication in Africa: Concept, application and prospects* (pp. 14–28).Ghana University Press.
Ashong, C., & Ogaraku, H. (2017). Content preference among online and hardcopy newspaper readers in Imo state. *Journal of New Media and Mass Communication, 4*(1), 1–15.
Charlesworth, A. (2009). *The digital revolution*. DK Publishing.
Chinweuba, G. E., & Ezeugwu, E. C. (2018). Culture and change: A critical analysis of Igbo cultural alienation in Chinua Achebe's "Things Fall Apart." *Philosophia: Journal of Philosophy and Culture, 19*, 115–29.
Chukwu, J. C. (2015). Traditional Igbo humane character: Nature and application. *Journal of Culture, Society and Development, 10*, 9–17.
Cutlip, S. M., Center, A. H., & Broom, G. M. (2006). *Effective public relations* (9th ed.). Pearson Prentice Hall.

Depaepe, M., & Simon, F. (2001). Reconstruction and interrogation of classroom pedagogy: Journals and textbooks as sources for teachers educating and teaching in the classroom in Belgium 1880s to 1960s. *Social Sciences History of Education, 2*(2), 68–79.

Ejiogu, E. C. (2015). Age-old democratic social authority patterns: The bases of Igbo identity and politics. In T. U Nwala., N. Aniekwu, & C. Ohiri-Aniche (Eds.), *Igbo nation: History and challenges of rebirth and development* (Vol. 1, pp. 505–37). Kraft Books Limited.

Emenanjo, E. N. (2006). *Language and communication: Myths, facts and features.* E-Frontiers Publishers Nig. Ltd.

Ezekwugo, C. (1989) Igbo worldview and contemporary realities in V. Nnabuchi Ndidiamaka (2010). *Worldview and culture* (Assignment on Rel -501: *Principles and Methods of Research in Religion*).

Flynn, T. (2014). Do they have what it takes? A review of the literature on knowledge, competencies, and skills necessary for twenty-first-century public relations practitioners in Canada. *Canadian Journal of Communication, 39*(3), 361–84.

Grunig, J., & Hunt, T. (1984). *Managing public relations.* Holt, Rinehart, and Winston.

Gupta, R. (2019). *Public relations strategies and tactics.* Random Publications.

Herbst, D. G. (2014, October). Public relations in the digital world: Global relationship management. In *Proceedings of the 2014 International Conference on Digital Media and Social Inclusion*, Istanbul.Istanbul. Oxford. (Pp. 67–87).

Ibagere, E. (1994). Taxonomy of African traditional modes of communication. In J. Tosanwumi & H. Ekwuazu (Eds.), *Mass communication: A basic text* (pp. 80–96). Caltop Publishers.

Igwe, I. C. (2017). Egbe belu ugo belu: The Igbo African approach to the principle of letting-be in Martin Heidegger's philosophy. *Igede Igbo: A Journal of Igbo Studies, 3*(1), 42–58.

Iroegbu, P. (1995). *Metaphysics: The Kpim of philosophy.* International Universities Press Ltd.

Iwunna, P., Ndukwu, E. C., Dioka, B. O., Alaribe, O. C., & Alison, J. O. (2021). History of Igbo people and education: A psychological implication. *Historical Research Letter, 53*, 51–61.

Ledingham, J. A., & Bruning, S. D. (1998). Relationship management in public relations: Dimensions of an organisation-public relationships. *Public Relations Review, 24*(1), 55–65. (Spring).

L'Etang, J. (2013). Public relations: A discipline in transformation. *Sociology Compass, 7*(10), 799–817.

McKie, D. & Sriramesh, K. (2017). Public relations. In D. S. James (Ed.)*The International encyclopedia of organisational communication. Palgrave* (pp. 1–18).

Nduka, U., & Ozioma, N. G. (2019). Chinua Achebe's things fall apart and the role of women in Igbo traditional religious culture. *Open Journal of Social Sciences, 7*, 272–89.

Nigussie, H. (2016). Indigenous communication forms and their potential to convey food security messages in rural Ethiopia. *Indian Journal of Human Development, 10*(3), 414–27.

Nnoruka, S. I. (2009). *Solidarity: A principle of sociality.* Living Flames Resources Publishers.

Nsereke, B. G., & Papamie, B. (2022). Historical development and transformation of the Nigerian indigenous communication media. In B. Mutsvairo & N. Ekeanyanwu (Eds.), *Media and communication in Nigeria: Conceptual connections, crossroads and constraints* (pp. 55–69). Routledge.

Nwala, T. U. (2010*). Igbo philosophy: The philosophy of the Igbo-speaking people of Nigeria* (3rd ed.). Triatlantic Books Ltd.

Nwoye, C. M. A. (2011). Igbo cultural and religious worldview: An insider's perspective. *International Journal of Sociology and Anthropology, 3*(9), 304–17.

Obasi, V. A., Obi, S., & Ndukwu, E. C. (2017). Effect of moral bankruptcy on education. In A. Akuma (Ed.), *Contemporary issues in education* (pp. 62–79). Hystab Publishers.

Obukoadata, P. R., Uduma, N., & Aniefiok, M. (2022). Technologies, media and the transmutation of public relations and advertising in Nigeria. In B. Mutsvairo & N. Ekeanyanwu (Eds.), *Media and communication in Nigeria: Conceptual connections, crossroads and constraints* (pp. 161–71). Routledge.

Ogaraku, H. C. (2015). Media threat: The Internet versus the newspaper. *Benin MediaCom Journal, 9,* 120–35.

Ogaraku, H. C. (2020). Social media and political communication: Use of facebook by two Nigerian political parties (APC and PDP) in the 2015 general election. Retrieved from http://www.researchgate.net/publication/338596026.

Ogbalu, F. C. (1974). *Omenala Igbo: The book of Igbo customs.* University Publishing Company.

Ogbuoshi, L. (2010). *Understanding traditional African communication systems.* Linco Enterprises.

Okafor, E. N. (2016.) The concept of Igbo spirituality and environment. *Prajñā Vihāra, 17*(2), 145–62.

Okoro, A. E., Eze, H., & Ofoegbu, F. (2017). Cultural rationality and the Igbo society. *Journal of Research in Humanities and Social Science, 5*(3), 88.

Onyibor, M. I. S. (2016). Igbo cosmology in Chinua Achebe's arrow of God: An evaluative analysis. *Open Journal of Philosophy, 6,* 110–19. https://doi.org/10.4236/ojpp.2016.61001.

Panford, S., Nyaney, M. O., Amoah, S. O., & Aidoo, N. G. (2001). Using folk media in HIV/AIDS prevention in rural Ghana. *American Journal of Public Health, 91*(10), 1559–62.

Porter, L. V., Sallot, L. M., Cameron, G. T., & Shamp, S. (2001). New technologies and public relations: Exploring practitioners' use of online resources to earn a seat at the management table. *Journalism and Mass Communication Quarterly, 78*(1), 172–90.

Rodman, G. (2006). *Mass media in a changing world: History, industry, controversy.* McGraw-Hill.

Ryan, M. L. (2004): *Narrative across media: The languages of storytelling.* University of Nebraska Press.

Ryan, M. L. (2006): *Avatars of story. Electronic mediations* (Vol.17). University of Minnesota Press.

Sriramesh, K., & Verčič, D. (2003). *The global public relations handbook: Theory, research and practice.* Lawrence Erlbaum Associates, Inc.

Sriramesh, K., & Verčič, D. (2009). *The global public relations handbook: Theory, research and practice. revised and expanded edition* (2nd ed.). Routledge.

Turay, T. M. (2002). Peace research and African development: An indigenous African perspective. In G. J. S. Dei, B. L. Hall, & D. G. Rosenberg (Eds.), *Indigenous knowledge in global contexts: Multiple readings of our world* (pp. 248–63). University of Toronto Press.

Ugboajah, F. O. (Ed.). (1985). *Mass communication, culture and society in West Africa.* K. G Saur.

Unah, J. I. (2010). *Metaphysics.* University of Lagos Press.

Ushe, M. U. (2010). *The mortgage culture of Tiv death and burial rights.* Vast Publishers.

Wang, G., & Dissanayake, W. (1984). *Continuity and change in communication systems: An Asian perspective.* Ablex Publishing Corporation.

Ward, K. L. (1998). *Evaluating public relationships.* The Institute for Public Relations.

Wilson, D. (1982, April). Traditional mass communication: Towards a redefinition of concepts. A Paper presented at the inaugural conference of Nigerian mass communication association, Lagos.

Wilson, D. (1987). Traditional media in modern African development. *African Media Review, 1*(2), 17–29.

Wilson, D. (1990). Traditional communication media system. In E. D. Akpan (Ed.), *Communication arts: Principles, applications and practices* (pp. 80–81). Modern Business Press Ltd.

Wilson, D. (1998). A taxonomy of traditional media in Africa. In K. Ansu-Kyeremeh (Ed.), *Perspectives on indigenous communication in Africa: Theory and application* (pp. 2–19). School of Communication Studies Printing Press.

Part III

ENDURING RELEVANCE OF AFRICAN INDIGENOUS COMMUNICATION SYSTEMS IN THE DIGITAL AGE

Chapter 9

Traditional Town Criers in Kenya and Nigeria

Enduring Relevance in the Digital Age

Shamilla Amulega, Unwana Samuel
Akpan, and Eddah Mbula Mutua

The honor of celebrating the work of a renowned African communication scholar Des Wilson goes beyond personal accolades to include recognition for scholarly contributions needed to move the field of African communication forward. Des Wilson's work offers scholars opportunities to engage in theory building about features and functions of African indigenous communication and media systems. Similarly, communication development practitioners find relevance in use of these indigenous systems in their role to disseminate information intended to improve livelihoods in many rural areas in Africa. In the big picture, Des Wilson's work is pivotal in "situating knowledge systems" (Chilisa, 2020, p. 1) in contemporary African communication environment. As an ethnocommunicologist, Des Wilson has influenced scholarly thinking about communication through African indigenous knowledge. Together with numerous scholars influenced by Wilson's work spanning over four decades, we have learned more about the taxonomies of African indigenous communication and trado-modern communication model and other theoretical frameworks that continue to extend frontiers of knowledge in the field (Wilson, 2015; Ogwezzy, 2008). In fact, this scholarship is not limited to understanding the traditional communication forms but also the structure of society, how social order is maintained and how cultural identities are sustained.

We find relevance in this book's focus on examining the role of indigenous communication in the digital age. This focus is important considering that misrepresentation of African communication and culture might arise due to failure to understand its relevance in society. Our contribution to ethnocommunication research involves investigating the relevance of town criers in the digital age. We relied on secondary research, newspaper articles, and informal discussions with individuals conversant with meanings assigned to the roles of town criers in African settings. This study provides valuable context and foundational knowledge about the functions of town criers in Kenya and Nigeria.

We are interested in the multiple roles that the town criers play in their communities and in the communication process. Wilson (2023, p. 218) avers that the role of town criers should not be restricted to simply disseminating information but also as information gatherers who offer feedback as they go round village paths and roads to deliver messages. Their role opens avenues to understanding ways that African indigenous knowledge shapes how African communication is structured and valued. Specially, we are interested in the manner in which town criers embody indigenous modes of communication namely instrumental (idiophones aerophones, symbolography, and membranophones); demonstrative (music and signal such a whistle or drum); and visual (colors) (Wilson, 2023, p. 219), all of which are the embodiment of African knowledge. Therefore, the question at hand is whether town criers have adapted to new modes of communication in the digital age. Are they still dependable channels of communication?

This chapter is organized into four sections. We begin with a review of literature on two topics: the history and role of town criers and impact of digitalization on traditional media. This literature allows for a clear problematization of the issues discussed in this chapter. Next, we describe how town criers perform their roles among diverse ethnic groups in Nigeria and Kenya. In keeping with scholarly efforts to ensure "survival" and success of African traditional modes of communication in the digital age, we discuss whether the digital age has affected this mode of communication. If so, how and if not, why? Responses to the questions will direct future research about ways to harness efforts to sustain the relevance of traditional forms of communication in the digital age.

THE HISTORY OF THE TOWN CRIER

The history of town crier goes as far in the past as the ancient civilizations, whereby designated persons used to make public announcements in the urban areas. In ancient Greece, heralds were paid to announce the crier in the agora—the city's leading marketplace and heart. In the same way, in ancient Rome, the role of the "praeco" was to proclaim official announcements and edicts to the public (Molto, 2023). During medieval times in Europe, town criers developed fame and became prominent figures in the local community.

The town criers were an extremely important factor in spreading the news to the public because widespread literacy and means of mass communication were lacking in those days. They were essentially autonomous figures tasked with enforcing peace by local authorities or guilds, some of whom were easily identifiable by their distinctive garments, including a bell, horn, or staff.

According to Malik et al. (2021), the town criers' duty was to inform the public about essential messages like royal decrees, market prices, and mundane public notices. In addition to the mere transmission of information, their roles also included the performance of duties as public entertainers and announcers of events such as fairs, festivals, and public executions. The town crier's loud and resonant voice was powerful enough to be heard even in the city's throngs, amid the hustle and bustle. Over time, the tradition of the town crier persisted into the early modern period and later evolved along with society and the newest ways of communication. The printing press and the rise of newspapers in the seventeenth and eighteenth centuries brought another revolutionary shift to the town criers (Idowu et al., 2022). Increasingly, information and news dissemination became the responsibility of the newspapers, reducing the role of town criers in some instances. Asemah et al. (2021) argue that historically, town councils relied on town criers to relay public announcements within the streets.

Akpan (2023a) explores the history of African indigenous media that explains colonial views circulated to downgrade or utterly obliterate African traditional media experiences. Until the late colonial period, prevailing among Western historians was the belief that Africa, mainly south of the Sahara, lacked any form of civilization and, consequently, had no historical significance. In fact, according to Nkwi (2018), some Western historians argued that even if there were events with historical importance, they remained obscured and inaccessible, given that African societies, for the most part, were predominantly oral and thus left behind no written records for historians to analyze. This perspective favored civilization and written documentation as the sole legitimate foundations for historical inquiry, thereby disregarding other forms of knowledge and oral traditions prevalent in African societies.

However, the 1950s to present bear witness to a burgeoning community of Africanists who vehemently contested this Eurocentric and anti-African historical worldview. Notable among them include Kwame Nkrumah (Ghana), Jomo Kenyatta (Kenya), Nelson and Winnie Mandela (South Africa), Herbert Macauly (Nigeria), Nnamdi Azikiwe (Nigeria), Obafemi Awolowo (Nigeria), Robert Mugabe (Zimbabwe), Patrice Lumumba (Congo), Julius Nyerere (Tanzania), Kenneth Kaunda (Zambia), Toussaint Louverture (Haiti), Jean-Jacques Dessalines (Haiti), Henri Christophe (Grenada), François Duvalier (Haiti), Aimé Césaire (Island of Martinique), Haile Selassie (Ethiopia), Edward Wilmot Blyden (Liberia), Robert Sobukwe (South Africa), Ahmed

Sékou Touré (Guinea), King Sobhuza II (Eswatini), Robert Mugabe (Zimbabwe), Thomas Sankara (Burkina Faso), Kwame Ture (Trinidad and Tobago), Dr. John Pombe Magufuli (Tanzania), Muammar Gaddafi (Libya), Walter Rodney (Guyana), Yoweri Kaguta Museveni (Uganda), Joseph Robert Love (Bahamas), Marcus Garvey (Jamaica), and Malcolm X (the United States), W. E. B. Du Bois (the United States), and Anténor Firmin (Haiti) (Akpan, in press). The historical context of the misrepresentation of African knowledge accelerates the agency to center the relevance of African communication forms in the digital age.

ROLE OF TOWN CRIERS

The literature on traditional modes of communication in Africa reveals widespread use of town criers across West, Central, and East African communities regardless of the circumstances (Obasi, 2023). The choice of healthy individuals ensured that they could effectively fulfill their duties. Nkwi (2018) describes the men in this role as well-built and often possessing excellent physiques and remarkable marksmanship skills upon recruitment. For example, the Bamenda society of Cameroon places significant importance on physical fitness of the town crier leading to the recruitment and employment of only robust, healthy men for this traditional role (Obasi, 2023). Nkwi (2018) asserts that town criers typically came from the lower echelons of society and gained higher societal status based on their role as town criers.

According to Enahoro (2022), in the Benin kingdom, crucial matters concerning the entire realm, requiring the attention of His Royal Majesty, the Oba (Traditional ruler), are typically deliberated at the Oba palace, where the Oba presides over these important decisions. Enahoro (2022) further asserts that for the various Dukedoms, gatherings take place either at the Odionwere's palace or at the Oguedion, the central meeting place of the community. The town crier plays a pivotal role in notifying communities of upcoming meetings and disseminating decisions and communiqués.

Town criers served as universal disseminators of general information, endowed with loud voices and tasked with broadcasting news to the local populace (Obasi, 2023). Chiefs and kings maintained control over this indigenous form of communication, utilizing town criers to disseminate information to serve information needs and promote harmony in the community. Ajayi et al. (2020) highlight the town criers' role as communication extensions of traditional rulers. They carried large conical metal gongs, attracting attention as they moved through the village to deliver urgent messages from royal palaces. The rhythm and intensity of the gong strikes conveyed specific messages. The resonant and repetitive beats of the town crier's gong drew immediate attention compelling individuals to halt their activities and listen attentively to information communicated. It is important to mention that the different communication modes used by town criers are specific to local contexts. For instance, the death of a prominent figure prompts the town crier to rhythmically strike the gong seven times in some communities (Enahoro, 2022). The persistent beats signal the news of a passing, leaving the community in suspense as they await details about the departed and the affected quarter or family. Enahoro (2022) reveals "in case of an emergency, the town crier also has a way of attracting the people's attention with the sound of his gong" (p. 1). These examples reveal that roles of the town crier are ingrained in local customs.

Ajayi et al. (2020) emphasize the eloquence and significance of town criers, describing them as authoritative voices of traditional authority. Their presence in the community, combined with their effective communication skills, ensured that important messages communicated were acted upon. Town criers operated strategically, often touring villages during the early morning or evening when the population was most accessible. According to Eze et al. (2021), town criers relayed information to villagers and compound heads simultaneously, facilitating the vertical distribution of messages through village leaders to family heads. Messages communicated varied widely, ranging from communal duties to political or social gatherings and reminding villagers of events. Special messages from higher government levels also circulated within villages, reaching both groups and individuals through vertical and horizontal communication channels.

Abdulai et al. (2023) outline the content of messages communicated by town criers that range from announcements about communal work schedules to updates on court proceedings in traditional courts. Typically, these messages broadcasted in the evenings, particularly during dinnertime, were to ensure maximum reach during quieter times of the day. The striking of a metal gong three times signaled people to pay attention to the forthcoming message or activity. For example, in the closely knit community of the Bamenda people, the town crier was pivotal in announcing designated days for communal work involving community members such as bridge construction and farm tilling (Wilson, 2023).

In some communities in Nigeria, town crier's role was more than a "newsman" in the local community. They assumed the role of a chief in some communities or being associated with a recognized age grade in others or acting as a PR officer of the traditional rulers. Understanding their roles, methods, and effectiveness can offer valuable insights into leveraging their potential for addressing pressing issues such as climate change, health awareness, and local intelligence gathering.

IMPACT OF DIGITIZATION ON TRADITIONAL INDIGENOUS MEDIA

Many communication methods have undergone profound transformation in the digital age (Gui & Büchi, 2021). The transformation continues to shape how individuals and communities interact and exchange information due to the widespread use of digital devices and the internet. Today, information is communicated instantly across vast distances. Beyond the technological advancement, the effect of digitization on the traditional indigenous media has raised concerns about cultural identity (Lipschultz, 2020). According to Alia (2022), digital technology is increasingly penetrating the world; hence, indigenous people find themselves at the crossroads of connectivity and cultural erosion. The internet and social media bring new communication channels for indigenous groups to have broader communications and present their claims to a global public (Tajvidi, 2020; Trilling et al., 2024). At the same time, the fear about possible erasure of one of the traditional roles of town criers as the embodiment of cultural heritage is a valid concern.

Furthermore, the digital gap between the information haves and information have-nots accentuates inequalities in opportunities for access to information and resources. In isolated and deprived indigenous areas, the internet's limited infrastructure and high connectivity cost increase the digital divide gap between the digitally connected communities and the digitally excluded (Stichel et al., 2019; Lipschultz, 2020; Barrowcliffe, 2021; Akhmetova & Musalitina, 2022). This, consequently, creates more hurdles in the way of marginalized communities' entrance into a digital economy, where they also fail to defend their rights and interests in an integrated world. Toth et al. (2018) note that the fast spread of digitization makes it possible to lose indigenous languages and oral traditions that are highly connected to identity and cultural heritage. In Africa, there is increased use of new technology by the younger generation who do not speak their mother tongue and are not conversant with their local traditions. According to Galla (2018), the initiative for language revitalization and cultural literacy promotion is a crucial point in the strategy of preserving linguistic diversity and forming intergenerational passing of traditional knowledge. This effort can serve to keep the relevance of traditional modes of communication alive in the digital age.

Similarly, there are concerns about cultural appropriation, copyright issues, and commoditization of indigenous cultural expressions in the digital age (Aubry et al., 2022). We are interested in exploring possibilities to keep traditional media alive. For example, Barrowcliffe (2021) provides an array of hope with the revelations that indigenous communities have seized digital opportunities to regain control of their cultural stories and affirm their sovereignty in the digital sphere to counter the aforementioned challenges. Digital narratives from indigenous groups such as those in Namibia utilizing social media campaigns at their grassroots levels and community-generated digital initiatives have today become strong instruments used by the indigenous activists and institutions to tackle stereotypes, foster cultural activities, and heighten indigenous voices to various issues like land rights, environmental sustainability, language revitalization, and self-determination (Stichel et al., 2019). Nowadays, these initiatives take indigenous perspectives and values into account where indigenous knowledge and cultural diversity enable an inclusive and equitable digital future. These successes resonate with our purpose for this study. It is valuable to know both the challenges and solutions the digital age poses for African communication systems.

THE ROLE OF TOWN CRIERS IN NIGERIA AND KENYA

As noted earlier, town criers are the embodiment of African knowledge, culture, and communication. In this section, we highlight their roles in articulating how African communication is structured, information needs are served, and generally, navigating the changing communication environment.

Town Criers in Nigeria

In Nigeria, various regions have unique names for the town crier, such as Otio-obe in Ora land; No'yawewe in Benin; Akede in Yorubaland; Okhue-Ibu in Esan; Amia mkpo isong among the Efiks, Annangs, and Ibibios; and Sankira in Hausa land. In Igbo society, the town crier, known as Oti-ekive, employs a distinctive flute resembling the military's bugle, capable of producing diverse sounds and rhythms. This specialized instrument enhances the communicative aspect of the town crier's duties. Specifically in ancient Yoruba communities, the town crier held a crucial role as the primary source of news referred to as "gbohùngbohùn," "akígbe," or "ajágbe." In this role, the town crier functioned as a local news channel, relaying vital information to the community.

The revered position of a town crier was bestowed upon an eloquent individual with authoritative presence. The town crier's voice carried a commanding weight, requiring all to fall silent when he spoke. Essentially, the town crier served as the embodiment of an ancient news broadcaster, disseminating news and announcements to the townspeople. Notably, the town crier also served as the public voice of the Oba (traditional ruler), transmitting essential information about current events directly to the common people. Typically, an adult male, the town crier functions akin to an information minister or PR officer for the community in rural Nigeria. One of the primary responsibilities

of the town crier is to call the community members to meetings. These gatherings may take place in various locations, such as the compound of the village head or even the Oba's palace. The specific venue often depends on the
customs and traditions of each community. For instance, in Igbo societies,
meetings are commonly convened in the market or village square. On the
other hand, in the Efik, Ibibio, and Annang communities, gatherings might
occur in specific places like "Afe isong" for Annangs and "Efe isong" for
Efiks/Ibibios. The role of the town crier was clearly defined and served to
connect the community and the traditional leadership with important updates
and maintaining a sense of unity and harmony.

Town Criers in Kenya

Traditional communities relied on town criers as an indigenous means of
relaying information from traditional leaders to the members in the community (Njomo et al., 2017). Indigenous traditional town criers in Kenya
are known by various names, reflecting the diverse ethnic groups across the
country. These individuals play a crucial role in keeping their communities
informed, connected, and harmonious. Among the Luo community, they are
known as "Jaluo Kamodho," while the Kikuyu people refer to them as "Gûtirî
wa Thî" or "Njoroge wa Ng'ang'a." In the Maasai community, they are called
"Olpayian," and among the Luhya, they go by the name "Omukolongolo."
Among the Akamba they are known as "mutumia wa kyivu" (chief's elder)
or "mutumia wa nguli" (the elder who blows the horn).

   The town criers play a crucial role in communication within their respective communities. Traditionally, they use distinct instruments such as drums,
horns, or even their voices to convey important messages. In the Luo community, Jaluo Kamodho often uses drums to signal community gatherings,
announcements, or impending events, acting as a communal beacon for
information (Obyerodhyambo & Wamunyu, 2023). Among the Kikuyu,
Gûtirî wa Thî was equipped with a horn or loud voice to announce gatherings, important decisions, or communal celebrations. Njoroge wa Ng'ang'a,
on the other hand, normally utilized rhythmic beats on a drum to convey
specific messages. The Maasai Olpayian, recognized for their elaborate beadwork, use distinct patterns and colors to communicate messages across their
vast territories. Whether it is signaling the arrival of important visitors or
announcing community decisions, their intricate beadwork serves as a visual
language. Within the Luhya community, the Omukolongolo often relies on
the resonance of a large drum to carry messages across villages. These messages may range from important communal announcements to summoning
villagers for meetings.

Town criers are indispensable messengers who bridge the gap between leaders and the populace. These heralds of information play a crucial role in disseminating news, announcements, and important messages within their respective communities. In essence, the roles of indigenous town criers in Kenya are deeply embedded in the cultural fabric of their communities, serving as both communicators and preservers of tradition. These roles extend beyond relaying information; they contribute to the communal identity and shared experiences within each ethnic group and promote harmonious relationships among diverse communities. Today, the role of town criers still exists. For instance, in Lamu Island and in Western Kenya, where the ancient Swahili culture intertwines with Arab and Bantu influences, the use of town criers are helpful in preserving traditional heritage (Praxides, 2022; Mutai, 2024). Town criers are essential figures in maintaining the unique identity of the region. They disseminate information about upcoming cultural festivals like the Lamu Cultural Festival, which celebrates the rich history, art, and architecture of the island. Likewise, in Western Kenya, town criers are instrumental in preserving the heritage of various ethnic groups such as the Luo, Luhya, and Kalenjin. They announce important ceremonies like traditional weddings, initiation rites, and community gatherings where oral history and ancestral traditions are passed down to younger generations.

CULTURAL ELEMENTS IN THE
ROLE OF TOWN CRIERS

In this section, we discuss key foundations of African culture and communication present in the roles played by town criers in Nigeria and Kenya. Traditional town criers share commonalities and variations in their roles that highlight the diversity of African culture. This is evident in the depth and richness of each community's cultural expressions. Undoubtedly, town criers remain living embodiments of Kenya's (read Africa's) oral heritage, weaving together the threads of tradition and modernity (Njoku, 2023). The town criers communicate and preserve the unique cultural identity of their respective communities.

Oral Traditions

Across numerous communities in Kenya and Nigeria, the transmission of information remains rooted in oral traditions. The town criers employ spoken words, often adorned with vivid storytelling elements, riddles, proverbs, and metaphors to convey messages effectively. They use spoken words to convey messages, ensuring that information is transmitted in a manner accessible to the community members. This oral approach not only preserves cultural nuances but also ensures that information is passed down from generation to generation. At the same time, while the basic role of town criers is universal, each community infuses its unique cultural elements into the way messages are delivered. Cultural specifics are emphasized to give credibility to information communicated. For instance, the Maasai, known for their distinct warrior culture, might incorporate martial symbolism and metaphors in their announcements, setting them apart from the more agrarian-influenced messages of the Kikuyu or Luhya town criers. In Nigeria, the town criers start their address by using a unique sound in drawing the attention of the people, and the sound is heralded by the sound of the gong. For instance, the "amia mko isong" in Akwa Ibom and Cross River communities might first start with an attractive folklore song that would arouse the interest of the people, and the song must be connected to the news about to be communicated. While the mode of communication in these communities is oral, the style and tone of messaging vary. The Maasai's Olpayian incorporate unique elements or storytelling techniques, setting it apart from how the Luhya's Omukolongolo conveys information.

Local Language/Symbolic Naming

Town criers communicate in the local language, fostering a sense of belonging and cultural identity. Additionally, each community assigns distinctive names to their town criers, reflecting the cultural meaning and significance of their role. For example, among the Kamba of Kenya, town crier is "mutumia wa kyivu," "mutumia" translates as "an old man or elder" and "mutumia wa kyivu" translates as "the old man sent by the chief." Mutumia wa nguli' translates as "the old man who carries the gong." These names encapsulate the essence of their duties and the cultural context in which they operate.

Attire and Symbols

Communities in Kenya and Nigeria have distinct attire and symbols associated with their town criers. Town criers often wear traditional attire that reflects the cultural aesthetics of their community. The Maasai, for instance, adorn colorful beadwork and distinctive warrior attire, creating a visual impact that complements their spoken messages. In contrast, the Luhya town crier's attire are influenced by the region's agricultural heritage. In Nigeria, the town criers dress to show their cultural affiliation. For instance, the "amia mkpo isong" in the Akwa Ibom and Cross River States communities tie wrappers characteristic of how men dress in that region, while in Yorubaland, the town criers wear "shokoto" and "iru."

Community Connectivity

Town criers in local communities in Kenya and Nigeria serve as a vital link between leaders, elders, and the general community. We use Bagale Chilisa's (2020) concept of "principle of relationality" that pushes to the center the need to build relationships in communities (p. 10). According to Chilisa (2020), building relationships with and in communities is at the core of African ontology. Town criers foster relationships in the community as entrusted conveyors of messages that range from important announcements to cultural ceremonies. This connectivity fosters a sense of community cohesion and engagement with communal affairs through communication. At the same time, community connectivity promotes what we call "community presence." Not only are town criers a visible and familiar presence in African communities but also key actors in facilitating communication. They often move through the villages or gather in well-known locations where they are easily accessible to community members. Their presence in the community makes information accessible at no cost, orally, in the local language and from familiar, reliable, and trusted sources.

Rituals and Ceremonies

The occasions on which town criers are deployed can vary among communities. Some may be associated with specific cultural ceremonies or events, while others may have a more regular and routine presence. The Maasai Olpayian, for instance, might have a significant role during rites of passage or communal gatherings, whereas the Kikuyu Gûtirî wa Thî may be more integrated into everyday village life.

Reverence

Among the Akamba of Kenya, the town crier or the chief's messenger is highly revered. For example, there is an expression that says "Mutumia ndaumawa" loosely translated as "the messenger is never insulated." This means the messenger must be respected even if you disagree with the message. In Nigeria, a town crier is appointed by the village council of elders based on his oratory prowess and knowledge of the community and the people.

The mandate to speak on behalf of the King or Chief meant upholding reverence to local traditions.

THE ROLE OF TOWN CRIERS IN THE DIGITAL AGE

We base our discussion about the impact of the digital age on the role of the town crier on existing literature that shows the interplay between traditional media and the digital age. In our prior discussion, we showed how town criers are still relevant among select communities in Nigeria and Kenya. It is without a doubt that the role of the town crier is no longer as it was before the digital age. Nonetheless, their role is still relevant—albeit with a different mode. Below are five major roles performed in the digital age.

Preservation of Local Customs and Fostering Continuity between Generations

Primarily, town criers are custodians of traditions and culture. For example, in Nigeria the town crier serves as a symbol of cultural pride for each community. Likewise, the role of Jaluo Kamodho in matters pertaining to death rites is very significant among the Luo. These two examples reveal that the presence of town criers at ceremonial activities and historical and cultural fests add a sense of truth and nostalgia, imprinting on the mind of the community the shared history and identity. In this way, town criers contribute to the preservation and celebration of local customs and traditions and foster a sense of continuity between past, present, and future generations.

Voice of the Community

Town criers remain the voice of the community (Toth et al., 2018). Even in rural areas or places where we do not have up to date digital facilities and internet connection, town criers act as sources of information and vehicles for community interaction. In Kenya and Nigeria, a town crier serves as the voice of the community at large. Their strong voices with an able presence give them a distinct ability to capture the attention of the community and deliver important messages like public safety announcements, invites for events, or the alerts, in an official and clear manner.

The Bridge between the Information Haves and Information Have-Nots

Town criers have moved to embracing modern forms of communication. For example, town criers publish their information through different online channels, websites, and newsletters to stay connected to the community and be more accessible in between their public appearances (Asemah et al., 2021). Such digital instruments empower town criers to share information swiftly and interactively, thus encouraging two-way communication and participation of bearers of different interests. The town crier can amplify their influence beyond the usual outlook by using the digital technology to connect with people who might not be physically present. According to Akpan (2023a), during the pandemic, town criers in Epe, Ikorodu, Badagry, and Ibeju-Lekki were able to use their unique traditional gowns and style of disseminating information, on some select radio stations in Lagos State, to create awareness of Covid-19, and elsewhere in Nigeria (Abaneme et al., 2021).

In Kenya, the services of the town criers were also employed to stem the tide of the virus (Barasa & Shitandi, 2020; Obyerodhyambo & Wamunyu, 2023).

Community Advocates for Local and Global Causes

Town criers are symbolic in giving a voice and bringing people together. They are advocates for the people and local authorities. As Nkwi (2018) asserts, the town crier's public presence and vocal advocacy for local interest groups or initiatives inspires the fanatical support and taking action by members of communities. For example, their roles in spreading the messages of protecting the environment, social justice, and cultural preservation takes on the role of advocates; they lift the voices of marginalized groups and advance the causes that benefit society. Thus, town criers enhance the democratic process by creating a well-informed citizen and civic participation which contributes to the well-being of society. Additionally, town criers are vital channels of communication for government policy campaigns about health and security and agricultural policies in rural areas in Kenya and Nigeria, respectively (Njomo et al., 2017; Ifukor & Omogo, 2013). In Kenya and Nigeria, town criers participated in efforts to sensitize members in their communities of the dangers and prevention of Covid-19. Studies conducted about the pandemic reveal that town criers played a big role in disseminating information about vaccination in the rural area (Abaneme et al., 2021; Akpan, 2023b; Obyerodhyambo & Wamunyu, 2023).

Admixture Model of Communication Forms and Practices

Although the ways of delivering messages by the traditional town criers and modern-day digital communication are fundamentally different, the two means of communication share a common goal of spreading information and creating a shared meaning among target audiences. In the first place, the town criers used to step into the streets and shout out the message verbally and use the sound of bells and drums to get it across to the local citizens (Abaneme et al., 2021). Today, town criers are able to utilize a wide variety of digital platforms such as social media, websites, email newsletters, and mobile apps. Town criers have moved to embracing modern forms of communication. For example, town criers publish their information through different online channels, websites, and newsletters to stay connected to the community and be more accessible in between their public appearances (Asemah et al., 2021). Such digital instruments empower town criers to share information swiftly and interactively, thus encouraging two-way communication and participation of bearers of different interests. The town crier can amplify their influence beyond the usual outlook by using the digital technology to connect with people who might not be physically present.

CONCLUDING REMARKS

In Kenya and Nigeria, the role of town criers underscores the enduring significance of indigenous media in preserving cultural heritage and fostering community harmony and resilience in the digital age. Thus, Des Wilson's clarion call to study the role of indigenous media cannot be overstated.

The effectiveness of town criers extending to their communication networks and protocols enhances the ability to perform multiple tasks in society. As discussed earlier, the roles of town criers in the digital age have evolved significantly during the Covid-19 pandemic. Town criers became an important go-between the government and communities enabling government authorities to leverage existing community structures for timely and effective communication during crises. They are trusted sources of information and demonstrate flexibility, employing social media and digital platforms to reach further audiences. Additionally, town criers embody the roles of messengers, newsmen, first responders, mediators, decision-makers, community development agents, and custodians of local culture. These roles continue to be particularly pertinent in the context of development efforts to mitigate, among other crises, climate change-induced disasters, where early warning systems and community mobilization are essential for minimizing risks and ensuring resilience (Collier et al., 2008). This is because town criers have been useful in local intelligence gathering and feedback mechanisms in addition to serving as intermediaries between communities and local authorities and to providing valuable insights into community needs, concerns, and priorities. Development practitioners can harness the multiple roles of town criers to enable more responsive and contextually relevant interventions, as evidenced during the Covid-19 pandemic. This could involve integrating town criers into community-based monitoring and evaluation systems or utilizing them as conduits for participatory decision-making processes. For example, town criers in the rural areas of Lagos acted as intermediaries between the government and the people in creating awareness about the pandemic (Akpan, 2023a,b).

Looking back at where we started, we must ask ourselves what our study reveals about town crier as a viable source of information and even more, as the embodiment of African communication and culture. Our study reveals that town criers in both Nigerian and Kenyan communities are resilient in preserving traditional culture and heritage. In keeping with scholarly efforts to ensure "survival" and success of African traditional modes of communication in the digital age, we are optimistic that the African indigenous media would continue to hold its significant place in the society. Despite the pervasive influence of digital technology, their enduring relevance of town criers is anchored in their unique ability to connect with communities at personal and community levels. As long as there are remote areas with limited digital access and a need for preserving cultural identity, the traditional town crier will continue to play an irreplaceable role in these societies. The town crier's continued relevance in Nigeria and Kenya is embedded in cultural, linguistic, accessibility, and trust-related factors. While digital technology has penetrated various aspects of modern life, the unique role and adaptability of the town crier ensure their continued importance in local communities.

Future research should focus on ways to harness efforts to sustain the relevance of traditional forms of communication in the digital age. Our study reveals that town criers have a role to play in the digital age. We are impressed by the ability of town criers to multitask in the digital space. The multitasking role of town criers surpasses the presumed role as "village newsman" (Wilson, 1987) to include function of stewards of culture and traditions, public announcers, digital communicators, development work agents, and community advocates all at the same time. All these roles make town criers occupy a unique and esteemed position not only in African indigenous communities but also in African communication scholarship.

REFERENCES

Abaneme, E., Nwasum, C., Chima, O., Elechi, O., & Uduma, N. (2021). Communicating COVID-19 to rural dwellers: Revisiting the role of traditional media in crisis communication. *Journal of African Media Studies*, *13*(2), 177–91.

Abdulai, M., Ibrahim, H., & Anas, A. L. (2023). The role of indigenous communication systems for rural development in the Tolon District of Ghana. *Research in Globalization*, *6*, 100128.

Ajayi, A. O., Adeloye, K. A., Olanrewaju, K. O., & Olayinka, K. O. (2020). Communication pattern used by community development associations: Empirical evidence from Ilero, Oke-Ogun, Oyo State, Nigeria. *ScientificPapers Seriesmanagement,EconomicEngineering in Agriculture and Rural Development*, *20*(3), 61–67.

Akhmetova, A. V., & Musalitina, E. A. (2022). Internet communication as a factor in preserving the traditional culture of indigenous peoples of the Russian far east.

In T. S. Bello (Ed.). *Business 4.0 as a subject of the digital economy* (pp. 791–94). Cham: Springer International Publishing.

Akpabio, E. (2023). *Indigenous communication: A global perspective.* Springer Nature.

Akpan, U. S. (2023a). Traditional African media: Looking back, looking forward. In U. S. Akpan (Ed.), *African media space and globalization* (pp. 3–51). Palgrave Macmillan. https://link.springer.com/chapter/10.1007/978-3-031-35060-3_1.

Akpan, U. S. (2023b). The role of traditional town criers using indigenous Yoruba language in COVID-19 awareness on radio for rural dwellers in Lagos. In P. Mpofu, I. A. Fadipe, T. Tshabangu (Eds.), *African language media* (pp. 127–39). Routledge. https://scholar.google.com/scholar?hl=en&as_sdt=0%2C5&q=Unwana+Samuel+Akpan&oq=#d=gs_qabs&t=1677615210434&u=%23p%3DzC-PgnRyI8wJ.

Akpan, U. S. (In press). Comparative analysis of Kunta Kinte in *"Roots"* and Okonkwo in *"Things Fall Apart"* as symbols of colonial and neocolonial defiants: Legacy of resistance and resilience against the white man's kraal in African tales. In U. S. Akpan (Ed.), *De-neocolonizing Africa: Harnessing the digital frontier.* Palgrave Macmillan.

Alia, V. (2022). *The new media nation: Indigenous peoples and global communication.* Berghahn Books.

Apata, T. G. (2019). Information dissemination and communication strategy using town crier in a traditional context in T. G. Zapata (Ed.). Southwestern states, Nigeria. *Applied Tropical Agriculture, 78–89.* Volume 1.

Asemah, E. S., Kente, J. S., & Nkwam-Uwaoma, A. O. (2021). *Handbook on African communication systems.*

Aubry, S., Frison, C., Medaglia, J. C., Frison, E., Jaspars, M., Rabone, M., . . . & Van Zimmeren, E. (2022). Bringing access and benefit sharing into the digital age. *Plants, People, Planet, 4*(1), 5–12.

Barasa, M. N., & Shitandi, A. (2020). Aspects of impact of Covid 19 on African traditional burial systems.: The case of the Bukusu of Kenya's North-Western Counties. *International Journal of Research and Innovation in Social Science, 5*(6), 388–97.

Barrowcliffe, R. (2021). Closing the narrative gap: Social media as a tool to reconcile institutional archival narratives with Indigenous counter-narratives. *Archives and Manuscripts, 49*(3), 151–66.

Carlson, B., & Frazer, R. (2021). *Indigenous digital life: The practice and politics of being indigenous on social media.* Palgrave Macmillan.

Collier, P., Conway, G., & Venables, T. (2008). Climate change and Africa. *Oxford Review of Economic Policy, 24*(2), 337–53.

D'Amata, S. A. (2020). *A case study of indigenous representation in film music: Smoke signals and dances with wolves.* Springer.

Enahoro, V. (2022). The town crier. *The Nigerian Observer.* https://nigerianobservernews.com/2022/10/the-town-crier/.

Eze, V. O., Okonkwo, U. U., Nnamdi Eke, S., Eze-Aruah, D. C., & Ukaogo, V. (2021). Modernity could not destroy them: Historicizing the African oral artist and the traditional means of communication in Nigeria. *Cogent Arts & Humanities, 8*(1), 2000556.

Galla, C. K. (2018). Digital realities of indigenous language revitalization: A look at Hawaiian language technology in the modern world. *Language and Literacy, 20*(3), 100–120.

Idowu, A. A., Aderemi, A. S., Olawale, A. I., & Omotayo, A. N. (2022). Assessing the impact of advertising agencies on effective advertising campaigns. *British Journal of Mass Communication and Media Research, 2*(1), 71.

Ifukor, M. O., & Omogo, M. (2013). Channels of information acquisition and dissemination among rural dwellers. *International Journal of Library and Information Science, 5*(10), 306–12.

Intahchomphoo, C. (2018). Indigenous peoples, social media, and the digital divide: A systematic literature review. *American Indian Culture and Research Journal, 42*(4), 85–111.

Kerkhove, R. (2021). Smoke signalling resistance: Aboriginal use of long-distance communication during Australia's frontier wars. *Queensland Review, 28*(1), 1–24.

Lipschultz, J. H. (2020). *Social media communication: Concepts, practices, data, law and ethics.* Routledge.

Malik, O., Perveen, A., & Khanam, M. (2021). Television advertising and its impact on children. *International Research Journal of Management and Social Sciences, 2*(2), 40–51.

Molto, L. (2023). Media sources. In *Conestoga english language reader 4.* Conestoga College.

Mutai, P. (2024). Feature: Communities in western Kenya still use village criers for critical messages. Palgrave.*XinhuaNet.* http://www.xinhuanet.com/english/2017 -08/24/c_136550111.htm.

Njoku, A. (2023). Modernization of African culture: The town crier and gender in Patrick Naagbanton's Writings. *Journal of Gender and Power* 20(2), 49–69. https://scholar.google.com/scholar?hl=en&as_sdt=0%2C5&q=town +crier+in+Kenya%2C+2023&btnG=#d=gs_qabs&t=1709047895582&u=%23p %3DG3scUDdAjgMJ.

Njomo, D.W., Masaku, J., Mwende. (2017). Local stakeholders' perceptions of community sensitization for school-based deworming programme in Kenya. *Tropical Diseases Travel Medicine and Vaccines,* (15), 1–8. https://doi.org/10.1186/s40794 -017-0058-9.

Njui, M. M. (2023). The place of the oral traditional techniques of communication in a digital era: The case of the Kenyang speaking Community. *Coou Journal of Arts and Humanities (CJAH) Formerly Ansu Journal of Arts and Humanities (AJAAH), 5*(4).

Nkwi, W. G. (2018). Communication in Africa: Talking drums and town criers in pre-colonial and colonial Bamenda Grassfields, Cameroon. *The Saber and Scroll Journal, 7*(2), 7–33.

Obasi, F. (2023). Another look at oramedia hypothesis. *Caritas Journal of Management, Social Sciences and Humanities, 2*(2).

Obyerodhyambo, O., & Wamunyu, W. (2023). The ogre and the griot: Culturally embedded communicative approaches addressing 'Deep Fake' COVID-19 narratives and hyperrealities in Kenya. In K. Langmia (Ed.), *Black communication in the age of disinformation* (pp. 105–29). Palgrave Macmillan. https://doi.org/10.1007/978-3-031-27696-5_6.

Ogwezzy, A. (2008). *A functional approach to African communication systems.* Concept Publications Limited.

Onuora-Oguno, C. K., & Ibekwe, E. U. (2023). Adaptation of the egwu ogene in a digital world: A study of Ejyk Nwamba. *Awka Journal of Research in Music and Arts (AJRMA)*, 16.

Patel, K. (2018, July). Impact of advancements in technological aids in communication media in bringing about social reformation. In *Proceeding of the Global Conference on Journalism and Mass Communication*, *1*(1), 1–5.

Praxides, C. (2022). Lamu town crier Shee keeps ancient tradition alive. *The Star.* https://www.the-star.co.ke/counties/coast/2022-01-28-lamu-town-crier-shee-keeps-ancient-tradition-alive/.

Rajput, A. S., & Sharma, S. (2023). An exploratory study of Indian scientists' perceptions of their roles and responsibilities in science communication. *African Journal of Science, Technology, Innovation and Development*, *15*(4), 415–28.

Sherry, S. Y., & Matsaganis, M. D. (Eds.). (2018). *Ethnic media in the digital age.* Routledge.

Shiri, A., Howard, D., & Farnel, S. (2022). Indigenous digital storytelling: Digital interfaces supporting cultural heritage preservation and access. *International Information & Library Review*, *54*(2), 93–114.

Smith, J. T. (2019). *The cries of London: Exhibiting several of the itinerant traders of ancient and modern times.* Good Press.

Stichel, B., Blake, E., Maasz, D., Stanley, C., Winschiers-Theophilus, H., & Afrikaner, H. (2019, June). Namibian indigenous communities reflecting on their own digital representations. In *Proceedings of the 9th International Conference on Communities & Technologies-Transforming Communities* (pp. 51–59). Association for Computing Machinery.

Tajvidi, M., Richard, M. O., Wang, Y., & Hajli, N. (2020). Brand co-creation through social commerce information sharing: The role of social media. *Journal of Business Research*, *121*, 476–86.

Thulla, F. Y. P., Koroma, A., Moriba, S., & Fofanah, I. M. (2022). Folk media: Existence, forms, uses and challenges in Mende indigenous communities of Southern Sierra Leone. *Research Journal in Advanced Humanities*, *3*(4), 13–25.

Toth, K., Smith, D., & Giroux, D. (2018). Indigenous peoples and empowerment via technology 1. *First Peoples Child & Family Review*, *13*(1), 21–33.

Trilling, D., Araujo, T., Kroon, A., Möller, A. M., Strycharz, J., & Vermeer, S. (2024). Computational communication science in a digital society. In T. Araujo, & P. Neijens (Eds.), *Communication research into the digital society: Fundamental insights from the Amsterdam school of communication research* (pp. 247–64). Amsterdam University Press. https://doi.org/10.1515/9789048560608-016.

Wilson, D. (1987). Traditional systems of communication in modern African development: An analytical viewpoint. *Africa Media Review*, *1*(2), 87–104.

Wilson, D. (2023). Relevance of Nigerian traditional communication systems in the digital space. In U. S. Akpan (Ed.), *Nigerian media industries in the era of globalization* (p. 213). Lexington.

Wu, J., & Chen, D. T. V. (2020). A systematic review of educational digital storytelling. *Computers & Education, 147*, 103786.

Chapter 10

Nurturing Indigenous African Communication Modes in a Digital Age

Performing Igbo Proverbs in Film for Advice and Warning

Ihuoma Okorie

Before the arrival of Western communication modes and channels, Africans had treasured traditional modes of disseminating information through which they maintained a stable society. This system of communication occupied a unique position in different societies. They delivered their content using African traditional instruments, mediums, and channels. The messages carried by these communication modes as stated by Manyozo (2018) "were largely passed through generations, and through the social structures and processes" (p. 395). To this end, the messages were timely and accessible to members of the society. For instance, Abdulai et al. (2023, p. 1) write that "storytelling, drumming, and the town crier provided an avenue for indigenous people to disseminate important information to rural communities in a language the local people were familiar with, and understand." This was a vital avenue for inculcating good ethical and moral values to the upcoming generation.

However, with the proliferation of media, occasioned by digital innovations, there has been an alteration of communication modes in traditional African societies; this, to a large extent, has jeopardized the purpose of indigenous communication modes and further hampered the growth and utilization of indigenous communication modes. Despite the stiff competition with the digital media, it is pertinent to note that digital transformation holds enormous opportunities in providing a wide range of information as it holds great potentials for indigenous communication. This calls for the need to refine and maintain indigenous communication in a way that would promote indigenous knowledge. The aim of this study is to adjudge the use of proverbs to communicate pertinent issues in the film, *Things Fall Apart*, an adaptation of Chinua Achebe's novel.

Since indigenous models of communication are numerous, this chapter focuses on proverbs because of the place they occupy in African communication. Proverbs enrich the understanding of African knowledge, value systems, and being (Izuogu, 2018). In different contexts, proverbs are used to give good advice or caution people against bad deeds. As a traditional mode of communication, proverbs serve to preserve, sustain, and transmit African culture from generation to generation. Through proverbs, the requisite wisdom and knowledge necessary for addressing personal and group challenges are inculcated into people in ways that are acceptable and functional. In the process of such interaction, the younger generation is expected to learn and imbibe the virtues of the rewards of personal sacrifice, purposeful leadership, and proper demeanor, among others. Considering the richness of African proverbs, this chapter examines ways to nurture Indigenous African Communication modes to continue their functions in the digital age. Specifically, proverbs in the film, *Things Fall Apart*, will be analyzed for their educational content.

METHODS

This chapter adopted the qualitative method of research. This research design aims at gathering primary data from documentary observation and secondary data from journals, dissertations, and seminar papers, among others. Documentary observation as a primary source of data in this chapter as defined by Bowen (2009, p. 28) is a form of qualitative research which allows for documents to be interpreted by the researcher, to give voice and meaning around the assessment topic. To ensure reliable results, O'Leary (2014) observes that the researcher must go through a detailed planning process (p. 191). To achieve this, the film, *Things Fall Apart, was* carefully watched with the intent of drawing out the proverbs used by some of the characters in different scenes. These proverbs were analyzed in relation to their context of use in the film. To further support the views drawn from the primary sources, this chapter deployed secondary data, particularly from journals, dissertations, and seminar papers. These sources contained articles on very specific subjects, which were related to the primary source. The intent was to interpret, or further explain the ideas and information, gotten from the primary source. This method is considered most appropriate because it focuses on the qualitative examination of both primary and secondary sources of data.

To further select the proverbs that were analyzed, the purposive sampling method, which is a type of non-probability sampling technique, was deployed. This is because it enables a more targeted and detailed exploration of the variables. The intent was to analyze ten proverbs for their moral and cultural values. Therefore, the findings will contribute to literature on indigenous communication modes and its merger with digital communication in a digital age. This is pertinent because African proverbs have epistemic relevance. Therefore, the usage of proverbs in any tribe or society implies the application of wisdom, truth, morals, experience, lessons, and advice as contained in such proverbs, to issues that enhance the living condition of the people for which the proverbs are couched. This helps them understand their world, and also, make progress. This explains why nurturing these highly revered modes of communication is germane in a digital age.

This chapter begins with the introduction which briefly explains the importance and purpose of indigenous modes of communication like proverbs, the methodology which elucidates on the research design and modes of data collection, a review of related literature on Indigenous Communication Modes in Africa, the Conceptual Framework which served as a tool of analysis, and the analysis of the film, *Things Fall Apart,* in relation to how proverbs were deployed, as well as its meaning, the findings, and conclusion.

INDIGENOUS COMMUNICATION MODES IN AFRICA

Indigenous communication is a form of traditional communication that is peculiar to a given culture or society. According to Ayangunna and Oyewo (2014), this system of communication existed before the arrival of modern mass media. The above simply connotes that it is a system of education that is predicated on African culture. On the other hand, Wilson (1987, p. 89) cited in Bussotti (2015) defines Indigenous Communication Modes as "a continual process of information sharing, entertainment, and education employed in communities that have not been significantly disrupted by Western culture or any other external influence, as many regions of the world have been." From the above, it can be garnered that indigenous forms of communication are specific to a particular society. It is a vital part of culture which is normally part of people's lives and their ways of making a living over a number of generations. This form of communication serves as a channel for messages in a manner that requires the utilization of the values, symbols, and ethos of the host culture through its unique qualities and attributes. Overtime, it has proven to be potent in the dissemination of information in rural communities. According to Adesoji and Ogunjimi (2015), these forms of communications "easily appeal to and connect with people's language, culture, beliefs, myths, legends, and custom." This resonates the idea of Izuogu (2018, p. 21) who states that:

> Every society has an identifiable system of communication that is peculiar to it, and such a system of communication could be organized, modern or traditional, verbal or nonverbal. Whatever the case, such systems of communication must originate from the societies being referred to, or must be the dominant ways of exchange of ideas amongst the people.

Therefore, the goals of indigenous modes of communication are news contents, directives, advertising, PR content, entertainment content, and educational content (Izuogu, 2018, p. 24). Again, Mundy and Laney (1992) opine that these media/channels are not but limited to folk, observation, interaction, oralmedia, informal media, storytelling, visual arts, concerts, gong beating, dirges, drumming and dancing, interpersonal channels and plays, use of proverbs, songs and dances, and use of native language and cultural resources. Therefore, despite the role of indigenous communication in educating people, both formally and informally, it serves as a custodian of the history, culture, and values of a people or society. African heritage is rich with proverbs that serve to inform and educate the people about a wide range of social issues. This brings to fore the importance and role of proverbs as an indigenous mode of communication.

PROVERBS

To begin with, it is pertinent to state that the debate about the actual definition of the proverb still persists. Although some scholars have successfully explained what proverbs are, it is not by any consistent definition but by identifying some dominant elements that usually constitute a proverb. Freyha (1974, p. 1) observes:

> Despite the many definitions put forth by different scholars as to how proverbs should be defined, none of it holds true of every proverb. The difficulty lies in the nature of proverbs, which contain all manner of ideas that touch upon the whole round of human experience.

Thus, while some definitions place emphasis on popularity others emphasize on role or content, an attempt to combine all these elements in a single definition is likely to result in wordiness and incomprehension. To further support the above claim, Taylor's (1931, p. 3) "classical study on proverbs" shows that there is no single definition of a proverb; however, later in his work, he tries to provide a more or less general definition for his readers which is that "a proverb is a saying current among the folk." Mieder (2004, p. 3) criticizes Taylor (1931) for not providing a proper definition, but at the same time acknowledges that his work has become famous and gained attention. Taylor's (1931) study on proverbs provides essential information about proverbs. Despite the earlier conceptual differences, it is expedient to state that scholars have hitherto achieved much in the sphere of proverb studies. According to Fakoya (2007, p. 13), proverbs are short and clever words full of wisdom, intended as rules of conduct and behavior. Here, proverbs are seen as tools that offer conventional wisdom which are usually short, expressing a general belief or a traditional code of conduct. In the words of Kewulezi (2004, p. 17), a proverb is a tool used for the purpose of rhetorical adornment and persuasion. They are used to express the morals as well as the ethics of the society. From the above, it can be deciphered that proverbs are valued for what they reveal about the wisdom and culture of a people.

A more developed definition of proverbs is given by Methangwane (2003, p. 408) in (Odebunmi, 2008, p. 2) who considers them as "relatively short expressions, which are usually associated with wisdom and are used to perform a variety of functions." From the above definitions, this paper acknowledges that proverbs perform different functions in the society. Thus, this study conceptualizes proverbs as contextually dependent words of wisdom which tell the story of the nonmaterial culture, and relevant in expressing, reflecting, and promoting the values of a people and society. Proverbs are trusted sources of wisdom. They are didactic, memorable, and passed down from one generation to another; hence, its role in disseminating cultural values.

In traditional societies, Ellman (1973) states that proverbs more often than not celebrated the ideals of the society to which it belonged. This simply suggests that through proverbs the cultural background of a group of people is ascertained. Mubina (2001) states that "a society's proverbs reflect its social, economic, and political institutions." Particularly, Mubina (2011) states that proverbs are an expression of values, perceptions, and aspirations of the people about whom the proverbs talk about. Thus, in relation to its social function, Bamukunda (2017, p. 18) states that proverbs played a huge role in institutionalizing checks and balances and also played a didactic role by addressing relevant issues in society, whether good or evil. In view of the conceptual framework provided to understand proverbs, it is pertinent to conclude this section by stating that proverbs embody the expectations of society and exist to promote virtues, condemn vices, and pass weighty messages in a mild or gentle way.

CONCEPTUAL FRAMEWORK

This paper is anchored on the concept of folk-hermeneutics as conceptualized by Okorie (2023). The concept is a medley of folkism, propounded
by Sam Ukala, and Hermeneutics, by Hans Gadamar. Folkism was coined
as a response partly to the prevalent criticism of Nigerian literary plays as
irrelevant and unpopular and partly to the findings that the unpopularity and
relative irrelevance of Nigeria literary plays derive from their unfamiliar
dramaturgy which are alien to the folk and much of the supposed educated
audience. In view of the above, Ukala (1993) states that:

> Nigerian literary plays draw their subject matter from the histories and cultures
> of Nigerians and yet many of them are not accessible to the populace because
> of their difficult language, their distortion of source material beyond recogni-
> tion, complex sentence structure, and mode of presentation that is foreign and
> strange. Because of these, the audience finds it difficult to comprehend and
> identify with the plays. (p. 285)

It is therefore the quest to perform typical folkloric plays in an original
environment that informed the use of folkism. Ukala (1993) defines folkism
as the tendency to base literary plays on history, culture, and concerns of the
folk and to compose or perform them in accordance with African conventions
for composing and performing plays in accordance with the people. This is
to say that folkism must be grounded in the culture and mores of the people.
Folkism is therefore an emergent aesthetic principle noted for its clear communication and its popularity among the folk (a people/culture).

Hermeneutics is the theory and philosophy of understanding and interpretation derived from Hermes, a son of Zeus, who interprets messages from
the Greek gods (Tomkins & Eatough, 2018). However, three key personalities that have championed, written, and contributed extensively to modern
hermeneutics are Schleiermacher (1998) who reviewed the origins of modern hermeneutics as an activity of interpretation and Heidegger (1962) and
Gadamer (2004) who view hermeneutics as a philosophy of understanding.
The above suggests that the field of hermeneutics has two main branches:
one concerned with the activities of interpretation and the other concerned
with the philosophy of understanding. Therefore, since hermeneutics as
a methodology of interpretation is inseparable from the cultural and discursive setting in which—and from which—the cultural features emerge,
the interplay between folkism and hermeneutics brings to life the concept,
folk-hermeneutics.

Consequently, folk-hermeneutics is conceived as a method of analysis
which focuses on interpreting and understanding the contextual local features

that are common to a people as documented in a play text or film within the context depicted. The film or play text must be centrally related to Africa, must be rooted in African culture, and should portray the history and cultures that the folk value. It deals with understanding a folk in a preconceived society in the text. Proverbs form the gist of what cultures consider of real concern to them (Lawal et al., 1997, p. 636). This suggests that proverbs are associated with what a folk document is important, common, and popular among them. However, as a folk element, it requires a tool that can be used to interpret and further understand the meanings embedded therein—this is where hermeneutics comes to play. Since proverb is an indigenous element, the following were key indicators for the analysis of proverbs sourced. They include the philosophy and the moral and cultural values inherent in the proverbs.

Since philosophies are communicated in proverbs, a critical examination of proverbs with the intent to highlight the indigenous wisdom communicated through the interpretation of the proverbs shall be brought to fore. This is because proverbs embody a large proportion of African philosophy. As such, the richness in divine wisdom was communicated. Morality or morals refers to what societies sanction as right and acceptable. Thus, the context from which the proverbs were used accounted for the morals laden in them. The lessons that were learned from the character's attitudes and behavior and the proverbs uttered formed the crux of analysis. Lastly, values are the core principles and ideals upon which an entire society exists. They are the elements or convictions common to a people which determine their way of being and further guide the behavior and decisions of individuals. This is imperative because proverbs are seen as effective teaching tools which help to unobtrusively enforce and develop an appreciation for the values; it is a verbal method of projecting values. Thus, the theory of folk-hermeneutics was used to contextually account for the philosophy, morals, and values of the cultures portrayed in the proverbs, focusing on the light they shed in the societies from which the proverbs originate.

NURTURING PROVERBS IN A DIGITAL AGE: PERFORMING PROVERBS IN FILM *THINGS FALL APART* (1971)

One of the most important features of recent developments in proverbs is the move away from oral compositions as a pivotal element toward the notion of performance. Performance is simply defined as the term used for public presentation that employs anything more than an embellished reading or saying. Okpewho (1985, p. 9) sees performance as a stage play, hence the performer has to support his words with the right movement of his body or control his voice so as to make an effective impression. How then can proverb, as an indigenous communication, be performed? In a bid to respond to the above, Ukozor and Etumnu (2022, p. 55) assert that:

Some of the challenges of indigenous communication in the modern era include the poor attitude of Nigerian children toward understanding indigenous modes of communication, which constitute a threat to its survival. Again, the rate at which some rural areas are being urbanized destroys communal life among the people that appreciate the use of folk media. This act poses a challenge to indigenous communication. The new generation's lack of pride in indigenous traditions and values is a big threat to the indigenous communication system in modern age.

The above sentiment brings to the fore concerns about exponential rise in advancements in technology as a threat to indigenous communication. Film is a powerful medium of mass communication which can be used as a potent weapon to nurture and project indigenous communication modes in Africa. This can be achieved by engaging in an aggressive pro-local approach to film packaging, infusing elements of culture in scripts or programs. For instance, this is exemplified in the way technology is harnessed in the filmic representation of the novel, *Things Fall Apart*, to ensure the continuity of the unique cultural heritage of Africans. Thus, it can be averred that indigenous communication is not fast losing its place to Western culture or communication, rather both can be utilized as a tool to further nurture and project these ways of communication that are relished by Africans.

The Film *Things Fall Apart* is an adaptation of literature about the culture and arts of the Igbo people. Thus, the filmic adaptation of this literary classic written by Chinua Achebe (1958) is a way of nurturing and propagating the cultural values of the Igbo people in Nigeria. The novel is laced with proverbs, usually considered as folk knowledge. The filmic representation of the novel was released in 1971, thirteen years after the novel was written. It was first produced in the United States. In this production, there was a blend of *Things Fall Apart* with Achebe's second novel, *No Longer at Ease*. The joint Nigerian, German, and American production was initially titled *Bullfrog in the Sun* and later renamed *Things Fall Apart,* directed by Jurgen Pohland, with Fern Mosk as executive producers and Francis Oladele as co-producer (Ugochukwu, 2014, p. 171).

Considering the fact that it was an adaptation from script to film, the film made up eleven clusters of scenes and was constructed around a continual shift in context, some presented as flashbacks that provides and exposes the impact of Western civilization on Africa. Ugochukwu (2014, p. 176) writes that the film looked at some of the events in the novel and read them in a unique way, quite different from the novel. This is exemplified in certain scenes that were enlarged, and some shrunk or expunged. Though the film was not completely faithful to the novel, the place of proverb was well documented.

Plot—*Things Fall Apart* (1971)

The film began with the coming of the missionaries (whom the people call Albino) to Mbanta to win the people to Christ. The people who are so attached to their gods refused to heed the Whiteman's request to quit serving their gods. However, a few adherents from Mbanta chose to follow the god of the Whiteman; as such, they were referred to as outcasts. To further deter the Whiteman from preaching in their land, they offered a huge amount of land (evil forest) to the Whiteman; this is with the intention that they will not survive. On the other hand, the Whiteman in partnership with some of the indigenous settlers joined forces and annihilated the people of Abame on their market day, except the aged, the sick, and children who were in their houses. This made the people of Umuofia, the neighboring community, scared. However, Ebubedike (Okonkwo), the only one with the courage to lead them, had been sent to exile. The chiefs decide to have a discussion on the next step to take seeing that the neighboring village has been attacked. They consider bringing back Okonkwo to help lead the warriors in defense of their community, but they also recall that he has just spent two years in exile out of the seven years. Therefore, they decide to send Obierika, his good friend, to intimate him on the happenings in their land. Though he is saddened because of his inability to return, he enjoins Obierika to gather the youths and inform them to stand in defense of their fatherland. This is to retain its name as "The Town of Warriors." The film uses many proverbs to communicate different aspects of Igbo society. However, I purposively sampled and chose to analyze ten proverbs for their moral and cultural values.

Proverb 1: *There Is Nothing to Fear from a Man Who Shouts*

Meaning: Know and learn when to apply silence.
Context: This proverb was uttered by Ogbuefi Uchendu when he was told the story of how the Whiteman obliterated the people of Abame. He utters this proverb to let Okonkwo and Obierika know that the people of Abame are to blame. This is because they allowed the Whiteman to have a feast on them without launching any form of attack. To him, the Whitemen invaded because they already knew nothing much would happen. This proverb sheds more light on the concept of strength and weakness as defined by culture. The traditional measure of strength for the Igbo people includes physical strength and fighting skill, while weakness connotes the inability to

stand up and win a fight or allow others to control you. Generally, the Igbos are resilient and dogged. Considering the aforestated, Ogbuefi through this proverb expected the people of Abame to display their physical strength by standing up in defense of their fatherland. The notion of silence is important in many indigenous cultures, but for him, silence was wrongly applied. This is because the Igbos are known for their strength and tenacity.

Moral: Apply wisdom when dealing with people. Know when to stand up for your right and also know when to be silent.

Cultural Value: Wisdom.

Proverb 2: *Anyone Who Refuses to Heed the Warning, Calls for His Death*

Meaning: Warnings are given to prevent danger.

Context: This proverb is uttered by Obunze during his discussion with Okonkwo regarding the obliteration of the Abame people. He blames them for refusing to heed the warning given by their ancestors to always protect the community from external attack when they notice any negative moves from people who are not part of them. The people noticed signs of an attack when they saw the Whiteman, accompanied by some settlers, spying through their community, rather than act, they took it with levity. It is clear that the people noticed signs of an attack, but refused to make plans on how to defend their land. Such telltale signs should have spurred the people to act.

Moral: Every action or inaction has a consequence. Strive to act rightly.

Cultural Value: Strive to prevent danger if it is within your reach.

Proverb 3: *Nothing Is New under the Sun*

Meaning: Expect the worst from trusted allies.

Context: This proverb was uttered by Amikwu when he discloses to Okonkwo that his son, Nwoye, has joined the Whiteman's religion. While still discussing with Obunze, Amikwu walks into the scene worried. They both approach him to ask what the problem is but Amikwu refuses to say what it is. This instigates the proverb by Amikwu, emphasizing the cyclic nature of human beings, and the need to be calm and take things easy. In the Igbo language, it is translated as "Onweghi ihe bu ihe ohuru n'okpuru Anyanwu."

Moral: Do not be disappointed when a trusted ally betrays you.

Cultural Value: Cautiousness.

Proverb 4: *The Hen Protects Her Chicks from the Cannon of the Hawks*

Meaning: Parents are meant to protect their children from danger.

Context: This proverb was uttered by the Chief priest while communicating with the goddess in the Shrine. He was spotted trying to appease her because she has been calm and refused to respond positively to his appeals and calls. From the happening in the scene, it is clear that the goddess sensed danger, a sinister move by someone; this made her weak, helpless, and unable to protect her people because she wonders why someone will choose to harm her despite how good she has been to them. In the Igbo culture, it is a cultural expectation for the goddess, called *alusi* (Deity), to protect her people, however, she is silent. The worship of this goddess is further captured by Agu (2003, p. 16) who states that "besides Nnobi society like many others, Anambra State is a patrilineal society with a strong female deity." The Chief priest reminds the goddess through this proverb that she is meant to protect the people of Umuofia, but seeing that she has been silent, he wonders what the problem is. A hen is to her little chicks a cover of safety; this explains why the chicks beneath the wings of the hen look excited when crowded. When the mother-bird spots a hawk in the sky, she gives her chicks a peculiar cluck of warning and quickly, they come and hide beneath her wings for safety. This cultural expectation of care for the helpless is embedded in everyday life ethos of society.

Moral: The place of parents and elders in loving, guiding, and protecting the young from any harm cannot be overemphasized. This is exemplified through giving advice, warning, and guiding them on the right choices to make as they grow older.

Cultural Value: Guidance, protection, and care.

Proverb 5: *When the Gray Hair Senses Danger and It Does Not Speak, It Is Death to Him*

Meaning: An elder is the first to be affected when he sees a wrong vice and does not speak up.

Context: The same context as above. The Chief priest, still trying to find out the reason why the goddess, is quiet. He reminds her of the fact that if she decides to be quiet, she will be the first to be affected if anything eventually happens. The Igbos tend to be communally resilient in protecting their land and its people. The goddess is seen and perceived as a figure of protection for some communities in Igbo land; however, if she decides to be silent when danger lurks, she will not escape the impact it will have. Her role is equivalent to that of parents and elders whose duty is to protect those who are feeble.

Moral: The place of parents and elders is to protect the land and its people.

Cultural Value: Guidance.

Proverb 6: A Man Will Starve If He Only Has One Kitchen from Which He Feeds Himself

Meaning: Having multiple sources of wealth and benefits guarantees one's peace of mind.

Context: This proverb is uttered by Okonkwo during his discussion with Obierika about his son Nwoye joining the Whiteman's religion. When Nwoye returns, Okonkwo in anger chokes him by the neck, demanding where he has been; however, Uchendu orders him to let go of the boy. Nwoye leaves his father's compound and travels to a school in Umuofia to learn reading and writing. Nwoye is further drawn to Christianity and feels himself exiled from the community; however, the church offers refuge to all those the society has cast out. Okonkwo wonders how he could ever have fathered an effeminate, weak son like Nwoye. This instigates the proverb.

This proverb further reveals the concept of extended family system, a well-known practice in Igbo land. Though, in Igbo culture, the core of the family is the nuclear family, that is, the parents and their children, they see a lot of advantages in the extended family system. This is because of the security it offers especially in the aspect of birthing many children, who they can rely on, should in any case, one falters. This is exemplified in the words of Nwokocha (2007) who states that "The persistence of high fertility among the Igbo of Nigeria is linked to the relative strength of the pronatalist tradition among them." This is the case with Okonkwo who has three wives and many children. When he is asked what he would do, he quickly responds with the proverb, reminding Obierika that he has more than one kitchen to feed from.

Moral: Do not depend on a single person or plan of action. You may be disappointed in the long run/do not risk everything by committing to one plan or idea.

Cultural Value: Wisdom.

Proverb 7: An Animal Rubs Its Aching Flank against the Tree, but a Man Asks His Kinsmen to Scratch His Back

Meaning: The place of kinsmen in the survival and prosperity of a person cannot be overemphasized.

Context: This proverb is uttered by Ogbuefi Uchendu during the feast prepared by Okonkwo the night before his return to Umuofia after completing his seven years of exile. Okonkwo thanked the chiefs for accommodating him in their land when he was excommunicated by his people. As a way to emphasize the importance of having Kinsmen, he utters this proverb. This is a pointer to the fact that the Igbo traditional society thrives on community life. This according to Nduka and Ozioma (2019) underlines the philosophical principle of "Igwebuike" (Unity is strength). This simply means that the community gives meaning to an individual's existence. They share a deep sense of communalism and solidarity; hence, a high sense of oneness and cohesiveness. Thus, the Igbos believe that they are better than animals because they have kinsmen.

Moral: Treat close family members and friends with love and respect.

Cultural Value: Mutuality.

Proverb 8: He That Has Children and Health Also Has Wealth

Context: Same context as the latter and uttered by the same character, Ogbuefi Uchendu. Children are considered the greatest blessing of all by the Igbos. This is exemplified in names like Nwakaego (A child is worth more than wealth), Nwabuikem (Children are my strength). Any name beginning with "Nwa" portrays the worldview of the Igbos about childbearing. Thus, a man who has many children is considered wealthy and influential. Shifting away from the above, it is pertinent to state that "the health and wealth" attached to this proverb is dependent on how well parents bring up their children. Thus, children who are properly brought up bring both health and wealth to their parents.

Moral: The health and wealth of a family are dependent on the children's training and discipline.

Cultural Value: Genuine nurturing.

Proverb 9: A Child Does Not Pay for His Mother's Milk

Meaning: Sometimes, it is difficult to repay both small and big deeds of kindness.

Context: He uses this proverb during the ceremonial breaking of the Kola nut among his relatives from Mbanta. This proverb is uttered by Okonkwo when he appreciates the chiefs for accommodating him at the end of his exile in his motherland of Mbanta. They were gracious hosts and helped him out as he adjusted to life in Mbanta. He recognizes that the way they have assisted him is invaluable and his attempt at hosting them to a feast is not to reward but to thank them. He compares their assistance to a mother nursing a child. Thus, the place of gratitude in the Igbo culture cannot be overemphasized.

Moral: Always appreciate those who are kind to you.

Cultural Value: Gratitude.

Proverb 10: When a Man Calls His Kinsmen to a Feast, He Does Not Do So Because They Are Starving

Context: Same as above, Obierika states that it is good for kinsmen to gather because loving and cherishing one another in true brotherly love is important. This makes them stronger than their problems. He considers the support given to kinsmen as the defining characteristic of humanity. Therefore, a family feast is not thrown to meet a family's need for sustenance; it is a loftier event than that. It is a celebration of the family's kinship. This brings to fore the importance of bonding and speaking with one voice, as a united body that acts for the good of all.

Moral: The importance of coming together occasionally to feast strengthens family and community ties.

Cultural Value: Family/Community ties.

NURTURING PROVERBS IN THE DIGITAL AGE

Proverbs play an important part in the communication and cultural life of the Igbos. The economy of words gives beauty and meaning and further strengthens the culture portrayed. They communicate the cultural heritage and values of a society and are also used to inculcate and underline standard of behavior. The use of proverbs in the film *Things Fall Apart* infuses it with a uniquely Igbo perspective on different subjects ranging from the importance of gratitude, mutuality, family/community ties, genuine nurturing, and guidance, among many others. Considering the richness of this cultural heritage, digitization becomes pertinent. Therefore, the importance of digitizing the proverbs lies in its preservation for posterity because the corresponding philosophical meanings assist greatly in the instruction of the younger generation on their cultural heritage.

The film's role in digitizing these proverbs assisted in reflecting the cultural values, beliefs, and wisdom of the Igbo African societies, providing insight into their history, customs, taboos, and way of life. Before now, these proverbs were often used in storytelling as a way of conveying the messages, lessons, and wisdom embedded in them to listeners; however, its use in the film has helped to bring these proverbs to a wider audience, as instructional vehicles through which cultural values are imparted. Thus, filming holds a great potential in assisting in their digital documentation for posterity. More importantly, preserving the information contained in proverbs in digital form is germane because the traditional generational knowledge transfer has been interrupted as a result of migration to cities by the younger generation.

Considering the great potential inherent in digitizing proverbs through film, young filmmakers should strive to incorporate African proverbs into their dialogue so that the audience can tap into the cultural significance of these proverbs. This can help to create a more memorable and impacting message that will resonate with the audience. Furthermore, these proverbs can be used to tell compelling stories that reflect and reinforce the cultural values of Africans. This lies in the fact that pertinent cultural values are often reflected in proverbs. Through this, diverse audiences will be connected. However, they must be careful not to misinterpret the proverbs while deploying them. The film's success reflects a significant and strategic global expansion of the Igbo culture. Therefore, film as a digital media can be positioned for projection of culture. Overall, the power of nurturing African Igbo proverbs through digitization cannot be overstated. Therefore, there is the need to further explore the use of proverbs in films to unlock the potential of proverbs as a cultural tool that can be used to project the ways of life and cultural values of Africans.

CONCLUSION

This paper took a critical look at proverbs as an indigenous form of communication and how it can be nurtured in a digital age via the use of film. Proverbs were conceptualized as indigenous mediums of communication intended to assist learning either formal learning or informal, family, or folk learning. This characterizes proverbs as an acceptable form of communication in and out of cultural contexts, providing meaning and explaining phenomena. Proverbs in the film *Things Fall Apart* were analyzed using the concept of folk-hermeneutics which focuses on analyzing the local features inherent in a play text or film, with the aim of revealing the moral and values embedded in the proverbs sourced. The study discovered that proverbs were used to state a general or acceptable truth and often used to advise, warn, and sometimes, clarify an idea. In this era of globalization, proverbs become a medium of education when performed using digital media. Here, the audience does not participate passively, they are involved both psychologically and emotionally. With this, there is no doubt that indigenous communication modes such as proverbs can be harnessed with technology to reveal the culture and values of a people. This is one viable way of nurturing it for further generations.

REFERENCES

Abdulai, M., Ibrahim, H., & Anas, A. (2023). The role of indigenous communication systems for rural development in the Tolon District of Ghana. *Research in Globalization*, *6*, 1–9. https://doi.org/10.1016/j.resglo.2023.100128.

Adesoji, S. A., & Ogunjimi, S. I. (2015). Assessing the use of indigenous communication media among rural dwellers of Osun State, Nigeria. *American Journal of Experimental Agriculture, 7*(6), 405–13. https://doi.org/109734/AJEA/2015/9743.

Agu, O. (2003) Female Goddesses, male Priests: An anthropological study in role complementarity and women empowerment among the Igbo. *Global Journal of Humanities, 2*(1&2), 16–20.

Ayangunna, J. A., & Oyewo, B. A. (2014). Indigenous communication, religion and education as determinants of attitudes toward STIS/HIV/AIDS education in Igando Community, Lagos State, Nigeria. *African Journal of Social Work, 4*(1), 59–77.

Bamukunda, H. (2017). *The thematic significance of proverbs toward child upbringing: A case study of selected primary schools in Mbarrara municipality* [Unpublished BA thesis]. Makerere University.

Bowen, G. A. (2009). Document analysis as a qualitative research method. *Qualitative Research Journal, 9*(2), 27–40.

Bussoti, I. (2015). Short reflections on the history of African communication. *Historian Communication Social, 20*(1), 205–22. https://doi.org/10.5209/rev_HICS.2015.V20.NL.49556.

Ellman, R. (1973). *The Norton anthology of modern poetry*. WW Norton & Company.

Fakoya, A. (2007). Sexually grounded proverbs and discourse relevance: Insight from Yoruba. *California Linguistic Notes, 2*(2), 1–29. www.academia.edu/5111672/sexually-groundedproverbs.

Frayha, A. (1974). *A dictionary of modern Lebanese proverbs*. Librairie du Liban.

Gadamer, H. G. (1996). *Truth and method*. (J. Weinsheimer & D. G. Marshall Eds.). Continuum.

Gadamer, H. G. (2004). *Truth and method*. (J. Weinsheimer & D. G. Marshall Eds.). Bloomsbury Academics. (Original work published 1960).

Izuogu, K. C. (2018). Westernization and indigenous modes of communication in a traditional African setting, assessment of the Igbo cultural heritage. *International Journal of Arts and Social Science, 1*(3), 5–19.

Kewulezi, D. (2004). *Selected Igbo proverbs and idiomatic expressions*. Kkoruna Books.

Lawal, A., Ajayi, B., & Raji, W. (1997). Pragmatic study of selected pairs of Yoruba proverbs. *Journal of Pragmatics, 27*, 635–52.

Manyozo, L. (2018). The context is the message: The theory of indigenous knowledge communication systems. *Javnost, 25*(4), 393–409.

Mieder, W. (2004). *Proverbs: A handbook*. Greenwood Press.

Mubina, H. K. (2001). *Oral literature of the Asians*. East African Educational Publishers.

Mundy, P., & Lloyd-Laney, M. (1992). Indigenous communications. *Appropriate Technology, 19*(2), 103–5.

Nduka, U., & Ozioma, N. G. (2019). Chinua Achebe's things fall apart and the role of women in Igbo traditional religious culture. *Open Journal of Social Sciences, 7*(12), 272–89.

Nwokocha, E. E. (2007). Male-child syndrome and the agony of motherhood among the Igbo of Nigeria. *International Journal of Sociology of the Family, 33*(1), 219–34.

Okorie, I. (2023). *A study of proverbs for the portrayal of cultural values in the plays of Femi Osofisan and Ahmed Yerima* [Unpublished doctoral dissertation] Ahmadu Bello University.

Okpewho, I. (1985). *The heritage of African poetry*. Longman.

O'Leary, Z. (2014) *The essential guide to doing your research project* (2nd ed.). SAGE Publications, Inc.

Orere, D. (1971). *Things fall apart*. Nigeria Television Authority.

Taylor, A. (1931). *The proverb*. Harvard University Press (Rpt, as *The Proverb an index to the proverb*. Hatboro, Folklore Associates).

Ugochukwu, F. (2014). Things fall apart- Achebe's legacy, from book to screen. *Research in African Literature, 45*(2), 168–83.

Ukala, S. (1993). Folkism: Towards a national aesthetic principle in dramaturgy. *A Monthly International Literary Journal of Writers Resort, 79*, 11–38.

Ukozor, N. F., & Etumnu, E. W. (2022). Indigenous communication and the prospects for survival in the modern era in African communication systems. In N. *The Era of Artificial Intelligence*. Rhyce Kerex Publishers.

Chapter 11

Implications of the Two-Step Flow Theory on Traditional Leadership in the Digital Age

The Case of Annang People in Akwa Ibom State in Nigeria

Iniobong Courage Nda

Every living being communicates—plant, animal, and man coexist with unique ways of engaging in the art and act of communication. Our lives revolve around communication, hence the saying "communication is life." We communicate intrapersonally (communication within oneself), interpersonally (communication between two or more persons), publicly (communication with an enlarged group of people), and massly (communication to a widely dispersed audience through the aid of technology). Through these different communication settings, human beings are able to interact and share meanings with their environment. At the same time, individuals are exposed to a wide array of information communicated via diverse communication modes. In the digital age, the advent of the internet and social media has skyrocketed the amount of information people are exposed to through different social media handles. Potter (2013, p. 5) pointed out that "the challenge is no longer accessing information; instead, the challenge is organizing it so that we can make meaningful use of it rather than letting it drown us in chaos."

Among the Annang speaking people of Akwa Ibom State Nigeria for instance, there exists a form of communication which the people hold close to their culture, that is, opinion leadership.

The Annang people occupy seven of the local government areas of Akwa Ibom State, Nigeria. They are artisans who are bonded by their uniqueness and accord great honor to their traditional leadership. The traditional leadership among the Annang speaking tribe is a revered position of key personalities accorded high respect and authenticated as dependable sources of information to rural dwellers. They are usually firsthand opinion leaders the rural people rely on for up-to-date information on issues of local, state-wide, national, and international concerns. This process of information flow resonates with the two-step flow theory. The success at disseminating information and communicating then becomes hinged on the traditional leadership who act also as opinion leaders to the people as they in turn look upon them for up-to-date information. Of interest to this study is how the two-step flow theory still holds sway among the rural people. The goal of the study is to analyze the implications of the two-step flow on traditional leadership among the Annang people.

INSTITUTION OF TRADITIONAL LEADERSHIP

In Africa, traditional leadership is community and culture based. Here, the legitimate authority comes from the traditions and customs of a particular area. Consequently, leaders at this level of governance owe the people guidance, direction, and motivation. This is the oldest system of governance in Nigeria. Traditional institutions are formed to play a vital role in society. They are there to serve the people first, not people to serve them. The traditional rulers are traditionally, the head of their ethnic group, clan, or community. They hold the highest executive authority in such communities and are appointed to the position in accordance with the peoples' culture, custom, and tradition. Leaders in traditional institutions are recognized by the government as the leader of the people and are seen as managers of the people and their affairs. They are also conflict managers at this level and must ensure peace and stability in their areas. Some of the notable roles played by the traditional leaders include: custodian of the land, link between rural people and the government, advocates for government political education and mobilization policies, custodians of culture, champions of national identity, peacemakers within their communities and neighboring communities, agents of the national government at the local level, and custodians of law and order.

The traditional leadership of the Annang people is modeled along the principle describing traditional leadership as an institution. It expresses the standpoint of the two-step theory, which suggests that the mass media exudes influence and information which flows from it to its audiences in a two-step format. This implies that certain individuals who are called opinion leaders are able to relay information to the community. Opinion leaders are well informed in society. Since most of the residents in the Annang speaking territory are basically not exposed to media messages, and those who do, do not have in-depth understanding of the issues in the news, they resort to these traditional leaders who have interest and engage in public affairs. As a result, they (traditional leaders) absorb media messages, interpret them, level or sharpen these messages where necessary, and share them with members of their community who are sometimes disinterested, distracted, or unaware of happenings around them. Through this approach, they have a stronghold and influence on the people as the people depend on them for information.

STATEMENT OF THE PROBLEM

One common art that binds humans together is the ability to communicate. Communication does not discriminate; whether you are learned or unlearned, schooled or unschooled, black or white, religious or irreligious, rich or poor, or tall or dwarf, you possess some abilities to relate with yourself, others, and the environment you find yourself through communication. The Annang-speaking people of Akwa Ibom State are not left out; they daily engage in the art and act of communication and express strong dependency on their opinion leaders in a bid to get details of the gist as well as take a position as to any issue at hand.

Consequently, one would think that with the emergence of modern communication platforms and techniques, there will be a decline in reliance on traditional leaders (opinion leaders) in the twenty-first century among the Annang tribe. Reasons being that the twenty-first century has brought with it enormous platforms for receiving and sending information, distance notwithstanding. Consequently, the two-step flow theory which emphasizes the strength of interpersonal interactions as perpetuated in this regard by the traditional leadership seems threatened in the digital age especially with the emergence of several digital communication platforms. It is on this framework that this work intends to find out the implications of the two-step flow on traditional leadership in the digital age: the case of the Annang people in Akwa Ibom State in Nigeria.

OBJECTIVES OF THE STUDY

The following are the objectives of the study:

1. To find out whether the two-step flow theory still hold sway in the Annangland,
2. To determine the relevance of traditional rulers in the information authentication process as opinion leaders in the Annnagland,

3. To find out how the Annang speaking people fare in the face of modern communication channels,
4. To find out whether the emergence of modern communication channels erodes the reliance and believability of information from traditional leaders as opinion leaders by the Annang people, and
5. To determine if the modern communication channels pose any threats to two-step flow communication among the Annang people.

RESEARCH QUESTIONS

The following are the research questions drawn from the objectives of this study:

1. Does the two-step flow theory still hold sway among the rural Annang people in the digital age?
2. Are traditional rulers still relevant in the information authentication process as opinion leaders among the rural Annang people?
3. How do the rural Annang people fare in the face of modern communication channels?
4. Has the emergence of modern communication channels eroded the reliance and believability of information from traditional leaders by the rural Annang people?
5. Are the modern communication channels posing any threats to two-step flow communication among the rural Annang people?

TRADITIONAL RULERS IN OPINION LEADERSHIP

According to Igwubor (2020), traditional rulers are leaders of the people and custodian of the people's culture and tradition are highly respected and revered by the people within and outside their domain. Their words are laws and opinions on issues highly respected due to their perceived role as intermediaries between the people and the gods. As the arm of government closest to the people, they promote peace; foster cohesion; and mediate between the people and the government. In conflict situations, traditional leaders are a major force in maintaining peace and order in their areas of command. Furthermore, they are bridge builders used by the local government to maintain peace and cement existing relationships among community members. They also act as opinion leaders to keep their subjects abreast with happenings and directives.

Opinion leaders are active media users who engage and interpret the meanings of media messages and contents to those who either do not have access to the media or are lower-end media users. They are those who are held in high esteem by their subjects especially for the contents they provide. For the rural Annang people who sometimes may not readily have access to the media or may be seeking clarity and understanding to media messages, they get their information through a mediated process where highly placed individuals like the traditional rulers provide. This means that information from the mass media sometimes does not flow directly to the people but is sieved by opinion leaders.

Several of characteristics traditional rulers as opinion leaders possess that make them influential in the decision-making include:

1. Ability to share knowledge and wisdom.
2. Possess strong media presence.
3. Possess power and influence from their network of followers.
4. Demonstrate charismatic leadership.
5. Ability to mobilize communities.
6. Reliable, trusted, credible, and knowledgeable sources of information.
7. Possess effective communication skills.

According to Patura and Potolia (2017), opinion leaders are individuals who exert a significant amount of influence within their network and who can affect the opinions of connected individuals. The traditional leaders in opinion leadership play a role in the two-step communication flow where information is passed from the mass media to the public in a two-step—firstly information is transferred from the mass media to the traditional leaders, and secondly, information is passed from the opinion leaders to their followers.

Opinion leaders are individuals with social influence within groups who typically serve as the hub of interpersonal communication networks (Carpenter & Sherbino, 2010). They also include village chiefs, community leaders, age grades, women group leaders, and other influential persons in the community and are attuned with happenings in and around them. Persons in this category wield a lot of influence and hence have followers who depend on them for information. These followers attribute so much credibility to opinion leaders and hence accept whatever they say on any subject matter.

TWO-STEP FLOW THEORY IN THE DIGITAL AGE

The two-step flow theory holds that communication flows from the media to the opinion leaders who share the same with people in their downline. It was first introduced by sociologist Paul Lazarsfeld in 1944 and later elaborated by Elihu Katz and Lazarfeld in 1955. The two-step theory postulates that most people are not directly influenced by the mass media but derive media messages which in turn influences their opinion, from a set of persons (opinion leaders) in the community who interpret media messages for their understanding and decision. Consequently, they become followers and dependents of the opinion leaders especially as regards information. Furthermore, the opinion leader after receiving media messages absorbs and digests them. In the process, the messages pass through a filtration process where they are leveled, sharpened, recast, reinterpreted, and later pass the finished product to their audiences who oftentimes are disinterested and unaware of happenings far and near. The fear here is the tendency to misinform their followers as they could in the process of disseminating information, water down its worth.

The emergence of digital technology has initiated an aggressive transformation in communication. The world has moved millions of steps ahead of history with groundbreaking technologies that have taken place in such a short time. With these innovations and inventions, one then wonders the fate of opinion leadership in rural areas, and the extent to which the availability of modern technology impacts lives. In the digital age, opinion leaders are obligated and have had to reevaluate their roles to remain relevant in the community. They must go the extra mile to perform their duties lest the new forms of technology override their role. In the traditional Annang setting, the traditional leaders are also opinion leaders. This is because they are exposed to diverse communication tools and channels which shape their opinions and influence their behaviors as they also influence, shape the perception, and spread the information to their downlines. This information could be from the television, radio, newspaper, magazine, and social media, among others, in the form of news stories, reviews, features, advertisements, and so forth. The traditional leaders as elites at the local level are exposed to several channels of information through which they impact people around them.

MEDIA CHANNEL

With the primary function of keeping the masses abreast with events around them, the media has the speed and reach to be able to do so. Accordingly, the traditional leaders have varied platforms to get media messages, compare reportage from one medium to the other, watch or listen to news analyses, and in the long run form opinion. As early adopters of innovations, they are able to effectively communicate the same to others. O'Shaughnessy and Stader (2011) define the media as "a whole host of modern communication systems, for example cinema, television, newspapers, magazines, advertisements, and radio. They also include video games, computers, phones and mobile phones, ages, texters, iPods, interactive multimedia, and most importantly, the internet." The media is still witnessing some transformation with the development of new forms of communication technologies for producing messages.

With the overwhelming number of messages from the diverse media channels, the outpouring of different angles/slants to stories, the increasing flood of information, and the likes, an opinion leader is faced with the challenge of determining through the process of filtration, what information to pay attention to, and through which channel. These messages are everywhere after all, and people cannot avoid the glut of information aggressively seeking their attention. However, the opinion leaders rely heavily on the channel or source that aligns with their culture and carries with its ingredients that they can identify with.

The media in turn according to O'Shaughnessy and Stader (2011, p. 34) do the following:

(a) *Representation:* The media—radio, television, cinema, and so on—have become the arenas through which people receive most of their entertainment and information about the world, so they are the primary sources for how we see the world.
(b) *Interpretation:* In their representations, the media give information, and then explanations, ways of understanding the world we live in. They take on the interpretative role, teaching people how to make sense of the world, of other people, and of ourselves.
(c) *Evaluation:* In so doing, they consistently privilege some issues and identities while devaluing others, thus giving an evaluative framework, a judgmental view of the information about the world that we receive.

From the foregoing, it is observed that the media gives many different explanations of the world and the traditional leaders who also act as opinion leaders sieve these explanations from the media. Although the media is not the only social force through which an individual makes sense of the world, nor do they have absolute control over how media audiences see and think about the world, they combine with other forces of socialization—family, religious, educational systems, opinion leaders, and so forth. As human beings progress in life, they are exposed to other views about how to behave; social morality; and political, cultural, and social forces, among others in the media, which are further strengthened through opinion leadership.

THEORETICAL FRAMEWORK

This work is hinged on two theories—the uses and gratifications theory and the two-step theory. Propounded by Blumler and Katz (1974), the theory is an approach used to understand why people seek out media information, how they seek it out, and what gratifications they derive from doing so. The argument here is that people use the media for varied purposes and not the reverse. According to Folarin (1998), the focus has shifted from media production and transmission functions to the media consumption function. For instance, instead of asking: "what kind of effects occur under what condition and for what reasons?" the question becomes "who uses which contents from which media, under which conditions and for what reasons?" The theory sees the audience as an active recipient of mass media messages as they select and consume media messages based on the gratifications they get from it.

The two-step theory propounded by Paul Lazarsfeld and Elihu Katz in 1944, on the other hand, says that most people form their opinions under the influence of opinion leaders who in turn are influenced by the mass media. According to Lazarsfeld and Katz, mass media information is channeled to the masses through opinion leadership. Persons in this category have more access to the media and are more literate in the understanding of media contents and can explain and diffuse the same to others. According to this model, people are directly influenced by the mass media, but instead base their opinions on opinion leaders who interpret media messages and put them into a context they understand. Opinion leaders are those who are exposed firsthand to media messages and contents, interpret it based on their own opinions and understanding, and infiltrate this opinion to those in their circle who follow them for such information.

Otherwise known as word-of-mouth communication, opinion leadership influences people's actions and attitudes informally. This goes on to buttress the fact that communication messages flow from a source through the mass media channels to opinion leaders who in turn pass on the same to their followers. Since they are considered trustworthy, their opinions are respected by their followers. They have an influence over their subjects, hence the heavy reliance on them for information and its authentication.

METHODOLOGY

This study required the qualitative research method. Senam (2020, p. 4) describes the qualitative research method as a method concerned with quality, attributes, or differentials. It is often adopted in studies relating to human behavior or attitude. To this end, the focus group was adopted as the instrument for gathering data for the study. This is a data collection technique where a group of people are brought together to bare their minds and give in-depth analyses on the subject of discourse. It affords the researcher the opportunity of getting a firsthand view on the experiences and opinions of the audience on the said topic. A set of five-point questions were asked to the respondents which are:

1. Does the two-step flow theory still hold sway among the rural Annang people in the digital age?
2. Are traditional rulers still relevant in the information authentication process as opinion leaders among the rural Annang people?
3. How do the rural Annang people fare in the face of modern communication channels?
4. Has the emergence of modern communication channels eroded the reliance and believability of information from traditional leaders by the rural Annang people?
5. Are the modern communication channels posing any threats to two-step flow communication among the rural Annang people?

The focus group discussion consisted of seven males and three females who were strong influences in their domains. The discussion lasted for four hours. This method afforded the researcher the opportunity to get firsthand and in-depth information as regards their relationships and interactions with their community members. The essence was to gather qualitative information from purposively selected respondents who bare their minds on the use of the media and their roles in spreading information derived from the media.

SAMPLING PROCEDURE

To draw the appropriate sample for this study using focus group discussion, ten participants were drawn from the different Local Government Areas making up the Annangland based on their transparency, experiences, roles played in the community, and knowledge about the subject matter. Each of the participants who were selected upon recommendation by members of their communities were given equal opportunity to express their thoughts on the implications of the two-step flow theory on traditional leadership among the Annang tribe in twenty-first-century Nigeria.

Focus Group Discussion Report

The focus group discussion report was done based on the research questions seen below:

Research Question 1: Does the two-step flow theory still hold sway among the rural Annang people in the digital age?

Findings derived from the focus group discussion indicate that the two-step flow theory is still prevalent among the Annang speaking people of Akwa Ibom State Nigeria. Focus group participants attributed this leadership among rural dwellers. They trust the roles opinion leaders perform especially in regard to their candid perspectives on local, state, national, and even international concerns. Although many people may perceive the digital media as a threat to opinion leaders, this is not the case as revealed by the Annang people. The reason being that the opinion leaders in the two-step flow pattern of communication act as bridge builders between information received from the media and the Annang-speaking people. According to some of the respondents, "opinion leaders are a vital source of information to the people who depend on them to stay informed." Another respondent noted that "the traditional leaders are a link between the people and happenings in the society."

It is a well-known fact that the pattern of communication has changed all over the world. To this end, people now have a wide variety of options to choose from when in need of information. They know where to get what and at what volume, space, and time. When in need of the more details as regards an urgent issue of national concern, they know the medium of communication that will serve such function. The point of buttress here is in the fact that even with these options, the Annang people still hold opinion leadership in high esteem especially for the function they play, while still paying attention to other mediums of communication. Some of the respondents noted that "although some of the Annang people are exposed to some medium of communication like radio, they still depend on opinion leaders to expatiate on the information they heard in the media."

Research Question 2: Are traditional rulers still relevant in the information authentication process as opinion leaders among the rural Annang people?

Findings from the focus group discussion reveal that traditional rulers are still relevant in the information authentication process as opinion leaders among the rural Annang people. This is because the office they hold accrues respect, power, and credibility which endears the people to them. In some cases, the Annang people do not act on information until they have received some authentication from persons in this category. With their exposure and influence as an authority, these traditional rulers possess the ability to relate with information and better express it in ways the rural people will understand. It is in doing so that they wield followership with the rural people who will stop at nothing to get authentication on any information before they can embrace or digest it.

Consequently, these traditional rulers who also play the opinion leaders role, by virtue of their personal dispositions are trusted by the people as credible sources for information and knowledge. Because of the offices they possess, they are able to relate with the people and share messages and information deemed beneficial for the community. According to one respondent, "imagine what would have been the fate of the rural people in the absence of opinion leaders; they are indeed a reliable partner to getting verifiable information at the local level." To another, "because of the power residing in their offices, the people believe in them and whatever information that comes from their end."

Research Question 3: How do the rural Annang people fare in the face of modern communication channels?

Focus group discussion showed evidence of their connection to other communication channels. For instance, they all possessed phones which had the ability of linking them to radio stations around them. Some of them also had phones that were internet compliant. With this, they could link the world and also stay attuned with life events all over the world. With the explosive growth in the telecommunication sector, one may think that the two-step communication flow will lose its relevance. Contrarily, this is not so as they (opinion leaders and modern communication channels) work hand in hand and the people derive gratifications from them all. Furthermore, this goes on to buttress the uses and gratifications theory which states that people pay attention to media channels based on the gratifications they derived from the said medium.

Consequently, Opubor (1975) noted that mass media are strong in creating awareness but weak in persuading people to adopt change. Traditional leaders therefore are an important conduit of change whose influences can be wielded on the people because of their information richness. This is a clear indication of the need for a blend of both the traditional and modern communication channels if the needed change must ensure. It is in this light that Wilson (1987) described traditional communication as a continuous process of information dissemination, entertainment, and education used in societies which have not been seriously dislocated by Western culture or any other external influence. This, according to the scholar, is called admix of the traditional and modern form of communication that exists side-by-side.

Every modern communication media channel requires an audience. According to Attallah and Shade (2006, p. 49), "media imply audiences and audiences imply media. Indeed, without an audience, there's no real point to the media's efforts. The audience confers meaning upon the activities of the media." This stresses the need to get an appropriate mechanism to reach the actual audiences for any medium of communication. The importance placed on media audiences is an indication that the rural people too are media audiences and should be accommodated as such. Modern communication channels should be inclusive in addressing issues that bother people in this category. For those who are "neglected," opinion leaders should accommodate them and also keep them abreast with happenings around them. This calls for a blend of both the traditional and modern media coexisting for the betterment of communities.

Research Question 4: Has the emergence of modern communication channels eroded the reliance and believability of information from traditional leaders by the rural Annang people?

Findings from the focus group discussion reveal that the emergence of modern communication channels has not eroded their believability of information from traditional leaders but rather create an avenue wherewith they authenticate the information they receive from these opinion leaders. For instance, some of them maintained that it was through the media that they heard firsthand of the emergence of Covid-19 before opinion leaders in their communities buttressed the information they earlier received on the scourge. According to them, it was the opinion leaders who fed them with detailed interpretation of information they heard about the virus from the media. From the foregoing, it can be said that the traditional leaders play a complementary role with the modern media as the rural Annang people do not toy with their mediatory role especially with regard to very important information. Sadly, some of the respondents feared that some opinion leaders could, apart from feeding the people with relevant information, contrarily deny the people access to some information that will displace their mediatory roles. Although not all rural Annang people have access to modern communication channels, there still exists a high dependency on opinion leaders for information as they continue to believe and depend on the traditional leaders. According to a female respondent, "our traditional leaders apart from the duties their offices saddle them with also act as our sources of information and give more insight to the information we receive from the media." To yet another respondent, "we still trust our traditional leaders for up-to-date information even with the emergence of modern communication channels."

Research Question 5: Are the modern communication channels posing any threats to two-step flow communication among the rural Annang people?

Responses from the respondents indicate that although the opinion leaders have not relented in their information dissemination function, the coming in of modern communication technologies do not pose a threat to their survival but rather complements the efforts of the opinion leaders. Most of the respondents reported that the two forms of information dissemination work hand-in-hand with one complementing the other and vice versa. According to Pearson et al. (2011, p. 83), "complementing is different from repetition in that it goes beyond duplication of the message in two channels, it is also not a substitution of one channel for the other." The modern media and the traditional leaders add meaning to their messages at the receiver's end.

The advantage the two-step flow communication however has over the modern communication channels is hinged on the characteristics possessed by the opinion leaders, hence their relevance even in the face of modern systems of communication. This is because the people have the physical advantage of seeing and receiving information firsthand from traditional leaders who are knowledgeable in their communities and can ask questions where necessary. This offers them the opportunity of witnessing all the vocal and bodily aspects such as the tone of their voices, gestures, bodily movements, and facial expressions of the traditional leaders, which adds up to strengthening the information received from the media. Participants at the focus group discussion noted that "although the modern communication channels do not pose any threat to the existence of two-step flow communication between the traditional leaders and the rural dwellers, they still depend on the traditional leaders because they live among them." Others also stressed that "the use of modern communication channels is dependent on several factors like availability, accessibility, electricity, among others. However, they can easily reach out to the traditional or opinion leaders at no cost."

CONCLUSION

This chapter set out to investigate the implications of the two-step flow on traditional leadership in the digital age: the case of the Annang people in Akwa Ibom State in Nigeria. Using the two-step theory and the uses and gratifications theory, the findings demonstrate several themes about the relevance of opinion leaders in the digital age to include:

(a) Two-step theory of communication is still prevalent among the rural Annang people.
(b) The traditional leaders also act as opinion leaders and relate to the rural Annang people information they gathered from modern communication channels.
(c) Their closeness with the rural people establishes a bond among them that enhances information sharing.

(d) Even with the prevalence of modern information sources, the rural Annang people still rely on the traditional leaders to interpret the issues in the news.

From the foregoing, a message that is perfectly clear and meaningful to the sender may not register with the receiver. This is why the sender's message must be constructed with the receiver's concerns, ideas, and perception in mind (Sommers, 2009). As true as this may sound, this is oftentimes a challenge for the rural Annang people because they may not at all times understand media messages due to the absence of face-to-face contact and the absence of nonverbal cues on the part of the sender. The role of opinion leaders still remains in the community where they are deeply embedded in the local ways of life as well as aware of the outside "world" of the Annangland. As trusted and credible members of the community, opinion leaders are able to communicate information needed in the community. The strong relationships maintained over generations through this tradition helps to facilitate communication in a manner acceptable to societal expectations. Moreover, the ability to use modern communication channels alongside traditional forms of communication is beneficial to society. It is valuable to members of the community without access to modern channels of communication.

Consequently, the two-step theory still holds sway even in the digital age especially as it is accommodating the rural audiences. It is a veritable means of reaching them with developmental information that will help them make informed decisions as well build them up for the future. The government as well as expatriates who try to penetrate rural areas with developmental information can utilize the services of opinion leaders to reach the rural audiences. By doing so, the two-step flow communication alongside other modern communication channels can work hand-in-hand to serve the information needs of the rural people.

RECOMMENDATIONS

The study recommends:

1. Since the two-step flow theory still holds sway in the Annangland, opinion leaders should stay abreast with happenings around them and therefore feed their followers with up-to-date information. How? Communication scholars, practitioners, local NGO workers, and government officials should work closely with opinion leaders to disseminate vital information given that their role in the digital age is still revered.

2. They should authenticate the information at their disposal before churning out the same to the rural audience.

3. Modern communication channels should be utilized side-by-side with opinion leadership. A complementary role should be encouraged. Communication scholars and practitioners should prioritize the admix communication model that emphasizes a blend of both modern and traditional channels of communication.

4. Modern communication channels should not erode the reliance and believability of information from traditional leaders as opinion leaders by the Annang people but should strengthen and recognize its existence. Encourage modern communication professionals to recognize the value of traditional communication channels such as opinion leaders.

5. Threats encountered in the use of modern communication should be checked by communication experts so they can serve as a balancing point prior or after exposure to media messages. The government should also make possible conducive environments where modern technologies are encouraged, for example, through the availability of electricity.

6. As mediators between modern communication channels and the people, opinion leaders should serve truthfully and so increase their credibility and dependability.

7. Since some of the rural audiences do not have access to modern communication channels, the opinion leaders who assume the function of disseminating information should be factual, in-depth, and expressive in their information dissemination function. They should understand the rudiments involved in sharing information and adhere to them.

REFERENCES

Attallah, P. (2006). *The audience and mediascapes: New patterns in Canadian communication* (2nd ed.). Thomson Nelson.

Carpenter, C. R., & Sherbino, J. (2010). How does an "opinion leader" influence my practice? *Canadian Journal of Emergency Medicine, 12*(5), 431–34.

Folarin, B. (1998) *Theories of mass communication: An introduction.* Stirling-Holden Publishers (Nig.) Ltd.

Igwubor, J. (2020). Traditional institution and nation building: The role of traditional rulers in the maintenance of national security for sustainable development. *Unizik Journal of Arts and Humanities, 21*(4), 201–14.

O'Shaughnessy, M., & Stader, J. (2011). *Media and society* (4th ed.). Oxford University Press.

Opubor, A. E. (1975). *An ideological perspective for African communication research* [Paper presentation]. West African Regional Conference on Mass Communication.

Pearson, J., Nelson, P., Titsworth, S., & Harter, L. (2011). *Human communication* (4th ed.). McGraw-Hill.

Potter, W. (2013). *Media literacy* (6th ed.). Sage Publications.

Senam, N. (2020). *Essentials and ethics of communication research.* Inela Venture & Publishers Limited.

Sommers, S. (2009). *Building media relationships* (2nd ed.). Oxford University Press.

Wilson, D. (1987). "Traditional Media in Modern African Development". *African Media Review, 1*(2), 87–104.

Chapter 12

Survival of Musical and Nonmusical Indigenous Namibian Media in the Digitized Age

Perminus Matiure

The advent of digitalization, together with other modern technological approaches, has on the one hand ameliorated the lives of communities in Namibia and on the other posed threat to the survival of some of the indigenous ways of living. To some, digitization entails a departure from the traditional principles and a gravitation toward Westernization. However, the rate at which this paradigm shift is moving is alarming, especially in urban settings all over Africa. A slow encroachment into the rural areas, where technology is still behind is quite glaring. Of concern to this chapter is the issue of whether the indigenous Namibian media survive in this digitalized era. The chapter discusses the survival of the musical and nonmusical indigenous Namibian media in the digital age. It will start by reflecting on the indigenous means of communication during the precolonial period. This will be followed by a theoretical framework and then a discussion on nonmusical and musical indigenous Namibian media, and the impact of digital media. The discussion will include how the majority of the people, including those in rural areas, are now able to own cellular telephones, radios, and televisions, which are a result of the digitization system, and how this has significantly improved the communication system among local people and even with the international world. Discussions around how some indigenous forms of media are being transformed and merged with the modern technological demands, especially those that fall under cultural lag like dance, folk music, and the horn would also be explored.

Before the influence of modern technology, globalization, and digitalization, Africa had its indigenous ways of dealing with media issues. As we know, the media has something to do with the dissemination of information from one point to another. Humans are homogenous, and one factor that keeps their homogeneity intact is the sharing of information. During the precolonial period, the commonest means of sharing information was orality. Orality involves the use of speech rather than writing or any other technological means to communicate (Nordquis, 2019). Digitalization has registered its hegemony on almost all aspects of humanity. Its transcendent characteristic has influenced all sectors of the economy from agriculture, mining, trade, tourism, education, media, and also the creative industry. Namibia is a country located in the Southeast of Africa. As a multicultural nation, comprising the Himba, the Damara, the San, the Herero, the Mbukushu, and many more, they have their indigenous ways of sending information from one individual to another and from one area to another. They also have means of communicating with their ancestors.

The indigenous African media have been in use from time immemorial. They were used to transmit information, norms, values, and ethos. They were also used to alert each other about impending danger. Some of the traditional means of communication are the use of smoke, use of songs, use of musical instruments, traditional theater, dance gestures, drumming, use of voice, village theater, town criers, folktales, proverbs, ululation, whistling, clapping, rock paintings, and use of signs and symptoms. The list demonstrates how rich the indigenous media system is. Most of them go beyond communication. They also strengthen the social bond. However, the advent of modern technology has brought sophisticated ways of media in the form of print and radio. As much as the new technology has made life easy today, it has its setbacks, some of which are detrimental to health and safety. The questions that come to mind are: does the African indigenous media continue to operate normally in the digitized world, what aspects have changed and what has continued, and what is the future of the African indigenous media system in the digitized world? The chapter interrogates these concerns with particular reference to the Namibian situation.

THEORETICAL FRAMEWORK

The ever-growing technology has reached a level where the world is better understood through the lenses of globalization and digitalization. Digitalization can be theorized if some reference is made to globalization. Cheng (2000) in Bakhtiari (2006, p. 95) postulates that globalization "may refer to the transfer, adaptation, and development of values, knowledge, technology, and behavioural norms across countries and societies in different parts of the world." It is an irresistible and benign force for delivering economic prosperity to people throughout the world (Bakhtiari, 2006). Globalization can also be referred to as denationalization. It involves the internationalization of cultural products. It is a pervasive process of expanding awareness and linkages between nations on an international level. Globalization is the process by which ideas, knowledge, information, goods, and services spread around the world (Robertson et al., 2007).

Digitalization can be defined as, "the process of conversion of different information into digital language" (Seethal, 2019, p. 140). Digital technology has enabled easy and fast processing and sharing of information globally. It has also boosted research through the introduction of online facilities in Namibia. Our music curriculum should strive to be de-Westernized and decolonized. Digitalization is part of technological development, which is the in-thing in this modern world. Autio (2017) defines digitalization as the application of digital technologies and infrastructures in business, economy, and society. Nations that have embraced digitalization have become more technological and visible globally. However, digitalization comes with its challenges, and a major one is the lack of resources in countries in the so-called Global South. Institutions are struggling to put in place infrastructure and equipment suitable for boosting digital technology. This approach is contrary to the indigenous communication systems in Africa.

Before theorizing indigenous communication systems, there is a need to touch a bit on what communication is and how it evolved in societies. Communication can be taken to mean the universal process of sending and receiving verbal and nonverbal symbols and signs that are decoded by members of the same media framework. There must be a source of information or signal, a process of sending and the receiving end. However, communication can take the following forms: intrapersonal, interpersonal, group, public, and mass communication (Neff, 1990). Intrapersonal refers to a monologue form of communication done within one's self. It is also called soliloquy which makes use of reflective thinking. Interpersonal communication is the communication that takes place among people who are mutually bound by common social ties. Group communication involves several people talking to achieve a common goal. Public communication involves one individual addressing the public like at a meeting or rally. The last one which is mass communication involves communicating to many people usually through print or electronic media. Some sources maintain that communication systems evolved due to the homogeneity and communalistic nature of societies. Poe (2011) postulates that the evolution in communication corresponded with a shift to a more settled, agrarian way of life. Communication is enhanced by making use of media. Rosencrance (2023) defines media as all channels of communication, including everything from printed paper to digital data. There are different types of media which are indigenous African media, print media, broadcast media, internet media, out-of-door media, and social media. In this chapter, the focus is on the indigenous African media which has been in use among the Namibians since the precolonial period.

Indigenous African Media (IAM) is defined as any agreed form of an endogenous communication system that originates in a specific culture and operates as a conduit for relaying information verbally, nonverbally, or symbolically with the ultimate goal of enhancing the use of symbols, values, institutions, and ethos of that culture. IAM can also be referred to as the Indigenous African Communication System (IACS) which was strongly interrogated by Meribe (2015) who states that although technology has introduced some forms of media, the IACS is still eminent in most of the rural societies. Mushengyezi supports IACS by indicating that "Indigenous media and their role in communicating development messages in African societies and communities could be utilized as one of the most respected, trusted, and acceptable forms of development communication" (2003, p. 108). Indigenous media enable the relay of ideas and information among community members. The worldview holds that any society's development is highly dependent on the means of communication.

NONMUSICAL INDIGENOUS AFRICAN MEANS OF COMMUNICATING

Like any other African country, Namibia has some indigenous communication systems which I will unpack in this section. These means of communication are to be viewed as what constitutes the indigenous Namibian media. Most of them are oral while others are nonverbal. Whatever type, the main aim is to communicate with colleagues, especially those living in the same locality. The commonest means of spreading information during the precolonial Namibia was by word of mouth. One participant indicated that each chief had a messenger whose duty was to travel to other chiefs to pass information. He gave an example that if there was a war and one chief decided to stop the war, a messenger was sent with a white pigeon to present to the other chief as a symbol of peace. Oral communication is used to deliver information about marriage, funerals, or any social information. Alongside this system was also that of the town crier whose duty was to announce information by standing on a high place or moving around the village spreading the message by shouting. The system was adopted from baboons who have one special sentinel who sits on the apex to alert his fellow baboons when he sees danger by making noise. Town criers were responsible for calling for meetings, announcing the death of someone, and telling people about the readiness of traditional brew (*Ntombo*).

Whistling is another way used to communicate, though it is rarely used to address many people but to signal someone from a distance. Whistling is done using one's lips by forcing air through a tiny opening created by lips. According to one of the culture bearers, whistling is one of the oldest means of signaling someone from a distance. Some kind of whistling could be used to convey a certain message to colleagues. In Namibian culture, whistling is used to drive cattle or to call someone who is a distance away. Whistling is also used to sing and encourage those who are dancing or in sports. The use of smoke is yet another common indigenous media used by Namibians. We are all aware that when fire produces smoke, the smoke rises to the sky. The rising smoke can be seen from a long distance. This system was used by the Namibians to inform other people from a faraway village about death or war. One participant has this to say:

> Society has to agree on the meaning of the smoke. For example, it may mean that the chief has passed on. Ancient Namibian communities also used fire to send messages to other villages by passing a burning stick from one village to another until it reached the destination. (Interview, 25 November, 2023. Kwando Village)

In other words, if a message is generated at village one and is intended for village three, a messenger from village one is sent with a log of fire or a skin tied with a string to the receiving village which may be a hundred or so kilometers away. The log with fire or skin symbolized a certain message. The messenger takes it to village two and gives it to another messenger from the village and so on until the message reaches its intended destination. This system of passing information this way was adopted during the liberation struggle. However, the messenger will be carrying the information in the form of a letter instead of a log of fire.

One of Namibia's communities known as the San people is historically known for rock painting. Although there are no fresh paintings, those painted long ago can still be visible today. When the San created these paintings, the aims were to register that they passed through the area and to report on their hunting experiences by drawing the animals that they hunted in that area. This is considered to be part of what Mhiripiri (2008) refers to as visual media. Dance has always been part of Namibian cultural expression. Dances are as varied as the cultures. However, every dance is characterized by shared patterns and gestures in the community and improvised as an individual dance. In expressing their emotion through dance movements and gestures, dancers communicate certain information to onlookers. As such it is a means of communication and part of the media. One participant who is a dancer indicated that when she is dancing, she will be telling a story through her body using the head, arms, legs, and waist. This is in line with Rosencrance (2023) who defines media as all channels of communication. Because of the communicative nature of the dancer, it qualifies to be media.

Symbols are part of any given culture. They are not perceived as mere pictures and gestures, but are a key part of culture's identity and association with other cultures (Mamentove, 2023). They embrace signs, emblems, gestures, props, and traditional archetypes. From a hermeneutical position, symbols are a powerful media of communication. They are nonverbal means of conveying messages. Symbols represent abstract ideas and concepts in a society. Namibian cultures also make use of symbols as a way of conveying information. For example, the Herero women wear headgear that symbolizes cattle. Other cultures have costumes and props that symbolize their history. For example, the Mbukushu wear reed costumes as a way of telling who they are. Symbols are part of indigenous media used to carry and convey information. Under this means of communication, we can include totemism. Most of the Namibian cultures make use of totems for identification and also for avoiding marriages between relatives. Some totems are associated with animals like baboons, lions, buffalo, monkeys, fish, elephants, and so on. Once someone mentions their totem then they have communicated their entire genealogical history. In a way, totemism is part of the symbolic communication system.

MUSIC-RELATED INDIGENOUS NAMIBIAN MEDIA

Several Namibian media systems make use of music. These include folk songs and musical instruments. Folk songs are those songs that have been handed over from generation to generation as part of heritage. However, folk music is not a set of songs from a particular community, but it is more of a working practice (Stobin, 2011). Folk songs carry the facets of a society's culture. They validate the norms and values of the society. They also entertain and transmit emotional feelings for individuals and groups. Some Namibian songs talk about bravery, love, solidarity, and peace. When people sing these songs, messages are transmitted instantly. In this case, songs become a medium of expression and a universal language that is used to convey information among the community members. However, not all the songs have overt meaning. Some have hidden meanings that one has to analyze to unpack. These songs have both literal and contextual meanings. For example, a song that was identified by one participant has text that talks about how great lions drink water from Zambezi. In this song, the literal meaning refers to lions and the Zambezi River, but the hidden contextual meaning is that great people, like the rich, are associated with big things like beautiful mansions and luxurious cars.

Apart from folk songs, musical instruments are also used as media. Musical instruments have musical and nonmusical functions in communities. One of the nonmusical functions is communication. According to the participants consulted, musical instruments like traditional drums were played in a particular way known to the society which signals that there is bad news or good news. One participant indicated that every chief had someone whose duty was to beat the drum to inform everyone in the village to assemble for a meeting. One of the participants consulted indicated that the drum was used to alert people about war.

The other instrument used to gather people and also during rituals is the horn (*enghuma*). Mans (1997, p. 89) indicated that the horn was used by old women to signal rising and bedtime for girls during the change initiation ceremony. The horn was also used during the war by the Namas to alert people about the enemy. It was used by the Herero to warn people when there is something dangerous coming. The same author indicated that chiefs used horns to invite villagers to a gathering.

Most of the Namibian ethnic groups believe in ancestry. Their ontology of life is informed by the belief that there is a strong relationship between the living and their ancestors. As such they communicate with these ancestors through a spirit medium during sacred rituals. One participant explained that what makes communication between the two entities possible is the music that is performed, which then creates a devotional framework where manifestation of spirit possession in the spirit medium takes place. When the spirit medium is possessed, the ancestors can then speak directly to the living through the medium. The living people are then able to present their problems and ask for rain or anything needed in the community. In other words, the rituals and music performed during these events are a very important part of the communication system among the members.

DIGITIZED MEDIA

From one end, technological advancement has brought better life conditions and from another end, it has brought more harm than good. Technology has been with the Namibians since human creation. Examples of traditional technology among the Namibian ethnic groups are the mice trap which makes use of the liver system, bow and arrow weapon, and method of making fire by twisting a stick on a wooden log.

However, globalization and modernization have gradually improved to great levels where digitalization has become the technological means of operation.

Digitized media embraces social media, film, interactive media, video, electronic media, email, podcast, website, music, digital photographs, ebook, and print media. The use of these means of communication has brought a paradigm shift in the way people in Namibia share information. Technology is slowly finding its way to rural areas where indigenous means of communication have long existed as major forms of communication. Because of the massive spread of digital ways of communication, some of the indigenous forms are no longer in use. This being the case, however, some forms of communication are still relevant as discussed below.

INDIGENOUS NAMIBIAN MEDIA THAT ARE STILL RELEVANT

The preceding discussion reveals how digitalization has impacted indigenous Namibian forms of media. This section highlights findings that indicate forms of indigenous media which are still relevant and in use in conjunction with modern digitized media. Namibian communities still use village criers to announce certain information in the village. When I consulted one chief in Kwando village, he said that he has a security man who also acts as the village crier. Each time he wants his people to gather, the security man moves around the village informing people about the gathering. He also said that sometimes the government gives him food to share with his people. Again, the security moves around the village informing every member to gather at the chief's homestead. This was the case the day I visited the chief. The town crier was responsible for announcing the meeting to all people in attendance.

It is important to highlight the admixture of indigenous media and modern technology. The chief and other elders indicated that the function of a messenger has been improved by modern technology. Messengers now board buses or ride bicycles to travel to far places to deliver messages or are the administrator of a WhatsApp group which acts as a platform where announcements are given. This, of course, happens in communities where the majority have phones. This move shows how some indigenous media forms can adapt to or are incorporated into new media. The same can be noticed in the use of folktales. One participant confirmed that there are now very few storytellers in the villages. Printed works such as novels have augmented their role. Norms and values usually communicated through folktales are now transmitted through print media. As such, there are fewer folk song performances in the villages than were during the precolonial period. The songs have found space in the recording studios for audio, television, and music libraries for a wider audience reach. Folk song performances are common in TV media.

Another aspect that is still happening is the use of music, dance, and ritual in communicating with the spiritual world. According to the chief, the use of sacred music during rituals is slowly declining even though it is still in use.

Spiritual rituals are conducted alongside the dual reality of local traditions and Christianity. In all, the chief expressed concerns about the decline in the use of traditional media forms and the weakening of the traditional roles of the chiefs.

INDIGENOUS NAMIBIAN MEDIA THAT IS SLOWLY DYING AWAY

The data collected reveals that some indigenous media forms are no longer relevant, especially in urban areas. Digitalization has privileged the use of cell phones whose multiple functions render them multimedia facilities. Going back to the definition of media provided by Rosencrance (2023) media refers to all channels of communication, including everything from printed paper to digital data. Cell phones have become the greatest innovation in the area of media, especially smartphones based on their capacity to perform different computer features (Mill, 2021).

Namibia has increased its network coverage by putting boosters and transmitters everywhere including in rural areas. Following this development, rural people own cell phones which they use for communication. This facility has replaced the various indigenous media systems, especially the use of smoke fire, the drum, and messengers. Even the chief whom I consulted has a phone. He indicated that the increased use of cell phones leaves the village crier with the responsibility to only reach those who do not own cell phones.

Rock paintings used during prehistoric times have been adopted by visual artists who paint on walls, utensils, and frames used for tourism. Also, the horn is no longer used the way it was used before to communicate different messages such as to herald the death of an important person during funerals for politicians. Instead, it has found space in churches where it is blown to signify the climax of a song. Elsewhere it is blown by the police forces when a coffin is being lowered to show respect to a departed hero. However, the horn used is not the indigenous one from wild animals like the kudu, it is a Western horn.

One participant indicated that they rarely beat the drum to alert people in the other villages of the death of a village member. However, a method of announcing death still in use is alerting other villagers by crying. A participant described it as a "special way of crying" which symbolizes death.

CONCLUSION

The chapter focused on evaluating the status of indigenous Namibian media in the digital age. It opened by reflecting on the indigenous means of communication during the precolonial period. It then provided a theoretical framework after which the indigenous Namibian media that are nonmusical and those that are musical were discussed. The chapter then had a brief discussion of the digital media currently used in Namibia and then presented those that are still relevant and those that are slowly dying away.

The discussions of the data gathered concluded that indigenous media systems in Namibia are slowly dying away due to advancements in technological and digital media systems. The majority of people, including those in rural areas, are now able to own cellular telephones, radios, and televisions which are slowly replacing the indigenous media systems. This digitalization has connected communities previously distanced in space time and technology. Some indigenous forms of media are being transformed and merged with the modern technological demands, especially those that fall under cultural lag like dance, folk music, and the horn.

REFERENCES

Autio, E. (2017). Digitalisation, ecosystems, entrepreneurship, and policy. Perspectives into topical issues in society and ways to support political decision-making. *Government's Analysis, Research and Assessment Activities Policy Brief, 20.* https://www.researchgate.net/profile/Erkko-Autio/publication/321944724.

Bakhtiari, S., & Shajar, H. (2006). Globalization and education: Challenges and opportunities. *International Business & Economics Research Journal (IBER), 5*(2), 95–100.

Cheng, Y. C. (2000). A CMI-Triplization paradigm for reforming education in the new millennium. *International Journal of Educational Management, 14*(4), 156–74.

Linn, M. S. (2014). Living archives: A community-based language archive model. *Language Documentation and Description, 12,* 53–67.

Mamentove, A. (2023). *Significance of cultural symbols.* https://www.linkedin.com/pulse/significance-cultural-symbols-alexey-mamontov-ntsif/.

Meribe, N. (2015). Reappraising indigenous African communication systems in the twenty-first century: New uses for ancient media. *Journal of African Media Studies, 7*(2), 203–16.

Mhiripiri, N. A. (2008). *The tourist viewer, the Bushmen, and the Zulu: imaging and (re) invention of identities through contemporary visual cultural productions* (Doctoral dissertation, University of KwaZulu-Natal).

Miller, D., Abed Rabho, L., Awondo, P., de Vries, M., Duque, M., Garvey, P., . . . & Wang, X. (2021). *The global smartphone: Beyond youth technology.* UCL Press.

Mushengyezi, A. (2003). Rethinking indigenous media: Rituals, 'talking drums' and orality as forms of public communication in Uganda. *Journal of African Cultural Studies, 16*(1), 107–17.

Neff, B. D. (1990). *Mass communication, public communication, and interpersonal communication: A global model for international public relations.* Paper presented at the annual meeting of the speech communication association. https://eric.ed.gov/?id=ED330010.

Nordquist, R. (2019). *Orality: Definition and examples.* https://www.thoughtco.com/orality-communication-term-1691455.

Poe, M. T. (2010). *A history of communications: Media and society from the evolution of speech to the internet.* Cambridge University Press.

Rosencrance, L. (2023). *What does the media mean?* https://www.techopedia.com/definition/1098/media.

Slobin, M. (2011). *Folk music: A very short introduction.* Oxford University Press.

Seethal, K., & Menaka, B. (2019). Digitalisation of education in 21st century: A boon or bane. *Higher Education, 43*(196), 140–43.

Chapter 13

Digital Technology in Breaking Information Barriers and the Preservation of Musical Arts in Zimbabwe

Richard Muranda, Absolom Mutavati, Khulekani F. Moyo, and Almon Moyo

This study cum article commemorates Professor Des Wilson, an African scholar of academic influence in media communication. His aptitude permeates through the analogue and digital domains and his contribution to scholarship remains relevant to the past, present, and future. Like elsewhere in Africa, Zimbabwe has not escaped the impact of digital technology. Digitalization is a positive reality for many people and unattainable reality for some. The advent of social media through digital technology has been met with mixed reactions across the world. Some sections of the African community have embraced digitalization (social media) in some facets of life while others have no means to access it. Scholars of African communication need to be attentive to the changes taking place in the African communication milieu. For example, the digital revolution has brought a shift from the traditional analogue use of print music scores. Oral music and stories have morphed to the computer domains that use online resources with audio and motion pictures. The increased efforts to preserve musical arts are now a priority to assure continuity of practices and traditions. The analogue epoch offered cumbersome and rigorous options to record, archive, and disseminate musical arts to the public. However, the merit of analogue was the natural sound and invulnerability to piracy. Digital resources have brought tenable ways to record, archive, preserve, and publish musical arts to the public via cyberspace. However, it has given away security of ownership in the wake of piracy. Some musical art works are now synthetic and that defies the African instruments' identity that need not get lost. Although social media unlocked musical arts to the people, it is vital to preserve originality of musical arts, curb piracy, and ensure continuity in spite of unescapable changes resulting from digitization.

The field of African communication is rich with theoretical directions to preserve modes of African communication. The work of a renowned ethnocommunicologist, Des Wilson, has made contributions over the last forty years to African communication scholarship which remain relevant to how we study the past, the present, and the future of African communication modes. As we examine ways to preserve music as a form of African communication in the digital era, the work of Des Wilson offers hope. We resonate with his stance to view "African traditional media systems as those which have defied all efforts by western media to cannibalize them and perhaps supplant them" (1987, p. 89). In this light, we see our efforts to preserve African music using modern technology as a way to sustain many aspects of African culture communicated through music rather than think of a complete loss of African traditions. Des Wilson's work has exerted immense influence in media communication discourses spanning from the analogue to the current trends in the digital era. His work teaches us that we can be proactive to keep African traditional media systems alive in the digital age.

This chapter discusses the role of digital technology in the preservation of Zimbabwean musical arts and the barriers to the flow of information. In this chapter, we focus on how digital technologies break the barriers to information and the preservation of musical arts in Zimbabwe. Evolution of technologies has imposed inevitable changes which call for adaptation and guarantee continuity. The ubiquity of modern technologies has resulted in increased music production, promotion, instrument construction, consumption, recreation, and sales. The study centers on the evolution of modern technology to the point of the removal of barriers in the spread and dissemination of information. The chapter is organized in sections. The first section covers backdrop information on digital technology and musical resources, the philosophical context of our study and the research methodology which is largely qualitative in nature. The chapter unfolds with some concerted discussions on social media and the musical arts in Zimbabwe in light of how they benefit from digital technology. We also go further to engage in a discourse on digital technology and how it serves as a conduit to transfer knowledge from one place to another within the society. On a very critical note, we discuss the lived experiences of the key participants in as far as digital technology has impacted communication among the people within the study.

DIGITAL TECHNOLOGY AND THE PRESERVATION OF AFRICAN MUSICAL RESOURCES

The Covid-19 pandemic spurred the use of digital resources in the world (Tafani, 2023); however, globally and in the African region the advent of digital technology as a phenomenon has resulted in varied views, impressions, and reactions across the world (Fitzgerald et al., 2014; Barnwell, 2023). Some sections of the African community have embraced digitalization in several facets of life and others have snubbed it, while some are still indecisive with a slow pace at the uptake of digital resources (Helsper, 2021; Heeks & Taglietti, 2023). Hesmondhalgh and Meier (2018) inform that globally, digital technology has seen some companies in the music industry regarding the advent of technology as progress while others have lost business. The digital revolution brought some paradigm shift from the use of traditional analogue resources as in print of music scores, oral songs, and verbalized stories, these were morphed to the computer domain that utilize text, audio, and motion pictures (Chung, 2007; Qionggang, 2009). The increased efforts to preserve musical arts have been a priority in order to assure continuity of practices in musical traditions. However, preservation of musicals in the analogue era had some challenges on concerns of quality, originality, and performance playback. The analogue epoch offered burdensome and rigorous options to record, archive, preserve, and disseminate musical arts to the public. Tajtáková (2011) informs that some of the merits of analogue sound are its natural ambience, warmth, and resistance to piracy. Digital technology brought about reasonable ways to record, archive, preserve, and publish musical arts to the public via cyberspace. However, Taşkıran (2019) mentions that it also gave away the security of ownership due to widespread piracy. Some of the musical productions also depict artificial sounds instead of the natural timbre of the African instruments whose identity need not get lost. Although digital technology unlocked new ways to manipulate musical arts, we find it imperative to preserve the musical arts and curb piracy to ensure continuity in spite of some inevitable changes resulting from the utility of the emerging technologies in the current times.

The musical arts have undergone significant changes since the twentieth century to date. The diversity of music cultures is largely due to Africa's geographical size and many ethnic groups. New technologies have seen a reform in African music in terms of production, propagation, and preservation. Language as one determinant of diffusion in musical arts, most of African music has been fused with exotic languages to gain international acceptance. However, its tug in preserving the natural traits of the music remains in the fate of digital technology advancements. Numerous scholarly papers articulate the roles of modern technology in breaking knowledge barriers and preservation of musical arts. Chimbudzi et al. (2021) commended technology as a tool in changing Zimbabwean music, as a result giving birth to new genres in the music market. The researchers deem the role of digital technology as important in the preservation of musical arts.

Preservation of musical culture remains a significant and ongoing concern in ethnomusicology. Turino (2017) argues that the cultural importance of music is undeniable, and its preservation is critical for the maintenance of cultural diversity and identity. Similarly, Zhang (2021) emphasizes music as crucial to humanity, hence access and preservation guarantee continuity of traditional beliefs and practices. One approach to preserving musical culture is through documentation and archiving in the digital environment (Fantozzi et al., 2017). This is particularly important for marginalized and underrepresented musical traditions, which may be at risk of disappearing without documentation and preservation. In addition to documentation, transmission of musical knowledge from one generation to the next is essential in preserving musical arts. Ryan (2020) opines that the oral transmission of music from teacher to student is a vital part of musical culture, to disseminate it in its context as the traditions associated with it are conserved. Transmission of knowledge also involves the integration of new technologies and media, such as online platforms and digital media, to reach wider audiences in innovative ways. However, the above trajectory faces numerous challenges, including the negative impact of globalization and economic pressures which result in loss of some musical traditions (Stirr, 2018).

Political factors such as censorship and repression can also impact the preservation of musical culture, particularly in contexts where certain musical practices are viewed as subversive or threatening to the status quo. However, the power of social media pervades censorship, as long as the internet runs without intentional disruptions by those in power. We envision that the research examines how these barriers are circumvented through social media as a channel of communication and preservation of musical arts in the twenty-first century. In the next section, we delve into the philosophical underpinnings to the chapter's focal points.

PHILOSOPHICAL CONTEXT

As a philosophy and contextual stance for this research, we opine that the world is a place with ever-changing ways of doing things. The music production industry is not spared from the force of change. An undisputable observation is that digital technology has brought an evolution to the arts, an incessant process which moves with changing times (Petri & Julien, 2017; Ford & Mandviwalla, 2020). In view of the above impression, it is reasonable to say that the music industry can still stay relevant with prevailing and emerging technology trends. This in turn enables the industry players to tap into the gains of digital technologies.

Tajtáková (2011), Montenieri (2018), and Taşkıran (2019) posit that digital technology has removed the physical and political boundaries that restricted access to the musical arts by audiences. People across the world now wield the capacity to access any musical arts of their interest from the internet. Of course, they have to pay for such services. Nonetheless, the number of people benefiting from digital technology to access the arts has increased in the twenty-first century. The creators of music, promoters, and manufacturers of musical instruments and ultimate consumers are now able to communicate, ask for what they prefer, pay for their products, and also critique the quality of the goods and services through a wide range of media communication networks (Taşkıran, 2019). Yousaf et al. (2021) view the digital media as critical to the preservation and communication of the digital culture in the digital age. Yousaf et al. (2021) further hold that various digital platforms ensure musical arts content is generated to meet the expectations of a diverse digital public. From what the above authors are saying we hold that as the world is getting digitally driven, this means the populace should also strive to become a digital community with capacity to use digital musical arts. In this study, our view is that as the world strides toward embracing digitalization, all the sectors of the music industry including the musical arts will also change. The creative and performing arts, manufacturing and sales of music products, and music instrument construction are facing an upsurge in the acceptance of digital resources. The music industry has and is undergoing a revolution stimulated by the onset of the Covid-19 pandemic to fast-tracked deployment of the new technologies in the musical arts. Music education and academia at tertiary institutions also need to keep pace if they are to produce relevant graduates that meet the demands of the digital age. We believe that promotion, preservation, and consumption of the musical arts have changed with the advent of technology; hence, all stakeholders need to keep pace with the alluded developments in order to survive (Petri & Julien, 2017).

METHODOLOGY

According to Creswell and Creswell (2018), we chose qualitative research to enable us to investigate into the details of the lived experiences of the participants purposely sampled for the study. We delved into the current trends to observe the practices in the creative arts. Purposive sampling was preferred to avoid inclusion of redundant participants into the study (Creswell & Poth, 2016). About ten music artists, twelve music producers, eleven music educators, eight entertainment promoters, and twenty music students were selected from three universities that offer studies in music in Zimbabwe. The participants were drawn from Bulawayo, Gweru, Harare, Mutare, and Masvingo—the major cities of Zimbabwe which are located in five provinces.

In concurrence with Woodyatt et al. (2016) and Reisner et al. (2018), we contacted some focus group discussions with university students and music educators at university and teachers' colleges to interact with participants who shared the same interests. The rest of the participants were subjected to the semi-structured interview to solicit for their experiences and ideas. The semi-structured interview enabled us to collect in-depth data. We complemented the data with some document analysis to explore policies that governed promotion, practice, and preservation of the arts in Zimbabwe. In particular, the following documents Information Communication Technology (ICT) policy, Broadcasting Authority of Zimbabwe (BAZ) statutes, POTRAZ reports, and the Cyber Security Act together with the Copyright and Neighbouring Act and The 2017 Visual Performing Arts primary and secondary syllabus. The data were collated and analyzed through the thematic approach to derive meanings (Lune & Berg, 2017). We presented the data with some citations of some critical lived experiences of participants to reinforce the findings and establish the historical and prevailing trends in the study. In this study as the researchers we aimed to establish ways in which digital technology can be a tool for musical arts preservation, knowledge transfer, and a key causal factor to issues of change and continuity of traditional musical practices and culture. It is vital to see how the musical arts are affected in view of the emerging digital technologies and how access to information has become a widespread and ubiquitous resource. The forthcoming segment takes the readers to social media in the context of the music industry mainly to appreciate how it influenced social interaction among the people. We discuss social media in light of the influence imposed on propagation, sales, consumption, and recreation of musicals including the musicians, music producers, and their fans.

SOCIAL MEDIA

Social media has become an essential tool within the music industry, allowing performers and fans to interact and engage in new and significant ways. This has resulted in a variety of global and regional trends at the convergence of social media and musical arts (Taşkıran, 2019). One global trend is the emergence of social media influencers in the music industry. Social media influencers are rapidly taking on the role of the music industry celebrities by wielding significant influence over music tastes and trends. The rise of social media influencers in the music industry is a global trend. This has resulted in a shift in how musicians and record companies approach marketing and promotion, with a greater emphasis on social media campaigns and influencer collaborations. Hesmondhalgh and Meier (2018) inform that the democratization of music production and distribution is another global trend. Musicians no longer need to rely on traditional record labels to get their music heard, thanks to the rise of social media. Instead, they can share their music directly to fans via channels such as YouTube, SoundCloud, and Bandcamp. According to music business specialists McLean et al. (2010), social media has returned power to the artist, allowing them to create and disseminate their music without relying on large machines. Social media has also had a huge impact on the music industry in Latin America. According to a report by the International Federation of the Phonographic Industry (IFPI), social media platforms like YouTube and Instagram help to connect artists with fans and propel the rise of genres like reggaetón and trap (IFPI, 2020). Overall, it is apparent that social media has had a significant impact on the worldwide music industry, resulting in new marketing, distribution, and audience interaction trends. Frith (2019) comments that social media has transformed the way musicians and fans interact, opening up new possibilities for creativity and expression.

One notable global development in the music industry is the increasing relevance of social media platforms for discovering and promoting new talent in the musical arts. Platforms like TikTok, for example, have become popular among youth as they look for new music. In addition, some music artists have found success as they produce content that resonates with their target audiences. Napier-Bell (2021) suggests that music artists can leverage social media platforms like Facebook, TikTok, and YouTube because they function as today's equivalent of radio. They use social media to reach new audiences and grow their fan base. Another recent trend is the increased use of social media as a means of live streaming music concerts and festivals. This is especially true in light of the Covid-19 pandemic, which forced many performers to cancel and/or postpone public performances. Despite the current absence of in-person concerts, musicians can still engage with their audience and earn money through streaming live music performances on social media platforms. Social media, for example, has played a significant influence in the spread of K-pop music in Asia. K-pop's enormous success on a worldwide scale can be attributed, in no small part, to social media's extraordinary capability to help fans engage with their beloved music idols and share the latest tracks with others. This, according to Benjamin (2021), has played a pivotal role in promoting the genre's popularity.

Social media has also had a huge impact on the music industry in the Middle East. In 2019, a study conducted by Arab Advisors Group revealed that social media has been instrumental in promoting Arabic music. With video-sharing sites such as YouTube and social network platforms like Facebook, musicians have expanded their global fan base, reaching new listeners from many corners of the world. It is evident that social media has revolutionized the music industry in the Arab world, providing artists with an opportunity to showcase their talents and gain international recognition (Arab Advisors Group, 2019). The use of social media as a conduit for the performing arts has brought about exhilarating advancements in both the local and global worlds. The above trends are likely to continue into the future years as social media platforms proliferate and improve service delivery. Musicians will then find a variety of ways to monetise their brands, connect with fans, and build their careers. In addition to the trends listed above, social media has influenced how musicians communicate with their audience. Many artists, for example, increasingly use social media sites such as Instagram and Twitter to provide a behind-the-scenes glimpse into their lives and creative processes. This has contributed to a more personal connection between artists and their fans, as well as a stronger sense of community within the music industry. A further recent development has been the use of social media to advocate social and political agendas through music. It is the view of the researchers that the Black Lives Matter movement, for example, inspired a lot of music artists to use their social media platforms to speak against racism and police brutality. Similarly, the #MeToo movement has raised awareness of sexual harassment and assault in the music industry, and many musicians have used social media to share their experiences and push for change. All these and others have broken the erstwhile communication barriers to pertinent information and that is owed to fluidity of digital technology.

Regionally, social media has also influenced how music is consumed and shared. Social media, for example, has aided the spread of electronic dance music (EDM) in Europe, with sites such as SoundCloud and Mix cloud allowing DJs and producers to share their music with a global audience (Kusek & Leonhard, 2005). Similarly, social media has played an important part in the development of genres such as cumbia and salsa throughout South America, with platforms such as YouTube and Facebook allowing artists to connect with fans outside of their home countries (Rabanal & Armesto, 2017). Overall, social media has had a significant impact on the global music production industry, resulting in new marketing, distribution, audience engagement, and social action trends. Bakhshi (2017) holds that, as social media evolves, we may expect even more changes in the music industry as artists and fans find new ways to interact and collaborate. There are also some regional trends at the junction of social media and musical arts. Social media, for example, has played a significant influence in the emergence of Afrobeat musical genres in Africa. Olorunyomi (2021), a music journalist, noted that a hybrid of indigenous genres and the modern beats has given birth to new genres. In

Zimbabwe, genres like Afro Jazz, Afro Fusion, Zim-dancehall, and Urban Grooves resulted from the advent of social media and the emerging music production technologies.

Statista (2021) highlights the increasing power of social media influencers in the music world, suggesting that social media influencers are swiftly becoming the new celebrities due to their ability to alter music tastes and trends and causing a shift in traditional celebrity culture. This ushered a new era of digital public. The digital community consumes and propagates digital information. According to Techzim (2021), around 14 million people in Zimbabwe have access to cell phone lines from the Econet, NetOne, and Telecel service providers. This in turn suggests that most of the cell phone owners have a chance to access social media platforms on their handsets as a paradigm shift from radio and television (Ford & Mandviwalla, 2020). According to Siddiqui and Singh (2016), as social media continues to grow in popularity, this trend will persist and become even more influential in the years to come. The next segment casts focus on the musical arts in as far as they draw from the utilization of social media to advance musical arts expressivity in a variety of forms and ways.

THE MUSICAL ARTS

Social media has become an essential component of the music industry, allowing performers and fans to interact and engage in new and significant ways. This has resulted in a variety of global and regional trends involving social media and musical arts (Tajtáková, 2011). Musical arts refer to arts expressions which include dance, spoken word or dialogue, acting, and songs. Under each category, there are subcategories which give further differences within a given musical art form. In African societies, these musical aspects exist in musical pieces as life experiences which are not prepared or rehearsed (Nzewi, 2007). At times, it is difficult to tell which art form dominates as they are performed with the same emphasis and artistic expression. Technology plays a pivotal role in breaking knowledge barriers and enhancing preservation of African musical arts. Migration from analogue to digital technology has its implications on the provision of knowledge and preservation of musical arts. Nzewi (2007, p. 56) points out that:

African art in all its ramifications and transactions, is a product of intuition researched and made concrete in human or societal experiences. That the logic of the musical arts explicates the lore of life is not a mystery, rather a mastery of the intuitive science that systematic sonic rationalizations can process the meaning of human life, death and society.

In simple terms, musical art's role gives individuals the ability to express themselves when they encounter different situations in their life experiences (Blacking, 1995). Experiences could be expressions of happiness, sorrow, dissatisfaction with authorities, praises, and many other life experiences. Mutero (2018) provided detail of how musical arts through social media were used during the late Robert Mugabe regime to air grievances and at the same time, how the masses were silenced by the government. This clearly shows how musical arts provide a voice to the subaltern to speak to those in power during times of suppression of dissenting voices. Siziba (2009) avers that African musical arts provide for the interesting application of cultural alternative theory. The theory emphasizes that cultural alternatives are choices that allow for differences in ideas, customs, and lifestyles. During suppression, people find alternative ways to express themselves, using African musical art forms as a tool to air their frustrations within a society and social media provides space for the abovesaid points.

Musical arts as a legacy contains knowledge art forms which provide knowledge about how to express or solve life's problems. Hence, the need for storage and transference to the next generation and digital technology becomes very important. The twenty-first century observed a prevalence of digital technology to impart, transmit, share, and preserve knowledge concerning these musical art forms. Matiure (2013) believes the effective way to preserve musical arts knowledge is skills transfer and collecting tangible artifacts for storage including the use of still graphics. In the twenty-first century, this is possible to execute using digital cameras and music production equipment in cost- and time-effective approaches for storage, live streaming, and transfer of such knowledge. Matiure (2013) advocates for preservation via active involvement in musical arts performances as a living archive of musical arts to ensure continuity of the cultural practices. In essence, musical arts performances ensure continuity of cultural beliefs systems relating to music and humanity.

DIGITAL TECHNOLOGY AND
KNOWLEDGE TRANSFER

Chimbudzi et al. (2021) churned a detailed treatise on the transition of recording from analogue to digital technologies. The aforesaid shift imposed a change on how musical arts information is shared and distributed. From the now obsolete vinyl records to analogue tapes, digital tapes, compact discs, memory cards/flash discs and now the media iCloud, TikTok, Facebook, YouTube, and many others. The digital radio and television broadcasting have also been overtaken by digital transmission of knowledge or information through the internet streaming. The population's sole reliance on the traditional radio and television broadcasting is increasingly losing grip as the masses access such services via their cell phones. In spite of the fact that the world has seen a migration and the adoption of digital technology in the broadcasting services, in Zimbabwe this has not yet been fully realized. The above technological changes exhibit a transition toward the dominance of digital technology and the replacement of human capital with artificial intelligence (Briley, 2001). His above advances made business tenable for partakers to advertise, sell, share, and or preserve musical arts knowledge. Once a dance performance, a song, or a musical video has been uploaded on the internet, it stays there for a lifetime and future generations will access it. The alluded details work as a way to preserve and share information. Moreover, videos about different musical arts as in dances, construction of musical instruments, tutorials on instrument playing, theory of music, and how to use music production software are available on the internet.

The skills transfer discussed owe credit to digital technology. However, a major worry could be the vulnerability of security of information which becomes prone to plagiarism and/or theft. In Zimbabwe piracy has proved beyond doubt that music hosted on the internet is given for free. Even if encryptions are used as a way of protecting the posted materials, the Zimbabwean community has accepted that piracy is now part and parcel of their day-to-day life and have adapted to it. The internet has played a very crucial role in the sharing and storage of musical arts information. This was not as easy during the analogue era. Huge expensive equipment which consumed space and time was used to transmit and store musical arts data and yet today people use small devices and still get the services required. Muranda (2017) supports the use of computer technology in the teaching of musical arts (*Nyunga nyunga* mbira).[1] The transfer of skills using computer technology demands massive computer distribution programs like the 2013 schools and college's computerization drive, even though it did not cover the whole nation of Zimbabwe. The New Curriculum of 2017 advocates the use of digital resources and the promotion of the musical arts. However, there is a critical shortage of computers in schools to meet this goal. The New Education Curricula 5.0 trajectory emphasizes the utility of digital resources for the development of skills and knowledge transfer, incorporation of the musical arts and heritage-based education through teaching, community engagement, research, innovation, and industrialization. A review of the education curricula penciled for May 24, 2023, was meant primarily to tackle a number of challenges, among them are the shortage of electricity power, internet connectivity, and computer technology hardware and software in schools.

Moral values and norms are at the core of the culture of a society (Hofstede, 2003). In some impressions of digital technologies, there is the view that the production of cultural and musical arts practices deemed esoteric is a threat to cultural values and norms. For example, some of the information available in the internet explicitly exposes drug abuse and domestic violence among the youth. Although modern technology is a driving force in shaping the digital cultural society, the idea of music as a free for all commodity is a cause for concern in our society. In view of the moral argument about preserving and upholding African/Zimbabwean culture, music videos and songs that are explicit with sensual and erotic content are deemed immoral and reflective of the downside to modern technologies.

We note that as much as technology has played a significant role in preserving musical arts, challenges persist. The ability to edit material posted online creates distorted information that kills the original meaning and intended goals assigned to a musical product. For example, a song can be edited and attached to a different video of another song as it happens with TikTok users. Modern technology is effective for the enhancement of the role of the musical arts in society but alas it has brought its own challenges. Certain sections of the society think that the alluded use of modern technology is a threat to moral values and beliefs. Hence, the need for conversations about moral and immoral cultural practices using cultural and/or human rights frameworks.

ZIMBABWE LIVED EXPERIENCES

Digital technologies played a major role in the enhancement of musical arts. In Zimbabwe arts practitioners and the consumers of the musical arts have experienced technological changes. Before the onset of recording technology, knowledge or skills transfer was done orally and through practice. Chimbudzi (2022) mentions that the advent of analogue recording technology was the first to bring major changes to the musical arts. Storage of musical arts pieces began with audio and later visual recordings. Preservation through oral means began to deteriorate. Further, the shift from analogue to digital also aggravated the evolution from oral traditions to pave way to emerging technologies. Consequently, that also began to choke the job market and revenue in the musical arts as piracy consumed most of the artist's revenue. The use of computer technology meant that musical arts could be accessed for free through the internet. This is quite evident in Zimbabwe where 13.5 million cell phone lines are used out of an estimated population of 15 million (Techzim, 2021). People are seen glued to their phones, tablets, and laptops consuming musical arts through various software applications. Several social media sites are hosted in cyberspace. Unscrupulous musical arts content is also posted on the internet; this is also coupled with unethical editing by visitors to such sites and that brings distortions and misrepresentations.

The participants in the study informed the researchers that the changes in technology came as a mixed bag of fortunes and misfortunes. One producer informed that,

> digital technology made music production to be tenable even though it has seen the rise of some lazy musicians who are no longer worried about perfecting their work before going to the studio. Furthermore, there is rampant piracy of music through the internet and file sharing of copyrighted music. In the analogue era the rate of piracy was quite low.

It should also be noted that each technological era brings about certain demands on consumers. Some of the elderly respondents bemoaned how their own storage devices, like vinyl records from the late 1980s and compact discs (digital), have become obsolete in a short space of time. There is a prevalence of computer technology skills that have become part and parcel of the day-to-day musical cultural practices. A musician informed, "today's musicians are not worried about playing musical instruments as they rely on digital recording software and that kills the real life experience that comes with performing music." They argued that this has killed the practicality of the musical arts. A digital culture has come, and there is a digital public within the digital arts industry. Since culture changes over time, people are also changing with the passage of time; hence, the consumption of digital arts has increased.

We confirmed Chimbudzi's (2022) observation that the main influencers of the musical arts were based in Harare the capital and Bulawayo the second largest city. In one interview, some long-serving music producer cum session artist who produced and participated in more than 1,000 music albums since the early 1980s informed that, "my studio thrives on both digital and analogue equipment my studio caters for various music productions in Harare where different ethnicities reside." Other participants submitted that they cherished the positive side of analogue sound, hence they relied on the analogue equipment as music producers. The majority of music arts personnel envied digital technology for the efficiency it brought into their practice, a view supported by Sawyer and Hodgson (2017). Some of the young music producers credited digital technology as it enabled them to break the knowledge barriers and enabled them to participate in music production. They were also quick to acknowledge that digital technology availed easy access to the requisite tools for music production, "I think digital technology has served me well as I have learnt a lot though informally I can do a lot of music productions using the available digital resources." However, they bemoaned the indispensable warmness of analogue music which they could not create in their studios. In view of the above, digital technology has scaled up the production processes, hence creating a double distinction in that promotion and preservation of African musical arts take place in one package.

According to the majority of participants' experiences, digital technology has proved to be a motivating force especially among the emerging music producers who cannot play musical instruments but rely on computer music programming. A producer who had worked with some of the popular music artists claimed that he did not play reputable musical instruments yet his productions had become popular nationally and beyond borders. He noted that, "I do not play any musical instrument but I only used the music production software effectively and preside over all the recording projects." The internet as a host to social media has enabled him to propagate his brand to fame in Zimbabwe. The above details show that digital technology has contributed in the removal of barriers in music arts and entertainment. A producer who also served as a music lecturer at one university said, "a band was no longer necessary on low budget projects since music can now be programmed using software plugins and a computer." A few music producers and performers among the respondents noted that the setback was the loss of innovation due to overdependence on digital technology for all the music production process. Digital technology was to blame for the demise of live bands and session musicians as they never left anything to chance as they did their work to perfection.

A number of music producers had specialized musical genres; they held that such a thing helped to ensure that quality was attained. Another producer said, "I provide the musical instrumental and the vocal rendition to my clients if they cannot do that on their own." Some producers claimed that they sang all the vocals from soprano to bass in some of the songs done at their studios. During the analogue, the above capabilities were not possible as that consumed more time than the multitracking. In the analogue time, everything was recorded at the same time and mistakes would be corrected by rerecording the song (Gervais, 2016). Most digital music producers claimed to have gained the knowledge to practice from the internet and observing the experienced producers doing their trade. They alleged that it was not easy to observe real live music producers during their working sessions because it was against their clients' privacy. The free tutorials on the internet made life easy and the producers continued to rely on them to explore new models of music production. The above point made digital technology appreciated in making work easier and faster. We noted that many studios had emerged in Zimbabwe because of digital technology as opposed to the restricted entry into the industry owing to complex and expensive recording equipment that was previously required. Today almost everything has become movable and portable.

Some public entertainment spot managers mentioned that live band performances at their premises no longer added value to sales since they were expensive to hire. One of them said, "one can provide entertainment without a live band if the music played is what the revelers like." Instead, the patrons enjoyed the music played through their sound system. They mentioned that Zim-dancehall artists were cheap to hire as they performed with few band members or as lone music artistes. The same money paid to the whole band would be a bone of contention because of the number of members who need to be paid. This shows the impact of digital technology to the reduction of human involvement in music performances. From the above observations, we realized that a lot of artists now use loops during performances in order to cut down the number of the band members and maximize on profits. However, during the analogue era this was not possible since it required all the instrumentalists to be on stage. On the same matter, some of the music artists mentioned the use of riddims as a great freedom to enable artistes to superimpose lyrics of their choice during stage performances. They mentioned that using various riddims they could freestyle on stage and last for a longtime. This is a different model from the traditional live performances which forced bands to stick to the selected repertoire.

NOTEWORTHY ISSUES

We have noted that the world has become techno savvy as the majority of the populace has become privy to a variety of digital resources that include social media. In Zimbabwe more than 13 million cell phone lines are in use and that demonstrates that the majority of the estimated Zimbabwe's population of 15 million constitute a digital public. Even though data is somewhat expensive, the use of Facebook, WhatsApp, and Instagram are on the increase. What this means is that the barriers to information are no longer as they used to be when people solely relied on radio and television broadcasting information. Since radio and television broadcasting can be accessed on the portable devices like cell phones and tablets, people can bypass censored material on the state-controlled radio and television stations. The twenty-first century has brought excessive freedom to information and that includes toxic and immoral material via that internet that comes as a negative factor.

In spite of some ills, we also observed that digital technology has improved the production and propagation of the musical arts in the world including Zimbabwe. The creators can actually advertise their brands via social media. The population can access recorded materials via the internet through authentic means and the creators can earn revenue from their literary works. Purchase of musical productions can be done within the comfort of the consumers' homes. Regardless of the threat of hackers, the arrival and use of social media has set the music business to run without restrictions of the geographical boundaries. People can visit any site on cyberspace to buy or sell or even shop for goods and services they require in the field of the arts. One setback though is that some of the information thus found on the cyber-spaces may not be credible and authentic because there are no checks and balances on issues of originality of content.

The role of social media in breaking information barriers to access musical arts and preservation of the same is critical since they keep changing with time. The digital public is supposed to keep pace with changes induced by the arrival of new technologies. Not all social media users wield the capacity to upgrade their devices to keep with current trends. In spite of the alluded set-back, the population reverts to oral tradition in order to share the information they acquire through social media to their friends and relatives. This usually works with politically specified information which cannot be broadcast on the state radio run media and yet there are no restrictions on social media. At the end of the day, the population ends up with the pertinent information that they may need to know.

While digital technology has offered opportunities to create improved quality of the musical arts productions, for others it was a loss as some equipment were rendered obsolete and outdated. The music producers who held on to the analogue modus operandi fell off due to their resistance to adapt to digital revolution. Digital technology has created a situation where music producers create music without using real instruments; rather, they use software (Chimbudzi et al., 2022). Largely music can no longer be created without computers and in trying to improve production the researchers were interested in scrutinizing its role in conserving musical arts. This has seen the blossoming of such genres as Amapiano, Afro fusion, Afro soul, and Urban Grooves which thrive on the use of prototypes of Western loops and plugins. The majority of the music producers in this regard are youthful specialists whose fan base are the youthful cohort. File sharing and illicit downloads of musical arts productions are rife among the youths in Zimbabwe and per-haps all over the world. The above-referred genres are being deemed to have originated from Africa; however, as a result of digital technology, they have spread to other parts of the world via social media.

What the details of the study show is that there is no longer any restriction to any information thus encrypted to the population's access. Considering that before the popular use of the internet in the 1980s to the late 1990s the people relied on radio and television information. Conversely, the majority of the populace did not own the radio and television sets. The government continues to impose censorship laws on radio and television broadcasts as if they do not take cognizance of the fact that the majority of people no longer care about radio and television as sole providers of information. They can always get the details from social media especially Facebook, WhatsApp, and

YouTube. People can access all information they desire to know as they do their chores and that empowers them to appreciate the current trends.

CONCLUSION

Social media has had a huge impact on the world population, resulting in new global and regional trends. These changes have altered the way people interact with their music artists. The arrival of social media opened new avenues for creation, expression, and involvement; subsequently, this promoted preservation of the arts. As social media evolves, society should expect more changes in the musical arts as musicians and fans find new ways to interact and collaborate. The preservation of musical arts is a crucial undertaking for ethnomusicologists and cultural advocates, hence change in technology is an aspect they also want to appreciate. We conclude that through documentation, archiving, and the transmission of musical knowledge, cultural traditions and practices can be preserved for future generations. For example, the song Nhemamusasa by Chiwoniso Maraire is based on a Zimbabwean traditional folk tune and has gained fame on social media due to digital technology (Lusafrica, 2016). Social media provides a worthy conduit for the passage of the musical arts. This in turn perpetuates such practices and the underlying traditions.

NOTE

1. *Nyunga nyunga* mbira is a Zimbabwean fifteen-key traditional musical instrument which originates from Kwanongoma college of music.

REFERENCES

Arab Advisors Group. (2019). *The impact of social media on the music industry in the Arab world.* https://www.arabadvisors.com/the-impact-of-social-media-on-the-music-industry-in-the-arab-world.

Bakhshi, H. (2017). Digital research and development in the arts. In V. M. Atteca-Amestoy et al. (Eds.), *Enhancing participation in the arts in the E.U.: Challenges and methods* (pp. 269–280). Springer International Publishing.

Barnwell, P. (2023). Embracing technologies with purpose. *Council Chronicle, 33*(1), 28–33.

BAZ. (n.d.). *Our functions.* Broadcasting Authority of Zimbabwe. http://baz.co.zw/about-baz/our-functions/.

Benjamin, J. (2021). The rise of K-pop and the power of social media. *Forbes.* https://www.forbes.com/sites/jeffbenjamin/2021/04/26/the-rise-of-k-pop-and-the-power-of-social-media/?sh=545e9c3e7c4d.

Blacking, J. (1995). *Music culture and experience. Selected papers of John Blacking.* University of Chicago Press.

Briley, A. R. (2001). *Network technology to digital audio.* Focal Press.

Chapter 26:05 Copyright and Neighbouring Rights Acts 11/2000, 22/2001 (S. 4)1.

Chimbudzi, W. (2022). *The impact of analogue and digital technologies on the evolution of music genres in Zimbabwe's recording industry* [MPhil Thesis]. Midlands State University.

Chimbudzi, W., Muranda, R., & Maguraushe, W. (2021). The evolution of music recording technologies in Zimbabwe. *Sabinet African Journals. The Dyke, 15*(1), 34–50.

Chimbudzi, W., Muranda, R., & Maguraushe, W. (2022). The evolution of the roles of producers in Zimbabwe's recording industry. In A. Salawu & I. A. Fadipe (Eds.), *Indigenous African popular music, volume 2: Social crusades and the future (pop music, culture and identity)* (pp. 395–411). Palgrave Macmillan Publishers.

Chung, S. K. (2007). Art education technology: Digital storytelling. *Art Education, 60*(2), 17–22.

Fantozzi, C., Bressan, F., Pretto, N., & Canazza, S. (2017). Tape music archives: From preservation to access. *International Journal on Digital Libraries, 18,* 233–249.

Fitzgerald, M., Kruschwitz, N., Bonnet, D., & Welch, M. (2014). Embracing digital technology: A new strategic imperative. *MIT Sloan Management Review, 55*(2), 1–13.

Ford, V., & Mandviwalla, M. (2020). Can digital engagement transform the performing arts? *Journal of Arts Management, Law, and Society, 50*(1), 46–62.

Frith, S. (2019). The impact of social media on the music industry. In R. K. Paterson (Ed.), *The Oxford handbook of social media and music learning* (pp. 23–36). Oxford University Press.

Heeks, R., & Taglietti, T. (2023). *Digitalization and digital skills gaps in Africa: An empirical profile.* Brookings Institution. https://www.brookings.edu/articles/digitalization-and-digital-skills-gaps-in-africa-an-empirical-profile/.

Helsper, E. (2021). *The digital disconnect: The social causes and consequences of digital inequalities* (pp. 1–232). SAGE Publications Ltd.

Hesmondhalgh, D., & Meier, L. M. (2018). What the digitalisation of music tells us about capitalism, culture and the power of the information technology sector. *Information, Communication & Society, 21*(11), 1555–1570.

Hofstede, G. (2003). What is culture? A reply to baskerville. *Accounting, Organizations and Society, 28*(7/8), 811–813.

IFPI. (2020). *Global music report 2020.* International Federation of the Phonographic Industry. https://www.ifpi.org/wp-content/uploads/2020/05/Global-Music-Report-2020-English.pdf.

Kusek, D., & Leonhard, G. (2005). *The impact of social media on the music industry. The future of music.* Berklee Press.

Lusafrica. (2016, August 8). Nhemamusasa. *Chiwoniso* [Video]. YouTube. https://www.youtube.com/watch?v=NTWgV7ih9Zw.

Matiure, P. (2013). *Archiving the cultural legacy of mbira dzavadzimu in the context of kurova guva and dandaro practices* [Doctoral thesis]. University of KwaZulu Natal.

McLean, R., Oliver, P. G., & Wainwright, D. W. (2010). The myths of empowerment through information communication technologies: An exploration of the music industries and fan bases. *Management Decision, 48*(9), 1365–1377. https://doi.org /10.1108/00251741011082116.

Montenieri, A. J. (2018). Digital streaming: Technology advancing access and engagement in performing arts organizations. *MD-SOAR, 11*(1), 1–12. https:// mdsoar.org/handle/11603/10980.

Muranda, R. (2017). *Implementation of a computer assisted method in teaching the Nyunga Nyunga Mbira* [Doctoral Thesis]. UNISA.

Muranda, R., & Maguraushe, W. (2013/2014). Sungura music's development in Zimbabwe: The emergency of trendsetters, emulators and copycats. *The Journal of Music and Meaning, 12*(2), 44–62.

Mutero, I. T. (2018). Muting voices of dissent: A case study of the rebel woman. In B. Chinouriri, U. Kufakunesu, & M. Nyakudya (Eds.), *Victors, victims and villains: Women and musical arts in Zimbabwe Past and Present* (pp. 200–215). University of Zimbabwe Publication.

Napier-Bell, S. (2021). The impact of social media on the music industry. *Music Business Worldwide.* https://www.musicbusinessworldwide.com/the-impact-of-social -media-on-the-music-industry/.

Olorunyomi, S. (2021). Afro beats: The rise of African music through social media. *CNN.* https://www.cnn.com/2021/02/25/africa/afrobeats-african-music-social -media-intl-cmd/index.html.

Petri, I., & Julien, F. (2017). *Digitizing the performing arts. Assessment report.* Canadian Arts Presenting Association and Strategic Moves. https://capacoaca/en/rese arch/digitizing-performing-arts.

Qionggang, R. (2009). *Application and research on digital music technology in music teaching.* 2009 IEEE 10th International Conference on Computer-Aided Industrial Design & Conceptual. http://dx.doi.org/10.1109/caidcd.2009.5375272.

Rabanal, J. P., & Armesto, D. (2017). Social media and the development of latin American music. *Latin American Music Review, 38*(1), 1–24. https://doi.org/10 .1353/lar.2017.0001.

Reisner, S. L., Randazzo, R. K., White Hughto, J. M., Peitzmeier, S., DuBois, L. Z., Pardee, D. J., & Potter, J. (2018). Sensitive health topics with underserved patient populations: Methodological considerations for online focus group discussions. *Qualitative Health Research, 28*(10), 1658–73.

Ryan, R. (2020). The transmission of musical knowledge. In A. K. Harding & T. N. Mitchell (Eds.), *The Oxford handbook of musical identities* (pp. 1–19). Oxford University Press.

Sawyer, H. R., & Hodgson, J. (2017) *Perspectives on music production: Mixing music.* Routledge.

Siddiqui, S., & Singh, T. (2016). Social media has its impact with positive and negative aspects. *International Journal of Computer Applications Technology and Research, 5*(2), 71–75.

Siziba, G. (2009). *Redefining the production and reproduction of culture in Zimba-bwe's Urban space: The case of urban grooves*. Council for the Development of Social Research in Africa CODESRIA.

Statista. (2021). *Social media influencers in the music industry*. https://www.statista .com/topics/4565/social-media-influencers-in-the-music-industry/.

Stirr, A. (2018). Music, globalization, and cultural heritage. In J. H. McDowell & J. A. Dubois (Eds.), *The Oxford handbook of music revival* (pp. 263–282). Oxford University Press.

Tafani, V. (2023). Embracing the change of digital world/digital disruption. *Ang-listicum Journal of the Association-Institute for English Language and American Studies, 12*(8), 31–41.

Tajtáková, M. (2014). *Theatre in the digital age: When technology meets the arts*. 9th International Workshop on Knowledge Management. http://www.cutn.sk/Library/ proceedings/km_2014/PDF%20FILES/Tajtakova.pdf.

Taşkıran, H. B. (2019). Digitalization of culture and arts communication: A study on digital databases and digital publics. In *Handbook of research on examining cul-tural policies through digital communication* (pp. 144–160). IGI Global.

Techzim, (2021). *2021 Zimbabwe telecoms reports by POTRAZ*. https://www .techzim.co.zw/zimbabwe-potraz-telecoms-reports/.

Wilson, D. (1987). Traditional systems of communication in modern African devel-opment: An analytical viewpoint. *Africa Media Review, 1*(2), 2–102.

Woodyatt, C. R., Finneran, C. A., & Stephenson, R. (2016). In-person versus online focus group discussions: A comparative analysis of data quality. *Qualitative Health Research, 26*(6), 741–749.

Yousaf, M., Yi, L., & Widodo, S. T. (2021). *The digital preservation and commu-nication of traditional Chinese tea culture and arts: A study of China's national tea museum*. Proceedings of the International Conference on Language Politeness (ICLP 2020).

Zhang, J. (2021). Traditional music protection from the perspective of intangible cul-tural heritage. *Learning and Education, 9*(4), 107–108. https://ojs.piscomed.com/ index.php/L-E/article/view/1689/1539.

Chapter 14

Vimbuza and Gule Wamkulu Traditional Dances as Enduring Malawian Indigenous Media Systems in the Digital Age

Jerry Rutsate

The ethnographic study for this chapter was conducted among the Tumbuka people in the Northern Region and the Chewa in the Central Region. Indigenous African people learn, educate, entertain, and disseminate knowledge and information about their social world through various modes of communication richly entrenched in local cultures. African indigenous media is a complex system of communicating and exchanging information (Adesoji & Ogunjimi, 2015) embodying language, folklore, songs, dances, instrumentation, poetry, drama, ritual ceremonies, and festivals which permeate all spheres of life. Performing arts are prevalent in Malawian indigenous media. Despite the country's history as a British colony for over sixty years, the use of indigenous media remains prevalent in rural areas. Even though modern media was superimposed on the existing national indigenous media, it has had little impact on the indigenous media of the majority population living in rural areas. As such, in postcolonial Malawi, the new media systems driving the digital world have not replaced the indigenes' means of communication.

Specifically, *Vimbuza* and *Gule Wankulu* dances are epistemological media that form the cultural fabric of Malawi people and have the capacity to positively contribute to development including Malawi's Agenda 2063 Vision *"An inclusively wealthy and self-reliant nation."*

African colonization by the West led Malawi to become a British colony for more than sixty years. Even though modern media was superimposed on the existing national indigenous media, it has had little impact on the indigenous media of the majority population living in rural areas. As such, in postcolonial Malawi, the new media systems driving the digital world have not replaced the indigenes' means of communication.

In the digital age, it is important to examine the place of indigenous media in a media ecology saturated with new forms of communication such as mobile phones, internet, YouTube, TikTok, and so forth. We believe that development efforts require both traditional and modern forms of communication to move any country forward given the expansion of the digital age. In this regard, the dances can be part of development efforts by embracing modern technologies and innovations to configure the documentation and dissemination of information including intangible cultural heritage of Malawi.

The essence of this chapter is to answer the question: Can the various African indigenous media systems be replaced by the new media driving the digital age? The chapter discusses this all-important question by attending to the Malawian traditional dances that represent many aspects of Malawian culture. We consider the *Vimbuza* and the *Gule Wamkulu* dances (*magule*) as vital parts of the indigenous Malawian media system that disseminate messages about societal ethos, values, and beliefs ingrained in the local culture. At the same time, these dances are critical cultural institutions and demonstrate communication through symbols and gestures of the Tumbuka and Chewa cultures. The study set out to explicate the attributes and qualities of both the *Vimbuza* and the *Gule Wamkulu* dances which readily appeal to and connect with the cultural heritage owners and performing experts. We also wanted to know more about ritual ceremonies where the dances are performed and their significance and meanings assigned to body movements that capture the spirit of the life force. By extension, the study solicited factors that supported the resilience of the dances in the constantly changing living environment of their exponents. The Tumbuka, also referred to as Kamanga, Batumbuka, and Matumbuka, are a Bantu ethnic group of people who reside in the Northern Region in Malawi. Chief among the values of the Tumbuka are: spirituality (communication with the ancestors); rituals such as initiation rites, healing, and celebration ceremonies; cultural materials including, but not limited to song, dance, use of drums, symbols, and gestures, as well as relationships among humans, ecology, and the spiritual realm. The Chewa, like the Tumbuka, are descendants of the Bantu people who are believed to have migrated from Malambo region in the Democratic Republic of the Congo and mainly settled in the Central and Southern Regions in Malawi. Essentially, the Chewa and the Tumbuka share the same values although the Chewa are also widely known for their use of masks for their Gule Wankulu dance.

The *Vimbuza* is a healing tradition (*n'goma*), which implies drums of affliction that ensnare the spirit of the life force. Drums prominently feature in the *Vimbuza* dance as well as the *Gule Wamkulu* dance. The effect of drumming in these dance traditions is aptly described by Nzewi (2007) as the science governing the material for making skin drums which establishes that the dry blood in a skin procured before decay sets in retains active energy that is transmitted sonically as a healing force into brain tissues and nerves in a performance. Egnew (2005) asserts that healing goes beyond the curing of illness in that it brings about harmony, understanding, and acceptance of things that one has no capacity to change. *Gule Wankulu* originated as a male Chewa dance communicating challenges of matrilineal relationships. The dance characters of the *Gule Wamkulu* express different forms of misbehavior in order to foster acceptable moral and social values. Dancers are believed to be representatives of the world of the spirits and the dead. Overall, the nature and character of *Vimbuza* and *Gule Wamkulu* dances can be defined as cultural heritage in Malawi. Kargho (2022) states that the life of an individual as a communicator starts with the assimilation of the norms and standards of one's cultural setting. This is the case with the Tumbuka people, and the Chewa embody what these dances represent in their lives.

This chapter is organized in four sections. First, we discuss the methodology and then move on to discuss the history and politics of indigenous and modern media; *Vimbuza* and *Gule Wamkulu* dance interpretation; and Malawian indigenous media in the digital age. We conclude by arguing that Malawian indigenous dances are a form of an enduring and effective communication system which is capable of harnessing modern and emerging communication technologies for community sustenance and national development.

METHODOLOGY

This chapter is an outgrowth of a systematic study of selected Malawian indigenous dances that have outlived the dominance of the modern communication systems into the digital era. The ethnographic study of the *Vimbuza* and *Gule Wamkulu* dances took a cultural lens of the Tumbuka and the Chewa people's perceptions and interpretations of their indigenous dance media heritages practiced within their communities (Fetterman, 2010). This ethnographic educational research employed participatory methodologies, theoretical engagement, and thick descriptions (Mills, 2019; Girtz, 1973). We observed the dances performed in their ritual contexts and thereafter had to conduct face-to-face interviews with the knowledge owners and performing experts meant to interpret the dance features and conventions. Among the targeted informants were two dance initiates (one from each culture) who also happened to be dance ethnography students. The techniques for gathering data involved research assistants, fieldnotes, and audio and video documentation equipment. We documented the culture owners' authoritative voices in vernacular and provided approximate English translations where possible.

HISTORY AND POLITICS OF INDIGENOUS AND MODERN MEDIA

The media and channels of communication used in each precolonial African society, especially in Sub-Saharan Africa, have been premised on the African veritable reality of fusing the epistemological and metaphysical modes of thinking to conceptualize, produce, and interpret means of interaction and strategies for survival in communities (Etim, 2019). The different creations have distinguished groups of people and their ways of living through which they associate and relate with their environments. In Malawi, for example, there are custodians of original dances which include the *Vimbuza* dance associated with the Tumbuka people and the *Gule Wankulu* of the Chewa people. Both the *Vimbuza* and the *Gule Wamkulu* dances were, in 2008, inscribed by the United Nations Educational Scientific and Cultural Organization (UNESCO) on the *Representation List of the Intangible Cultural Heritage of Humanity*. It is worth noting that cultures are not static and change overtime. This observation is relevant in any culture where the effects of the digital age cannot be ignored. For example, the highly elaborate movements, gestures, and costumes of the Gule Wamkulu dance have made it so popular that it has since become a part of Malawi's cultural tourism.

The Western purview of Africans and the subsequent subjugation of their indigenous media systems has been vehemently echoed by both African and Western scholars. Davidson (1972) notes that to many Europeans, during the nineteenth century, all that was there in Africa before the coming of the Europeans was savage and chaos which was fortunately resolved by the conquerors as they brought civilization to peoples against whom the Gates of Eden had barely closed. Bates (2012) further contends that negative perceptions about Africa date back to the dates of Herodotus who suggested that Africa was not only different, but also more dangerous than Greece. Adum et al. (2015) opine that according to Livingstone's dictum, the perception of Africa as a land of beasts and cannibals was justified as the reason for colonization which brought light in the form of Christianity, civilization, and capitalism. It is evident from the observations contained in the three citations that the perpetrators of Africa colonization had to condemn not only the dignity and knowledge systems of the Africans but also their creative geniuses to pave way for the imposition of the Eurocentric epistemology, ideology, and methodology. Des Wilson's (1987) categorization of forms of traditional communication exemplifies Afrocentric media knowledge and creative genius as follows:

- Idiophones; Membranophones (mainly drums);
- Aerophones (mainly animal horns);
- Symbolography (symbolic writing or representation);
- Signals: Signs (objects used to represent something);
- Objectifics (media presented in concrete forms); Color schemes (combination of colors to convey meaning);
- Music (songs, folktales, and instrumentation);
- Extramundane communication (communication between the living, ancestral spirits and Supreme Being); and
- Symbolic displays (gestures, voice qualities, and facial expressions).

This categorization further demonstrates a complex diverse system of communication that cannot be understood through Western lenses. Throughout history, Africans continue to utilize the traditional channels of communication that serve them well. In Malawi, the Eurocentric media continue to shape urban communication and lifestyle while the enduring traditions of oral culture are discernable among the Tumbuka and the Chewa people. This observation confirms Wilson's (1987) earlier submission—almost four decades ago—that indigenous media systems remain the sources of information that essentially sustain the survival needs of the 82 percent Malawian rural population out of the nation's total population (The World Bank data, 2022). Thus, reviewing the role of African indigenous forms of communication in the digital age underscores their resilience, endurance, and relevance in the everyday lives of African people. These forms of communication can be used to engage communities in matters about working toward self-actualization, community building, and national development (Mwale; Phiri, 2023).

VIMBUZA AND *GULE WAMKULU* RITUAL DANCE INTERPRETATION

This section begins by examining the meaning, nature, and purpose of African ritual as the basis for conceptualizing Malawian indigenous media through the lens of the *Vimbuza* and *Gule Wamkulu* ritual dances. A ritual is commonly defined as a solemn ceremony which is made up of a series of actions performed according to a prescribed order. In his article entitled Ontology of African ritual, Etim (2019, p. 23) observes that

> Ritual is seen as a culturally-patterned-symbolic action, thus bearing the label and image of a particular culture with its corpus of values and beliefs. Being the

conveyer of the value of society, ritual ought to endure. Actually, rituals span the entire spectrum of human life.

Drawing from Etim's interpretation of ritual in African thought, ritual can be viewed as the African creative genius that represents and expresses the reality of the mutual existence of the physical and the spiritual realms of life. This claim is substantiated by Olupona's (2015) assertion that African spirituality simply acknowledges that beliefs and practices touch on and inform every facet of human life, and therefore, African religion cannot be separated from the everyday or mundane. Ranger (1972) outlines the structure (nature and purpose) of ritual into four categories: (1) symbolic structure—an aggregate of symbols aiding adequate understanding of human society; (2) value structure—expressive of authoritative message about crucial values; (3) telic structure—performed for the sake of an end, and (4) role structure—product of interaction of different human actions expressing a common end. All these attributes and phenomena of ritual are clearly manifested in the narratives of the *Vimbuza* and *Gule Wamkulu* dances.

VIMBUZA DANCE

The knowledge owners and performing experts of the *vimbuza* assign two different meanings to this term. In one sense, *vimbuza* is a mental illness, and in another sense, it is a dance. The description and explanation of the procedure for treating vimbuza, which constitutes the manifestation of symptoms of the illness, diagnosis to confirm the illness, and treatment that Hastings Mwale provided appears hereunder:

Vinyake vyakukhwaskana na nthenda ya vimbuza viwonekero vinyake vya nthenda iyi muluwali wa Vimbuza wakuwavye khumbo la chakurya panji chakumwa chilichose. Pala wachichizgika kuti warye, wakukomoka. Pala wasisipuka, muluwali uyu wakuchemeska vyakurya ivo mizimu yamuphalira kuti warye pela nga ni misisi yakubaba chomene iyo banthu wanji wangarya chala. yamuphalira kuti warye pela nga ni misisi yakubaba chomene iyo banthu wanji wangarya chala. Panyengo iyi wakuyamba kupanga vithu nga wafuntha ndipo wakuyezgeka kuti bawone kuti panji wana vimbuza. Iyo ndiyo nyengo misisi kweniso vikwa vya Mkhaya na Chitongololo vikugwiliskika ntchito. Misisi na vikwa ivi kikudumulika panji kupulika mthuli nakutupikika mu maji ndipo muluwali wakupika kuti wamwe. Nyengo zinyake, misisi na vikwa ivi vikuotcheka pa moto ndipo muluwali wakudika chisalu nakunuska josi lakufuma pachipembo cha misisi yila. Josi lakufuma pa chipembo ndilo likuvundula vimbuza. Munthu wakwimikika kuwa na vimbuza pala thupi likunjekemera chomene, kuyowoya malulimi, wakuti wakuyowoya na mizimu kweniso pala wakuti wakuona njoka.

Pala wapimika nakusangika kuti wana vimbuza, baluwazgi wake wakuchemeska gule wa vimbuza. Panyengo iyi muluwali wakuvina pa Makala gha moto kwambula kupsa, wanji wakubika moto mumlomo kwambulaso kupsa. Muluwali wavimbuza uyu wakuchemeska chilopa cha mbuzi panji nkhuku yituwa, wakukola chiweto icho wapika nakuchiluma nakumwa ndopa/chilopa chake. Nyama ya chiweto ichi yikupika kubanthu kuti barye. (Mwale, 2023)

The patient loses appetite to the extent that he or she at all costs avoids foods or drinks given to him or her by guardians or relatives. If you force him to eat or drink, he or she faints or loses consciousness. After gaining consciousness, the patient demands eating foods as prescribed by spiritual ancestors and nothing else, for example, bitter plant roots and barks. At this stage, the patient is in a trance state. Following this stage, the patient is tested for *vimbuza*. This is the time when very bad smelling roots and barks of either the Mkhaya or Chitongololo or both trees are used. The roots and barks are carefully chopped or ground and soaked in a pot of water after which the drink is given to a patient. Alternatively, the roots and barks are burnt by a small fire and the patient inhales the smoke under special covering of the whole body by a cloth or blanket. The smoke or the drink acts like a catalyst. The patient is deemed to have *vimbuza* if he or she displays the following behaviors: strong body shaking; speaking in unknown languages; claims to communicate with ancestors; and claims to see snakes. This time, the patient will behave like a diviner. After the diagnosis, the guardians organize a ritual ceremony in which *vimbuza* dance is performed. This time some patients dance on fire without being burnt. Others put hot charcoal of fire in their mouth and suffered no harm. After the dance, the patient shows signs of normality. At this time, the patient may or may not make further demands according to what the ancestors have said to him or her. She may demand *chilopa* (blood) of a white goat or chicken. Then people have to go and find a goat or chicken of that color. The patient holds tightly and bites the nose of the goat and sucks its blood. This time, the patient is satisfied and relieved of the illness. The carcass is given to people for meat. The patient has nothing to do with the meat.

Philip Gausi complemented Mwale's narration of *Vimbuza* by giving the following account:

Kuluwala kwa nyengo yitali kwakusazgikana na mutu ukali,kubinya kwa thupi, thupi lakutomboloka, kutimbanizgika kwa mongo, kuyowoya malulimi, kubigha, kuchima kwakututuzgika na maloto na mboniwoni, kutandalira kugona. Matenda agha ghakukola chomene banakazi na banalume ba pa nthwengwa ba vyaka/vilimika makhumi gha nkhondi na ghatatu(80) kuyila pasi. Nthenda iyi yikupimika na kuchizgika na balalabalala ba mumuzi awo bana kamanyiro. Gule wa vimbuza wakuvinika nyengo ya usiku pala chakurya chakugonela

*charyeka. Kuchizga nthenda iyi kukukhumba thupi livine mwa nkhongono paku-
londezga nyimbo zakwimbika pakuwetha/kukuwa makowo, kulila kwa ng'oma
izo kanandi zikuwa zitatu panji zinayi (zakulila chapasipasi, pakatikati na
pachanya chomene), visekese na majembe. Muluwali wa vimbuza wakuvwala
Mangenjeza mumalundi ghake, wakuvwala Madumbo mchiwuno, wakuyegha
Litchoba m'mawoko ghake, wakuvwala Chisoti chakutozgeka na mahungwa
gha tuyuni.* (Gausi, 2023)

Vimbuza is a serious illness inflicted on people by evil spirits called
Mizimu. Symptoms include prolonged illness due to severe headaches, general body weakness, mental confusion, speaking in tongues, frequent burping
(*kubigha*), foretelling events awakened by dreams and visions, and prolonged
periods of bed rest. This illness affects especially married women and men
below the age of eighty years. It is diagnosed and healed by elderly and
experienced people of the village. The *Vimbuza* dance usually takes place in
the evening after supper. The healing process undergoes vigorous physical
dancing to the tune of songs accompanied by clapping of hands, drumming
(usually three African drums called *ng'oma* with low, medium, and high
pitches), beating metal hoes (*majembe*), and *visekese* (grass shakers with corn
inside). The patient wears Mangenjeza (metal balls encased in metal rings
tied around the lower legs from kneecaps), Madumbo (stripes of leather or
light metal worn around the waist), Litchoba (lower part of a cow's tail held
in the hand), and Chisoti (hat decorated with bird feathers).

The *vimbuza* narratives by Mwale and Gausi presented above reflect on
the Tumbuka perception of life which receives its fullest expression through
singing, instrumentation, dancing, and use of gestures and props. As such,
Friedson (2010) observes that in Tumbuka divination, medical technology is
part of musical experience, and musical experience a mode of being-in-the
world for both spirit and human. In addition, Friedson concludes that the
Tumbuka, music, dance, spirits, and trance penetrate the very fabric of everyday experience, an everyday where worlds are moved by spirits and spirits
are moved by music.

GULE WAMKULU DANCE

One of the renowned *Gule Wamkulu* (Great Dance) knowledge owners and
performing experts, Santhe Mthande defined the Gule as follows:

*Gule Wamkulu, gule wa chikhalidwe komanso chipembedzo cha mtundu wa
Achewa aku Malawi, Zambia ndi Mozambique, unazama muchikhalidwe
komanso chipembedzo chofunikira. Gule Wamkulu ndi chikhalidwe chofunikira chosonyezera umodzi, kugwirizana komanso kufunikira kwa mizimu ya*

makolo. Tione zinthu zomwe zili mu Gule Wamkulu monga kuyimba, kuvina, zida, mitundu ya zilombo, zigoba ndi matanthauzo ake ku chikhalidwe komanso kachitidwe kake pakati pa amuna ndi akazi. Tisanapite ku ntchito yomwe tikuyenera kuchita, ndi chofunikira kudziwa mayina ofananirana ndi Gule Wamkulu. Gule Wamkulu ali ndi mayina atatu odziwika bwino, koma dzina lirilonse limagwirizana bwino ndi guleyu. Poyamba, Gule Wamkulu amatanthauza gule wa akulu. Unalandira dzinali Kamba ka kukula kwake poyerekeza ndi magule ena. Mwachitsanzo, kutenga nawo mbali mu Gule Wamkulu umayenera kuvinidwa, chomwe chimasiyanisa guleyu ndi magule ena. Dzina lachiwiri la Gule Wamkulu ndi vilombo" zomwe zimatanthauzira kuti "zinyama" pa Chichewa. Dzinali limaunikira mitundu yosiyanasiya ya zinyama yomwe imaimiliridwa ndi Gule Wamkulu. Dzina la chitatu ndi "mizimu". Wotenga nawo mbali mu Gule Wamkulu amakhulupilira kuti guleyu anazama ndi mizimu ya makolo. Kuyimba: Kuyimba mu Gule Wamkulu kumakhudza mbali ziwiri: imodzi ndi mbali ya anyamata ndi ina ya amayi. Anyamata amatulutsa mawu apamwamba pakutulutsa mpweya m'kamwa mwawo, kuwonjezera nthabwala ndipo amasonyeza kukhalapo kwa Gule Wamkulu. Amayi motsogozedwa ndi Gule Wamkulu, amapeleka mlingo womwe ayimbire komanso amatsogolera nyimbo. Nthawi zina, membala wamwamuna kapena wamkazi wa gulu la Gule Wamkulu amatsogoleranso oimba. (Mthande, 2024)

The *Gule Wamkulu*, a traditional dance and ritual of the Chewa people of Malawi, Zambia, and Mozambique, embodies rich cultural heritage and spiritual significance. It is a vibrant expression of community identity, social cohesion, and ancestral reverence. Let us consider the dance features, including singing, dancing, instrumentation, species representation, masks, and their cultural meanings, as well as the gender dynamics involved in its performance. Before delving into the task at hand, it is important to note alternative names for *Gule Wamkulu*. *Gule Wamkulu* has three well-known names, each with significant connections to the dance itself. Firstly, "*Gule Wamkulu*" translates literally to "Big Dance." It earns this name due to its extensive involvement compared to other dances. For instance, participation in *Gule Wamkulu* versions requires undergoing an initiation ceremony, which sets it apart from other dances. The second name for *Gule Wamkulu* is "Zilombo," which translates to "wild animals" in English. This name is reflective of the diverse animal representations within *Gule Wamkulu*. The third name is "Mizimu," meaning "spirits" in English. Practitioners of *Gule Wamkulu* believe that these dances embody the spirits of their ancestors.

According to Mthande, the name of the *Gule Wamkulu* dance distinguishes itself from many other dances in that it embodies the holistic perception of the African worldview in which the physical and spiritual worlds interconnect for the well-being of humanity. The *Gule Wamkulu* dance sphere that incorporates initiation is secretive and it was originally meant for males only though Mthande reports that a few women to the present have been initiated. The Zilombo sphere of the *Gule Wamkulu* dance reflects on different human personalities which are characterized by various animals as a way of showing the connection between animals and humans.

An overview of the other *Gule Wamkulu* dance features was provided by Luka Phiri as outlined hereunder:

Kuyimba: Kuyimba mu Gule Wamkulu kumakhudza mbali ziwiri: imodzi ndi mbali ya anyamata ndi ina ya amayi. Anyamata amatulutsa mawu apamwamba pakutulutsa mpweya m'kamwa mwawo, kuwonjezera nthabwala ndipo amasonyeza kukhalapo kwa Gule Wamkulu. Amayi motsogozedwa ndi Gule Wamkulu, amapeleka mlingo womwe ayimbire komanso amatsogolera nyimbo. Nthawi zina, membala wamwamuna kapena wamkazi wa gulu la Gule Wamkulu amatsogoleranso oimba.

Kuvina: Kuvina mu Gule Wamkulu kumatsimikiziridwa ndi zinthu zosiyanasiyana, kuphatikizapo zovala. Chovala chilichonse chimakhala ndi kavinidwe kake kake. Mwachitsanzo, ovina ovala ngati nyama zakutchire amakhala ndi mavinidwe apadera poyerekezera ndi amene akuimira anthu. Kuwonjezera apo, kuvina kumasiyanasiyana malinga ndi zochitika; Pamaliro pamakhala mayendedwe osiyanasiyana kuposa kuyika mfumu. Ovina a Gule Wamkulu amavinanso mwatchutchutchu pofuna kutulutsa mizimu yoipa yomwe amakhulupirira kuti imavutitsa anthu.

Zida: Zida zazikulu zomwe zimagwiritsidwa ntchito mu Gule Wamkulu ndi ng'oma ndi zisekese. Zida zimenezi, zikaimbidwa mwamphamvu pamodzi ndi nyimbo, zimalimbikitsa kuvina kosangalatsa. Kamvekedwe ka zisekese kamayimira maso a Gule Wamkulu ndikutsindika kupezeka kwawo panthawi yovina.

[9]*Zigoba: Zigoba zomwe ovina a Gule Wamkulu amavala zimasonyeza khalidwe la anthu amene amawasonyeza. Mwachitsanzo, chigoba chochititsa mantha chimasonyeza ngozi, pamene chigoba chaubwenzi chimasonyeza kukhalapo kwabwino kwambiri. Kuphatikiza apo, zigoba zina zimakhala ngati zizindikilo za atsamunda, kuwonetsa anthu otchuka ochokera kumayiko akumadzulo monga Mfumukazi Elizabeth, Obama, ndi Bill Gates. Ena amatsanzira zinthu monga magalimoto, ndege, ndi njinga zamoto, n'cholinga chochotsa maganizo a anthu pa zinthu za azungu.* (Phiri, 2024)

Singing

Singing in *Gule Wamkulu* involves two aspects: one by boys and the other by women. Boys produce high-pitched sounds by vibrating air through their mouths, adding humor, and symbolizing the presence of *Gule Wamkulu*. Women, guided by *Gule Wamkulu*, provide key and lead the song.

Sometimes, a male or female member of the *Gule Wamkulu* group also leads the singers.

Dancing

Dancing in *Gule Wamkulu* is determined by various factors, including attire. Each costume has its own unique dance style. For example, dancers dressed as wild animals have a distinct dance compared to those representing humans. Additionally, dancing varies depending on the occasion; funerals entail different movements than the installation of a king. *Gule Wamkulu* dancers also perform specific dances to expel evil spirits believed to afflict individuals.

Instrumentation

The main instruments used in *Gule Wamkulu* are drums and shakers. These instruments, when played intensively alongside songs, enhance the mood of the dance. The sound of the shakers symbolizes the eyes of Gule Wamkulu and emphasizes their presence during the dance.

Masks

Masks worn by *Gule Wamkulu* dancers reflect the behavior of the characters they portray. For instance, a frightening mask signifies danger, while a friendly mask indicates a more benign presence. Additionally, some masks serve as symbols of decolonization, depicting famous figures from Western countries like Queen Elizabeth, Obama, and Bill Gates. Others mimic objects like cars, airplanes, and motorcycles, aimed at shifting people's focus away from Western influences.

In *Gule Wamkulu*, men are responsible for dancing, playing drums, and being the owners of the *Gule Wamkulu* cult. Men are much involved in the *Gule* because they are considered to be stronger enough to achieve energy and rigor which characterize the dance movements. Women are responsible for singing and clapping hands to enhance the *Gule* dancing.

MALAWIAN INDIGENOUS MEDIA IN THE DIGITAL AGE

As mentioned in the "Methodology" section of this chapter, two of the key informants, Rose Mwale for *Vimbuza* dance and Blessings Phiri for *Gule Wamkulu*, are Tumbuka and Chewa by descent. Presently, both of them are in the final semester of their four-year Bachelor of Arts degree in African

Musicology offered by the Bingu School of Culture and Heritage, Malawi University of Science and Technology. We reserved three questions which suited their dance ethnography studies in the digital age. Why are *Vimbuza* and *Gule Wamkulu* dances alive today? What makes *Vimbuza* and *Gule Wamkulu* relevant in the past, at present, and for the future? How can digital technology be harnessed to enhance Malawian indigenous media? The two etic dance ethnographers with lived experiences of the dances of their cultures were interviewed separately. With specific reference to the *Vimbuza* dance, Rose Mwale answered all the questions in chiTumbuka and English translations as detailed hereunder.

WHY IS THE VIMBUZA DANCE ALIVE TODAY?

Gule wa vimbuza wachali wmoyo ndipo wakuvinika mhanyauno kwakulingana na kuzirwa kwake ku mtundu wa banthu ba Tumbuka.Wukugumatizga banthu pamoza, wukuchizga pakutebeteska mizimu ya bazigogo. Nangauli wusinthikiro wasono wavyakuchitika naukhaliro muvikaya, Vimbuza vichali kutebeteskeka kufuma ku basekulu kukhirira pasi kwizira mu mafuko, kukhozga mtundu nakulera kukoleranako Kwa muvikaya. Kusazgilapo, nkhongono za kusungilira na kulutizga panthazi vyakuchitika vyapa mtundu vyasazgilako kukhalirira Kwa Vimbuza mu mtundu wasono wa ba tumbuka. (Mwale, 2024)

The *Vimbuza* dance remains alive and performed today due to its deep cultural significance and relevance to the Tumbuka people. It serves as a form of communal expression, spiritual healing, and connection to ancestors. Despite modernization and societal changes, *Vimbuza* continues to be passed down through generations, reinforcing cultural identity and fostering community cohesion. Additionally, efforts to preserve and promote traditional practices have contributed to its persistence in contemporary Tumbuka society.

WHAT MAKES *VIMBUZA* AND *GULE WAMKULU* RELEVANT IN THE PAST, AT PRESENT, AND FOR THE FUTURE?

Vimbuza vyaba vyakuzirwa kufuma papo kale nga ntchigaba chakulu Cha mtheto waba Tumbuka,pakugwiriskika ntchito munandi nga nkhuchizga Kwa masuzgo gha thupi na nthenda za mizimu, kumazga mbembe za pa mtundu,nakusungilira mtundu. Kwasono Vimbuza vichali kuzirwa pakujisankhira chigaba uko uli nakulutizga mtheto wa ba Tumbuka nanga kube vyakusinthika mu vikaya na ukhaliro wasono. Pakulabiska kunthazi , kuzirwa Kwa Vimbuza kutolelenge naumo vinthu vilili sono,chomenemene kusungilira mtheto, kukoleranako Kwa vikaya, na chakujimanyira mtundu ku mafuko ghamunthazi. (Mwale, 2024)

Vimbuza has been relevant in the past as a vital aspect of Tumbuka culture, serving multiple purposes such as healing physical and spiritual ailments, resolving social conflicts, and maintaining cultural identity. In the present, *Vimbuza* remains relevant as it continues to provide a sense of belonging and cultural continuity for the Tumbuka people, despite societal changes and modernization. Looking to the future, *Vimbuza*'s relevance may evolve as it adapts to contemporary contexts, potentially serving as a means of cultural preservation, community cohesion, and identity affirmation for future generations.

HOW CAN DIGITAL TECHNOLOGY BE HARNESSED TO ENHANCE MALAWIAN INDIGENOUS MEDIA?

Nthowa za Kuyezgayezga kusungilira nakulutizga panthazi Vimbuza nga ntchitewetero chankhongono chakudumbilana vyakhwaska vyakuchitika vyakupambanapambana vyakulingalinga kulutizga mudawuko wake na mulimo wake kuvyachitika vyanyengo yino. Ichi chakhwaska:
Viphikiro na vyakuchitika vya ukhaliro:
Kunozga Mwambo wa viphikiro navyakuchitika apo Vimbuza vikuwoneskeka vikupeleka mwabi kuti gulu lA banthu liwone nakukhutira. Mawungano agha ghakupeleka ku bavini kulongola gule,kugabana mbiri yake nakusambizga muwiro wa Sono za kuzirwa kwake.
Kulemba na Kafukufuku:
Basambiri bakutemwa mtheto papanga Kafukufuku nakulemba mbiri, mitheto kachitiro, na vilongolero vyakukhwaskana na Vimbuza. Kulemba uku kukovwira unenesko wa gule na kupelekeka virwelo vyakuzirwa vyakusambizgira mafuko ghakunthazi.
Nkhumano za Wupu na Visambizgo:
Pakuwikako nkhumano za wupu na nyengo za visambizgo pa ma wupu waba Tumbuka vikovwila kutandazga kamanyiro na kachitiro ka Vimbuza kufuma ku nkhwantha kuluta kubaniche. Zinyengo izi zikupereka kusambira luso lwa maboko nakulutizga vidumbilano vya fuko ku fuko kuwoneseska kulutilizga Kwa mdauko.
Kusazgikana na Masambiro:
Kusazga Vimbuza mu Visambizgo vyamasambiro vikovwila kubikamo ghanoghano la kujitemwa na chilolero chapadera Cha ukhaliro mu bana bachoko. Masukulu na mawupu ghakubona na za ukhaliro bangasazgamo gule wa vimbuza mumapulogilamu ghabo, kupelekeka ku basambiri kusambira nakujibikamo muvyakuchitika vya ukhaliro wa makolo. (Mwale, 2024)

Vya Makani na Unkhwantha:
Kutebeteska bavya Makani na Unkhwantha pakulongola Vimbuza ku banthu banandi kungovwira kukweza kupanikizga na khumbiro mu gule. Ichi chikusazgilapo kupanga mbiri kufuma pakwamba, kupanga vyakugwiriska ntchito pafoni nakugaba vithuzi/vidiyo ya maviniro pa Sosho Midiya. (Mwale, 2024)

Vimbuza can be harnessed through modern technology in several ways to enhance communication within and among the Tumbuka community while contributing to societal and national development:

Digital Documentation

Utilize digital platforms to document *Vimbuza* rituals, songs, dances, and traditional knowledge. This ensures preservation for future generations and enables broader access for Tumbuka communities worldwide.

Social Media Engagement

Create social media channels dedicated to *Vimbuza*, allowing Tumbuka people to share experiences, stories, and performances. This fosters community engagement, cultural exchange, and solidarity among Tumbuka individuals across geographical boundaries.

Mobile Apps for Education

Develop educational apps that provide information about the history, significance, and practices of *Vimbuza*. These apps can be used in schools and communities to promote cultural awareness and appreciation among younger generations.

Virtual Reality Experiences

Design virtual reality (VR) experiences that allow users to immerse themselves in *Vimbuza* performances and rituals. This innovative approach can provide a deeper understanding and appreciation of the cultural significance of *Vimbuza*.

Tourism Promotion

Use digital platforms to promote *Vimbuza* as a cultural tourism attraction, attracting visitors to Tumbuka regions and generating revenue for local communities. This contributes to economic development and preserves cultural heritage simultaneously.

Online Forums and Discussions

Facilitate online forums and discussions dedicated to *Vimbuza*, where community members can exchange ideas, share experiences, and discuss ways to support and preserve this cultural tradition.

By leveraging modern technology in these ways, *Vimbuza* can serve as a powerful tool for communication, cultural preservation, and socioeconomic development within the Tumbuka community and beyond. With particular reference to the *Gule Wamkulu* dance, Blessings Phiri answered all the questions in Chichewa and English translations as detailed hereunder.

WHY IS GULE WAMKULU DANCE ALIVE TODAY?

Gule wamkulu ndi gawo lofunika kwambiri pa mbiri ya chikhalidwe cha a Chewa. Pachifukwa ichi, anthu a mtunduwu amayesetsa kuteteza guleyu kuti mibado yobwerayo idzamupeze. Zina mwa njira zomwe zimagwiritsidwa ntchito popanga izi ndi monga kudzera mu; i) Gawo lalilkulu la chikhalidwe cha Chichewa cha Gule wamkulu limaphunzitsidwa kuchoka kum'bado wina kupita ku m'bado wina pogwiritsa ntchito mawu a pakamwa. Ana amaphunzira matanthauzo a zinthu, nkhani komanso kufunika kwa miyambo yachikhalidwe chawo kuchokera kwa akuluakulu a mmudzi mwawo poti ndi omwe amakhala ndi ukadaulo pa nkhani zotero. Iwo amafotokoza nkhani pofuna kulongosola mbiri ya Gule wamkulu, zizindikiro komanso maudindo a anthu ku guleko; ii) Ana amaphunzira Gule wamkulu kudzira mu kusonyeza mavinidwe kuchokera kwa omwe ali ndi ukatswiri pakavinidweka. Akaonera, naonso amayamba kuyeserera komanso kutenga nawo gawo pa zochitika zotere. Pakutero, iwo amayamba kukhala ndi chidwi ndi zinthu za Gule wamkulu monga mapatani a ng'oma, zovala za gule komanso mavinidwe ake, iii) Kwa omwe ali ndi chidwi ndi guleyu amayenera kulowa ku chinamwali cha Gule wamkulu ndipo iwo amadzakhala ovina atsopano. (Phiri, 2024)

An important part of the Chewa cultural legacy is *Gule Wamkulu*. In order to maintain their cultural identity, communities work hard to pass on their traditions to upcoming generations. The Chewa Community uses several ways to pass their *Gule* to other generations. These include (i) Oral Tradition: A significant portion of the *Gule Wamkulu*'s knowledge is passed down orally. Younger generations learn the meanings, stories, and significance of the ritual from the elders in the community, who are usually the guardians of this cultural legacy. They narrate stories to explain the dance's history, symbolism, and various character roles; (ii) Practicing the *Gule Wamkulu* is a common part of learning it. Alongside seasoned actors, younger community members watch and take part in the rituals. They pick up the nuances of the dance, such as the rhythms, costumes, and moves, via active participation; and (iii) Initiation and Training: For those who are interested in performing the *Gule Wamkulu*, they may occasionally be taught official initiation procedures. In these initiation rituals, more seasoned dancers and elders offer training.

A Chewa amakhulupirira kuti Gule wamkulu ndi gule wamizimu amene amavina pa miyambo yosiyanasiyani ya mtundu wa anthu a Chichewa. Iwo amakhulupirira kuti guleyu amalumikizitsa anthu a moyo ndi mizimu ya anthu omwe adamwalira. Anthu ovina komanso kuonerera guleyu, amakhala ndi chithuzithunzi chakutsamira pachikhalidwe chawo. Izi zimabweretsa pamodzi anthu a mtunduwu. Anthu ochoka maiko ena amakopeka ndi guleyu. Izi zimathandiza kupititsa patsogolo mbiri ya Gule wamkulu. (Phiri, 2024)

For the Chewa people, the dance has great spiritual significance. It is frequently performed at significant ceremonies like rites of passage, funerals, and initiations. It is thought to play a vital role in preserving spiritual harmony and balance by establishing a connection between the living and their ancestors and spirits. Both participants and onlookers experience a sense of belonging and community thanks to *Gule Wamkulu*. It fosters unity and strengthens ties between people, strengthening social ties within Chewa society. Travelers seeking to immerse themselves in traditional African culture are drawn to *Gule Wamkulu* and its ongoing effectiveness.

WHAT MAKES *GULE WAMKULU* RELEVANT IN THE PAST, AT PRESENT, AND FOR THE FUTURE?

Gule wamkulu wakhala wofunika kwambiri kuyambira kale, tsopano ndinso mtsogolo kaamba koti guleyu amagwiritsidwa ntchito pophunzitsa achinyamata makhalidw i)e abwino kudzera mu zinamwali. Kuonjezera apo, guleyu amaamalimbikitsa khalidwe loyenera pakati pa anthu a mtundu wa Chichewa kudzera mu njira izi; (i) Gule wamkulu ngati imodzi mwa miyambo ikuluikulu ya chikhalidwe cha Chichewa, guleyu amalimbikitsa kwambiri kulemekeza miyambo ndi zikhulupiriro zake; (ii) Anthu akuluakulu a mmudzi ndi omwe amatsogolera zochitika za Gule wamkulu. Iwo ndi omwe amapereka matanthauzo a zinthu zosiyanasiyana zokhudza guleyu zomwe zimaphuzitsa khalidwe loyenera ndikuthandiza kuti anthu azikhala wopindulira dsra lawo; (iii) Gule wamkulu amagwiritsa ntchito zizindikiro komanso nkhani zosiyanasiyana pophunzitsa khalidwe loyenera. Nkhanizi zimafotokoza za zotsatira za khalidwe losayenera pophatikiza pakulimbikitsa kukhulupirika, ulemu komanso kudalirika, (iv) iv. Gule wamkulu amagwiritsidwanso ntchito ngati chida chothandizira kuumba khalidwe la anthu a m'dera podzera mu zochitikachitika zodzudzula khalidwe losayenera pakati pa anthu. Chomcho guleyu amathandiza kuchepetsa mavuto akudza kaamba ka khalidwe losayenera. (Phiri, 2024)

Gule Wamkulu has been of great importance, it is today and it will be in future, especially in molding behaviors among boys as *Gule Wamkulu* is used to initiate boys among the Chewa. Similarly, *Gule Wamkulu* enforces morality among the Chewa in many ways: (i) Gule Wamkulu has a strong cultural heritage and tradition derived from the Chewa people. The ritual emphasizes the significance of honoring cultural norms and values, especially moral precepts passed down through the generations, by maintaining and celebrating these traditions; (ii) Respected elders or community leaders frequently supervise *Gule Wamkulu* performances, helping to interpret the moral lessons the ritual aims to impart. Their direction and wisdom serve to uphold moral lessons and give community members a sense of purpose, and (iii) *Gule Wamkulu* plays frequently use symbolic characters and stories to convey moral lessons. These narratives usually depict the negative effects of immoral behavior in addition to highlighting virtues like honesty, respect, and civic duty. The community has strengthened moral standards as a result of these performances, and (iv) *Gule Wamkulu* performances have the potential to function as a social control mechanism by means of openly addressing and critiquing behaviors that are deemed immoral or disruptive to the community. Through performances that depict particular behaviors or attitudes negatively, *Gule Wamkulu* works to dissuade community members from engaging in those kinds of behaviors.

Guleyu amagwiritsidwa ntchito pazochitika za chikhalidwe cha a Chewa monga miyambo ya maliro ndi zina zambiri. Iye amazindikiritsa anthu a Chichewa kwa alondo omwe abwera m'madera awo. Mulendo akafika ku dera la anthu a Chichewa amakhutira kuti afika kwawo kwa a Chewa pokhapokha ataona guleyu. Kudzera mu zinthu ngati zimenezi, iwo amafalitsa mbiri yawo kumadera ena ndinso mitundu ina ya anthu. Gule wamkulu ndi njira yodalirika yosungira chikhalidwe cha Chichewa kuchoka kumibado ina kupita kumibado ina. Mwachitsanzo, zovala za Gule wamkulu, miyambo yake, zikhulupiriro zake komanso mavinidwe ake zakhala kwa zaka zochuluka ndipo zidzapitirirabe kumibado ina ikudzayo. Gule wamkulu ndi njira yodalirika yobweretsera anthu pamodzi kudzera mu zochitikachitika za guleyu. Izi zimathandiza kuyanjanitsa anthu. Kudzera mu zinthu ngati zimenezi, anthu amagawana zochitika za chikhalidwe cha mitundu yawo komanso kulimbikitsa kulolerana ndinso kufalitsa uthenga koyenera ndi umodzi. (Phiri, 2024)

Gule Wamkulu is used in different cultural events such as funeral ceremonies and other rituals among the Chewa. *Gule Wankulu* shapes the identity of the Chewa people more than any other Chewa traditions in such a way that if visitors enter into the Chewa community, they will only appreciate their entrance upon seeing *Gule Wamkulu*. Through this, their cultural identity is shared with other cultures. *Gule Wamkulu* serves as one way of transmitting culture for the Chewa people from one generation to the other. This has been so from the past to present and will be the same in future. For instance, *Gule Wamkulu* costumes, traditions, beliefs, and performances have been there for years and still being passed to other generations to come. *Gule Wamkulu* is a great tool for bringing people together during performances which is very important in bringing unity among people. Through this, people share traditions as well as promote tolerance, effective communication, and oneness.

HOW CAN DIGITAL TECHNOLOGY BE HARNESSED TO ENHANCE MALAWIAN INDIGENOUS TRADITIONAL MEDIA?

Kusunga mbiri ya Gule wamkulu pogwiritsa ntchito njira zamakono za pambiri ya guleyu. Zinthu zamakono ngati zimenezi zili ndi ubwino ochuluka kuphatikizapo zotsatirazi: (i) Zinthu zomwe zajambulidwa zimaoneka zapamwamba komanso chilichonse chomwe chimayenera kuoneka, chimaoneka. Chomcho, kujambula zinthu monga zovala za Gule wamkulu, zotchinga kumanso komanso mautoto apakhungu la gule kumayenera zipangizo ngati zimenezi. Mitundu ya zovala za Gule wamkulu yomwe imapangidwa mosiyanasiyana malingana ndi mwambo omwe guleyu akukavina, ikhoza kuoneka bwino ngati itajambulidwa ndi HD Videograph: (iii) Mavinidwe a Gule wamkulu amakhala osinthasintha malo chomcho amafunika kujambulidwa ndi ma HD Videography kaamba ka mpata waukulu omwe amakhala nawo omwe umathandiza kuonetsa malo akulu ndipo akhoza kumasunthidwa pang'onopang'ono motsatira guleyo: (iv) Zipangizo zojambulira za HD zili ndikuthekera kujambula ngakhali zinthu zazing'ono kwambiri. Izi ndi monga zizindikiro za pakhope komanso ziyankhulo za zizindikiro zomwe zimasonyeza momwe wovinayo akumvera, and v) Zipangizo zojam,bulira za HD zimajambula mawu mwapamwamba zomwe zingathandize kujambula phokoso lapansipansi nthawi yomwe Gulw wamkulu akuvina, phokoso la mapazi ake povina komanso nyimbo. (Phiri, 2024)

To record and preserve *Gule Wamkulu* performances, make use of contemporary technologies like high-definition videography such as still videography. This is because of the following reasons: (i) Clear and detailed imagery can be captured in high-definition videos thanks to its superior resolution. Capturing the elaborate costumes, masks, and body paint frequently associated with *Gule Wamkulu* may require this; (ii) The rich hues and elaborate patterns of the traditional clothing and decorations worn during *Gule Wamkulu* ceremonies can be faithfully captured in HD videography: (iii) *Gule Wamkulu*'s dynamic dances and performances require high frame rates for HD videography to capture fluid movements: (iv) High-definition videography is capable of capturing minute facial expressions and body language, which translates the feelings and narrative that are intrinsic to *Gule Wamkulu* performances, and (v) High-definition videos frequently have excellent audio recording features, making it possible to capture the Gule's background noise, chants, and music in crystal clear details.

Kuphatikizira apo, njira zina zofalitsira uthenga zikhoza kugwiritsidwanso ntchito posunga mbiri ya Gule wamkulu monga Virtual Reality (VR) komanso Augmented Reality(AR). Izi zili ndi ubwino otsatirawu; (i) Munthu akhoza kuonerera Gule wamkulu pogwiritsa ntchito zipangizozi popanda kupita komwe guleyu akuvinidwira. Izi zingathandize kuti Gule wamkulu adziwike kumadera ambiri: (ii) Zinthu zokhudza Gule wamkulu zomwe zimavuta kuzimvetsa, munthu angathe kuzimvetsa pa nthawi yake kudzera mu kulumikizana komwe komwe kumatheka ndi VR komanso AR zomwe zimapereka mwayi opeza magawo osiyanasiyana ophunzirirapo chomwe munthu akufuna, (iii) Zolembalemba komanso zojambulajambula ndi zina mwa njira zomwe anthu amagwiritsa ntchito posunga mbiri ngakhale kuti izi sizingapereke chithunzithunzi choyenera cha momwe Gule wamkulu amachitikira. Komabe, VR ndi AR zili ndikuthekera kusunga mbiri monga ya Gule wamkulu mwa pamwamba komanso mopereka chithunzi chenicheni cha momwe guleyu amavinidwira. (Phiri, 2024)

In addition, other means of communication such as VR, and AR can be employed in documentation of *Gule Wamkulu*. This is because of the following reasons: (i) Without physically being there, anyone from all over the world may enjoy *Gule Wamkulu* thanks to VR and AR technologies. It is imperative that Chewa culture become more widely known and appreciated worldwide; (ii) *Gule Wamkulu*'s complexities can be explored at the user's own speed through interactive learning experiences provided by VR and AR platforms. Users have the ability to enlarge on certain aspects, discover the meaning behind the costumes and choreography, and interact with additional educational materials, and (iii) Written descriptions and photos are common forms of documentation, although they might not adequately convey the breadth and complexity of *Gule Wamkulu*. Conversely, VR and AR provide a more thorough and immersive method of documenting, giving a more true-to-life portrayal of the performances.

Pofuna kusunga mbiri monga iyi, zipamgizo za makono monga zimenezi zingagwiritsidwe ntchito ngati zida zophunzitsira mibado ya lero komanso ya mawa zokhudza Gule wamkulu.Kukhazikitsa masamba a mchezo a pa internet pophunzitsa anthu za Gule wamkulu. Malo monga awa mukhoza kumaikidwa zinthu monga nkhani, makanema komanso mafunso okhudza ndi Gule wamkulu.Izi zimathandiza kufalitsa zochitika za Gule wamkulu kwa anthu ochuluka kuphatikiza omwe sakanatha kuonerera. Izi zingathe kuperka mwayi kwa anthu kuonera guleyu nthawi yomwe akuvinidwa popanda iwowo kupita ku malo ovinirawo. Akhozanso kuonera zojambulidwa za Gule wamkuluyu nthawi yomwe iwo akufuna. Kugwiritsa ntchito njira za luso lamakono posinthana maluso a chikhalidwe pakati pa anthu a Chichewa ndi mitundu ina padziko lonse. Izi zingathandize kudziwitsa anthu ena za Gule wamkulu zomwe zingalimbuikitsenso kulemekezana pakati pa mitundu ya anthu. Kudzera mu zinthu ngati zimenezi, anthu akhoza kumadziwitsana zinthu zosiyanasiyana za zomwe amakumana nazo, nthano, komanso miyambo yawo. Kugwiritsa ntchito njira zamakono za sayasi pogulitsa chikhalidwe cha Chichewa monga Gule wamkulu. Izi ndi monga kulengeza zochitika zokhudza Gule wamkulu, kugulitsa malonda a Gule wamkulu pa masamba a mchezo a pa internet ndi zina zambiri zomwe zingathandize kupititsa miyoyo ya anthu patsogolo maka pa zachuma ndi chitukuko. (Phiri, 2024)

In order to preserve cultural knowledge and customs, these digital archives may be used as teaching tools for present and future generations. Create websites, mobile applications, or online platforms that offer educational materials about *Gule Wamkulu*, including its background, relevance, and symbolism. In order to inform and engage members of the Chewa community as well as people from other cultural backgrounds, these platforms might include interactive multimedia content in the form of articles, videos, quizzes, and virtual tours. Broadcast *Gule Wamkulu* performances to a larger audience, including people who might not otherwise have the chance, by utilizing live streaming technology. This would help people from all over the world have access to *Gule Wamkulu* performances and activities on real time, thereby having the real experience of it. Arrange for cultural exchanges between Chewa communities and other cultures worldwide by utilizing contemporary technology. This could entail online conversations in which people discuss experiences, tales, and knowledge about *Gule Wamkulu* and other cultural customs. Programs like this can encourage respect for one another, intercultural communication, and global citizenship. Make use of technology to assist community-led projects that protect and advance *Gule Wamkulu*. This could include online marketplaces for booking performances and cultural tours, as well as digital platforms for selling handcrafted dance-related crafts and costumes. These programs can support Chewa communities' economic growth and cultural sustainability by empowering regional artists and performers.

CONCLUSION

This chapter underscores the fact that indigenous media of communities which use bodies to dance and connect with the cosmos and the earth never die even when subjected to severe hegemonic forces such as colonial conquests. By embracing contemporary content into indigenous *Vimbuza* and *Gule Wamkulu* dances, the Tumbuka and Chewa creative genius has enabled the endurance of their valued means of communication. Both the documentation and digital transmission of indigenous media including the *Vimbuza* and the *Gule Wamkulu* since the colonial era have neither subdued nor replaced the performative means of communication that is upheld by most of the people living in rural communities and promoted such indigenous media which is highly esteemed for its efficacious communication.

REFERENCES

Adesoji, S., & Ogunjimi, S. (2015). Assessing the use of indigenous communication media among rural dwellers of Osun State Nigeria. *American Journal of Experimental Agriculture, 7*(6), 405–13.

Adum A. N., Emmanuel N. M., & Ojiakor O. E. (2015). Towards the media of Africa by Africans for Africans. *Journal of African Studies, 5*(1), 1–9.

Bates, R. (2012). *Africa through western eyes: The world's dark continent or capitalism's shining light.* Think Africa Press.

Davidson, B. (1972). *Africa: History of a continent.* Spring Books.

Egnew, R. (2005). The meaning of healing: Transcending suffering. *Annals of Family Medicine, 3*(3), 225–62.

Etim, F. (2019). Ontology of African ritual. *Advances in Applied Sociology, 9*(1), 1–14.

Fetternan, D. (2010). *Ethnography: Step by step guide.* Sage.

Friedson, S. (2010). *Dancing prophets: Musical experience in Tumbuka healing.* University of Chicago Press.

Gausi, P. (2023). *Formal communication.* Mzimba district, Northern Region Malawi.

Geertz, C. (1973). *The interpretation of cultures.* Basi Books.

Hammersley, M., & Atkinson, P. (2007). *Ethnography: Principles in practice.* Routledge.

Kargho, J. (2022). Diminishing African traditional systems of communication: Perception of a professional. *African Journal of Library Information Science Studies, 8*(4), 1–13.

Mills, D. (2019, January 15). *Using ethnography in educational research.* Oxford Bibliographies. https://www.oxfordbibliographies.com/display/document/obo-9780199756810/obo-9780199756810-0208.xml.

Mthande, S. (2024). *Formal communication.* Kasungu district, Central Region Malawi.

Mtinde, L., Bonin, M., & Nyamaka K. (1998). What is community radio? AMARC.

Mwale, H. (2023). *Formal communication*. Mzimba district, Northern Region Malawi.

Mwale, S. (2023). *Formal communication*. Mzimba district, Northern Region Malawi.

Nzewi, M. (2007). *A contemporary study of musical arts informed by African indigenous knowledge systems. Vol. 4. Illuminations, reflections and explorations*. African Minds.

Olupona, J. (2015). *The spirituality of Africa*. Harvard Gazette.

Phiri, B. (2023). Formal communication. Kasungu district, Central Region Malawi.

Phiri, L. (2024). Formal communication. Kasungu district, Central Region Malawi.

Ranger, T. (1972). *The historical study of African religion*. Heineman Books.

Syaputra, I., & Sabri, Y. (2023). The role and function of media institutions in society in the digital age: A case of Indonesia. *Journal of Social Media, Communication and Journalism, 1*(1), 63–67.

Wilson, D., (1987). Traditional systems of communication in modern African development: An analytical viewpoint. *African Media Review, 1*(2), 87–104.

The World Bank. (2022). *Data on African rural population*.

Index

About the Contributors

Abayomi Bamidele Adisa is a multitalented journalist, consummate writer, storyteller, and researcher. He has more than fifteen years of experience as a journalist in Nigeria and has worked in both local and international newsrooms. He presently works as a senior journalist for the British Broadcasting Corporation (BBC) in Lagos, Nigeria. He holds a first-class honors bachelor's degree and a master's degree in mass communication. He is an alumnus of the Radio Nederlands Training Centre in the Netherlands where he bagged an international certification in broadcast and multimedia journalism. Abayomi has more than forty professional courses in journalism and digital content production to his name from BBC Academy, Reuters, and LinkedIn Learning, among others. His research interest is in the multidimensional layers of disinformation in digital media and implication on societies and their democracies.

Paul Agada is a multisectoral communications professional and sustainable development advocate whose specialty spans across Public Relations, advertising, product marketing, journalism, broadcasting, publishing, social media management, and communications for development. Paul earned a first-class bachelor's degree in Mass Communications at the UNESCO rated Multimedia Centre of Excellence, the Department of Mass Communication, University of Lagos, where he emerged as the Best Graduating Student of the 2019/20 set. He is a proud alumnus of McKinsey Forward Program, Future Creative Leaders Academy, and Millennium Fellowship, among others. He is also a founding member of the Lagos SDGs Youth Alliance.

Unwana Samuel Akpan is a multidisciplinary media scholar-practitioner with over two decades of broadcast experience. He has been a visiting scholar at the Department of Communication, Culture and Media Studies, where he completed his postdoctoral studies in the School of Communication and Media Studies, Howard University, Washington D.C., the United States. He is the editor of the University of Lagos Communication Review. He started his career with The Federal Radio Corporation of Nigeria and was deployed to The National Broadcast Academy, its training arm, after obtaining his PhD in Mass Communication. He is presently a lecturer in the Department of Mass Communication, University of Lagos, Akoka, Nigeria. He has been a visiting scholar in the Department of Communication, Culture and Media Studies, Howard University, Washington D.C., the United States, where he completed his postdoctoral research. He has publications in the form of book chapters and research articles in prominent national and international journals. He has delivered several research papers at international conferences and has published journal articles, book chapters, and books in both prominent local and international journals and publishers such as Lexington, Palgrave Macmillan (Springer Nature), Routledge (Taylor and Francis), and Peter Lang. His classes are in research, teaching, and learning interface, and he is dedicated to making students succeed in the classroom and beyond. His research and teaching investigate and explore broadcast contents, sport communication, African communication systems, diaspora communication studies, and media aesthetic.

Shamilla Amulega is an innovative and value-driven communications leader and scholar with more than fifteen years of extensive experience shaping communications, public relations, and marketing strategies for highly visible organizations. She is an adept strategist with a proven track record of success driving influential campaigns while building and executing internal communication programs that champion the organizational narrative and vision. She is a two-time Telly Award recipient in television production. She is also a culture champion, published author, and global communications strategist across North America, Africa, and the Middle Eastern regions who cultivates a collaborative culture and executive trust by supporting cross-functional initiatives with powerful direction. Amulega earned her Bachelor of Arts degree in Journalism, Electronic edia (TV/Radio/Print/Film) at Daystar University, Nairobi, Kenya, a Master of Arts degree in Communications and a Post-Graduate Certificate in Teaching and Adult Learning from Bethel University, St. Paul, Minnesota, and her doctoral degree from Howard University Department of Communication, Culture and Media Studies in Washington D.C. Her communication research areas of interest are critical studies in media and global communications.

Herbert Batta, a professorial cadre academic, holds the headship at the Department of Information and Media Studies, University of Uyo, Nigeria, where he has taught since 2000. His research interests are in science, health, and environmental communication and media studies. He has published his research in over sixty-five national and foreign journals and book chapters. He holds (or held in the past) active membership in the African Council for Communication Education (ACCE, Nigeria, where he was National Treasurer and later, Deputy National Secretary); International Environmental Communication Association, Ohio, the United States; Public Communication of Science and Technology (PCST), Australia; European Communication Research and Education Association, Belgium; as well as the International Communication Association, the International Association of Media and Communication Research (IAMCR), Paris, and the Association for Educators in Journalism and Mass Communication. Batta has attended and presented papers in over thirty-six conferences held by these organizations and others in Nigeria, Ghana, Kenya, Italy, Sweden, Switzerland, Brazil, the UK, the United States, Russia, and Japan. He co-edited communication books including: *Communication and Africa's Development Crisis* (2010), *Companion to Communication and Development Issues* (2012), *Science, Health and Environmental Communication* (2013), and *Communication Education and Research in 21st Century Nigeria* (2018). Some of his scholarly articles have garnered more than a modest 305 Google Scholar citations. He participated in an effort to map the emergence of modern science communication in the world—a book project anchored by PCST published in 2020 by the Australian National University Press. That effort effectively placed Nigeria in that map.

Nnamdi Tobechukwu Ekeanyanwu is professor of International and Strategic Communications, University of Uyo, Nigeria. He obtained his first, second, and doctorate degrees in Mass Communication, specializing in International Communication. Prof. Ekeanyanwu is a Summer Study of the United States Institutes for Scholars (SUSI) Scholar and Winner of the 2011 U.S.-sponsored SUSI in the area of Journalism and Media Studies. He spent his fellowship tenure at the Institute for International Journalism, Ohio University, the United States. He is also a CIMARC Scholar. With the CIMARC Scholarship, Prof. Ekeanyanwu became a Short-Term Visiting Scholar to the University of Bedfordshire, UK. Prof. Ekeanyanwu is a Grantee, British Academy International Mobility Scheme Award for 2016–2017; TETFund Institutional-based Research Grant for 2017–2018 and 2019–2020; and currently a Co-Grantee of the prestigious National Research Fund Grant administered by TETFund for the 2020–2023 academic sessions. He has written over seventy peer-reviewed articles and books and spoken at various international conferences in the United States, Europe, Africa, and Nigeria. He recently co-edited a book on Media and

Communication in Nigeria with Prof. Bruce Mutsvairo which was published by Routledge.

Isaac Olajide Fadeyi is a lecturer of Public Relations and Advertising at
Redeemer's University, Ede, Osun State, Nigeria. His research focuses on
advertising, PR, and communication theory. He holds a PhD in Mass Communication with specialization in PR and advertising.

Aloysius Chukwuebuka Ifeanyichukwu is a doctoral student of Political
Communication and teaching assistant at the Department of Communication,
University of Delaware, the United States. His other areas of interest include
PR, cultural communication, and development communication.

Shirley Marang Kekana is a highly accomplished individual with an impressive academic background, having acquired five degrees, including a Doctor
of Music from the esteemed University of Pretoria in South Africa. Her doctoral research delved into the practices of early childhood music experts, with
a view to providing guidance for ECE tertiary training in Southern Africa. In
addition, she holds a Master of Music, a Bachelor of Music Hons, a Bachelor
of Arts—Culture and Media Studies Honors, and a Bachelor of Arts Music.
Kekana is currently employed as a lecturer and researcher at the University of
Botswana, where she has been engaged for a number of years. With over two
decades of teaching experience, she previously served as a Principal Education Officer II (Broadcasting), where she conducted research and developed
content for educational programs on radio and television, particularly in the
field of music education. Kekana's contributions to the field of music education are widely recognized, as evidenced by her research publications and
presentations at the annual Music Education International Conference. She
has also held the position of Vice President of the Pan African Society of
Music and Arts Educators (PASME)—West Africa Region, further attesting
to her expertise and leadership in this field.

Kehbuma Langmia is a Fulbright scholar/professor and chair in the Department of Strategic, Legal and Management Communication, School of Communications, Howard University. A graduate from the Communication and
Media Studies Program at Howard University in 2006, Langmia has extensive
knowledge and expertise in Information Communication Technology (ICT),
intercultural, cross-cultural and international communication, black diaspora
communication theory, decolonial media studies, social media, and Afrocentricity. Since earning his PhD in communications and media studies from
Howard University in 2006, he has published thirteen books, seventeen book
chapters, and nine peer-reviewed journal articles nationally and internationally.

In November 2017, Langmia was awarded the prestigious Toyin Falola Africa Book Award in Marrakesh, Morocco, by the Association of Global South Studies for his book titled *Globalization and Cyberculture: An Afrocentric Perspective*. For the last four years he has been selected by Howard University to act as scholar coach for the Howard University Summer Writing Academy. This year, he was selected among the thirty-five U.S. professors chosen from a competitive pool of over one-hundred applicants to serve in the Visiting Professor Program at Fordham University in New York organized by ANA. In addition, he regularly gives keynote speeches on ICT, black diaspora-mediated communication, and social media in prominent national and international universities, including the Library of Congress, the National Intelligence University (Department of Defense, USA), and National Defense University (Department of Defense, USA); Morgan State University (Maryland, USA); Bowie State University (Maryland, USA); Melbourne University (Australia); Buea University (Cameroon), Madras Institute of Technology (India); ICT University (Cameroon); Covenant University (Nigeria); Makerere, University Business School, MUBS, (Uganda); and Temple University, Pennsylvania. He was the 2017 Maryland Communication Association Keynote Speaker held at College of Southern Maryland, Waldorf, MD, and Communication Educators' Association Conference at Winneba, Ghana, in 2019. His most recent books are: *Black/Africana Communication Theory*, published in 2018 by Palgrave/Macmillan Press; *Globalization and Cyberculture: An Afrocentric Perspective,* and *Social Media: Culture and Identity* published in 2017 by Palgrave, Macmillan Press and the latter co-edited with Tia Tyree published by Lexington Books. He is presently editing two books. *Social Media: SafeSpacesor Dangerous Terrain* with Tia Tyree of Howard University, *Digital Communication at Crossroads in Africa: A Decolonial Approach* with Agnes Lucy Lando of Daystar University, Kenya, and self-authoring *Black Lives . . . and Cyber Culturalism* to be published by the end of this year. Website: drlangmia.net.

Perminus Matiure was brought up in a musical family. Perminus Matiure started playing mbira at the age of twelve and later studied it at masters and PhD levels. Out of these studies, he was able to publish several articles and book chapters in ethnomusicology and also presented papers at international conferences like ICTM, PASME, CIMCIM, Applied Ethnomusicology Study Group, and MESI. He founded the "Zvirimudeze mbira ensemble." He also produced six innovations on mbira. He can teach, construct, tune, and play mbira, chipendani, and ngoma. He also teaches music video production and archiving of tangible and intangible musical materials.

Almon Moyo is a lecturer in music at Midlands State University (MSU), he holds MSc Music Technology and BSc Music and Musicology degrees,

Creative Entrepreneurship Certificate (British Council), Innovator with MSU, and a manufacturer of traditional music instruments, and he has three pending publications.

Khulekani F. Moyo is a holder of an MSc in Music Technology, BSc honors in Music and Musicology (MSU), and PGD Education (ZOU). Moyo is a lecturer and music producer with more than several music productions on national and community radio stations in Zimbabwe. His research interests are music production and live sound and video production. He has two peer-reviewed publications.

Richard Muranda holds a BA education in music (Africa University), BMus and MMus both in Music Technology (University of Pretoria), and a PhD in Musicology (UNISA). Dr. Muranda wields thirty-six years of experience in teaching music. He is a senior lecturer at Midlands State University in the Department of Music Business, Musicology and Technology. He teaches and undertakes research in music technology, music pedagogy, performance, popular music, and ethnomusicology. Dr. Muranda supervises and examines honors and masters research. He has presented papers in Botswana, China, Finland, South Africa, and Zimbabwe. He has published twenty-five peer-reviewed articles.

Absolom Mutavati is a lecturer at Midlands State University, specializing in Music Technology. He holds an BSc honors degree in Music and Musicology and an MSc in Music Technology (MSU), he lectures music technology, music production, and live sound reinforcement. Absolom is actively involved in research and scholarly pursuits. He has authored and published four articles in the field of music technology.

Eddah Mbula Mutua is a professor of Intercultural Communication at St. Cloud State University, Minnesota. Her research interests include African communication education and scholarship, the role of women in grassroots peacebuilding initiatives in post-conflict societies in Eastern Africa, relations between East African refugee and host communities in Central Minnesota, and critical service learning as a pedagogical practice in peace education. Her work has received national and international recognition for an award-winning service-learning project. She is the co-editor of *Rhetorical Legacy of Wangari Mathaai: Planting the Future* and *Internationalization of the Communication Curriculum in an Age of Globalization*. Other publications appear in *Language and Intercultural Communication, Review of Communication, The Journal of Social Encounters, Qualitative Inquiry, Africa Media Review, African Yearbook of Rhetoric, Women & Language,*

Text and Performance Quarterly, and several edited intercultural communication books. She has served as a guest editor for *Africa Media Review* and *Journal of Social Encounter* and editorial board member of *Review of Communication.*

Iniobong Courage Nda is a lecturer in the Faculty of Communication and Media Studies, University of Uyo, Uyo, Akwa Ibom State, Nigeria, where she has taught communication and media studies since 2012. As a scholar who has garnered practical expertise from both the print (The Sensor Newspaper) and broadcast media (The Nigerian Television Authority), respectively, Nda has been able to integrate her field experience with the classroom demands for effective and efficient teaching of mass communication and has published her research in several national and international journals including contributing chapters to books. She is an active member of the African Council of Communication Education (ACCE), Nigerian Institute of Management (NIM), and the Nigerian Union of Journalists (NUJ). Her research interests are in business/organizational, health, and development communication.

Paul Obi is a media scholar and researcher interested in political communication and how the media and technology interact with elections, politics, and democracy; media influence of Africa's democratization; propaganda studies; misinformation and disinformation in Africa; autocracy and mediated authoritarianism; political participation; public sphere; and media law. He is co-editor/author of the book *Media and Nigeria's Constitutional Democracy: Civic Space, Free Speech, and The Battle for Freedom of the Press* (Lexington Books, an imprint of Rowman and Littlefield). Obi has also published more than a dozen publications in the above thematic areas in journals, edited volumes, and collections including *ESSACHES—Journal for Communication Studies* where he co-authored a journal article recently exploring the Russian–Ukrainian War impact on Dis/Misinformation in Africa. His co-authored book chapter, "Cyberspace as a Battlefield for Nationalists and Separatist Groups: A Study of Nigeria's Indigenous Peoples of Biafra Online Propaganda" appeared in the book *Digital Dissidence and Social Media Censorship in Africa.* In 2020, his paper "Insider Peddling . . ." on hate speech won UNESCO second best paper. Between 2009 and 2018, he was a journalist with This Day Newspaper, a leading publication in Africa and one of Nigeria's most authoritative newspapers of records. He is 2017 Fellow, ICFJ/ UN Fellowship on Migration/Climate. He holds a BA in English, University of Abuja, Nigeria, and an MA in Political Communication, from the School of Journalism, Media and Culture (JOMEC), Cardiff University, UK. Obi is currently a research fellow at The Abuja School of Social and Political Thought, Nigeria.

Henry Chibueze Ogaraku holds a BA in Communication Arts and a Masters in Mass Communication (print journalism) from the Department of Communication Arts, University of Uyo, Akwa Ibom State. He is currently a doctoral candidate in the Department of Linguistics and Communication Studies, University of Port Harcourt, Rivers State. Henry lectures in the Department of Mass Communication of Trinity University, Lagos. With several publications, both solo and collaborative, local and international, and one honorarium to his credit, his research interests lie at the intersection of the old (traditional mass media) and new media, among others.

Abigail Odozi Ogwezzy-Ndisika is the first female professor in the Department of Mass Communication, University of Lagos. At different times, she had served as the head of this department. She is an expert in development communication, Public Relations, and advertising, with research interest in the gender dimension to development and strategic communication. She has worked on multisector projects and with a number of international organizations across Nigeria. She is a recipient of ELF Petroleum Coy Ltd and British Chevening scholarships; laureate of the Council for the Development of Social Science Research in Africa (CODESRIA), laureate of the African Association of Political Science (AAPS)/Harry Frank Guggenheim (HFG); laureate, Pulitzer Center on Crisis Reporting, Washington D.C.; Erasmus+ Staff Mobility grant for teaching at Birmingham School of Media, Birmingham City University, Birmingham, the UK; and 1991 best graduating student in Department of Linguistics, University of Port Harcourt. In addition, she is a fellow of the Nigerian Institute of Public Relations (NIPR); Associate Registered Practitioner of Advertising (ARPA), member; Association of Communication Scholars & Professionals of Nigeria (ACSPN), and member, International Association for Media and Communication Research (IAMCR). She has attended various local and international conferences and published articles and books locally and internationally.

Ihuoma Okorie completed her Bachelor's and Master's degrees at Ahmadu Bello University, Zaria. She is presently a lecturer in the Department of Theatre and Performing Arts, Bayero University, Kano, and a fellow of the Global Arts in Medicine. She has published works in reputable journals and has attended several national and international conferences. Her primary research interest is in the field of textual analysis. She is also interested in writing and pedagogies of experimental writing. Her hobbies include teaching, writing, and dancing, among others. Ihuoma is presently a doctoral student in the Department of Theatre and Performing Arts, Ahmadu Bello University, Zaria.

Oyinloye Oloyede is a lecturer in the Department of Mass Communication, Redeemer's University, Ede, Osun State, Nigeria. His research interest focuses on media studies, human and mass communication theories. He holds a PhD in psychology of organizational communication with special focus on communication competence.

Chuka Onwumechili is a professor of strategic, legal, and management communication at Howard University in Washington D.C. (the United States). He is the author of more than ten books focusing largely on several communication issues that pertain to Africa. These books touch on varied subjects including sports, telecommunications, culture, and development. His most recent book is *Africa's Elite Football: Structure, Politics, and Everyday Challenges*. His other works on similar subjects have been published in peer-reviewed academic journals. Presently, he serves as Editor-in-Chief of the *Howard Journal of Communications* and serves on the Editorial Board of the *Communication & Sport* journal. It is important to note that before joining Howard University, Onwumechili served as Vice President for the Digital Bridge Institute in Nigeria where his brief included executive visioning, managing, and overseeing training programs at different levels for employees in both the Nigerian telecommunications industry and other interested markets.

Akinola Moses Owolabi is the Director, News and Current Affairs of the Television Service of Osun State Broadcasting Corporation. In the course of duty, he had undertaken local, national, and international assignments as well as undergone training, seminars, and conferences at national and international levels. Akinola is a prolific writer and biographer. He is presently pursuing a doctorate degree in mass communication. His areas of interest are political and indigenous communication.

Ibitayo Samuel Popoola is an associate professor of political communication and teaches at the Department of Mass Communication, University of Lagos. He has published widely in local and foreign journals with several chapter contributions in local and foreign textbooks. He is the author of *GSM as a Tool for News Reporting in Nigeria, Specialized Reporting: A Global Trend in Media Training Vol 1 & 2, Introduction to Mass Communication, Mass Media Law in Nigeria, a professional perspective, Public Relations, Advertising and Promotion, Parrot Journalism, A Guide in Investigative Journalism*, and many more.

Jerry Rutsate is a versatile music educationist and African music scholar. He is a senior lecturer in music and musicology, Malawi University of Science and Technology, Tjolo, Malawi. His academic qualifications include

BA honors in music and musicology, MA in music, and PhD in music (dance ethnography research focus). Professional qualifications include Certificate in Education and Bachelor of Education in Higher Education (music). Working experience involves teaching in primary and secondary schools, lecturing in primary and secondary teacher-training colleges of education, as well as teaching in universities in Zimbabwe, South Africa, and Malawi. Research supervision experience includes undergraduate and postgraduate studies up to doctoral levels to completion. External examination experience includes undergraduate and postgraduate programs, dissertations, and theses. He is actively involved in curriculum development and in crafting secondary school, diploma, honors, and masters music degree programs. His research area of interest is applied ethnomusicology.

Muhammad Hamisu Sani is a senior lecturer and the Head of Mass Communication Department at Baze University, Abuja, Nigeria. Before joining Baze University, he taught at several universities across the globe, including Queens University, Kingston, Canada; University of Winnipeg, Manitoba, Canada; Morgan State University, Baltimore, Maryland, the United States; the American University of Nigeria, Yola, Nigeria; and Bayero University, Kano, Nigeria. His research interests focus on media and conflicts, media and identity politics, media framing, African media space, and globalization.

Bernice Oluwalaanu Sanusi is an associate professor in the Department of Mass Communication, Redeemer's University. She holds a doctorate degree in mass communication with special interest in educational broadcasting and development communication. Before she joined the academic world, Sanusi worked in the print media as a journalist covering areas such as court, politics, as well as life and style.